NUMEROLOGY
PALMISTRY and PROSPERITY

Also by Dr. M. Katakkar
in UBSPD

- Encyclopaedia of Palm and Palm Reading
- Dial Your Birth Number
- Palmistry, Marriage and Family Welfare

NUMEROLOGY PALMISTRY and PROSPERITY

Dr. M. Katakkar

UBSPD

UBS Publishers' Distributors Ltd.

New Delhi • Bombay • Bangalore • Madras
Calcutta • Patna • Kanpur • London

UBS Publishers' Distributors Ltd.
5 Ansari Road, New Delhi-110 002
Bombay Bangalore Madras
Calcutta Patna Kanpur London

First Edition 1987
Second Edition 1992

ISBN 81-85674-52-3

Cover Design: UBS Art Studio

Printed at Ram Printograph, C-114 Okhla Industrial Area, Phase I, New Delhi-110 020

CONTENTS

Chapters		Page
	Part One : Numerology	
	Introduction	vii
1	1) The Study of Numerolgy : a) History of Numerology, b) Theory of Numerology, c) Utility of the study of Numerology.	1
	2) Importance of Numbers : a) Basic facts about numbers, b) Affinity of numbers, c) The Ruling number and the Fadic number, d) Influence of numbers and Rasis (Zodiacs) on the human body.	
2	Significance of numbers 1 to 9 How to find out the Ruling number and the lucky number	14
3	Number 1 : a) Character, b) Finance, c) Vocation, d) Health, e) Marriage and friends, f) Fortunate days, g) Lucky colours, h) Lucky jewels and stones, i) important years in life, j) Good qualities and drawbacks.	16
4	Number 2	21
5	Number 3	25
6	Number 4	29
7	Number 5	33
8	Number 6	37
9	Number 7	41
10	Number 8	45
11	Number 9	50
	Summary Chart of Numbers	54
12	The month you are born in Born in January	56
13	Born in February	59
14	Born in March	61
15	Born in April	63
16	Born in May	65
17	Born in June	67
18	Born in July	69
19	Born in August	72
20	Born in September	75
21	Born in October	77
22	Born in November	79
23	Born in December	81
	Summary Chart of Months	83

Chapters		Page
24	What does your Birth Date indicate ? Numerological Horoscope	85
25	What is in a name ?	90
26	The Day for a move : How to find out a lucky day for a specific purpose	93
27	How to find out the day of the week from the birth date	97
28	Tracing things lost	99
29	The Pyramid System	103
30	Horse Racing	106
31	Epilogue	108
	Part Two : Palmistry	
	Preface	111
32	Introduction : a) Causes of discredit, b) Origin and History of the Science, c) Utility of the study, d) Some of the standard objections and arguments raised against this science	116
33	Preliminaries	124
34	The Shape of the Hand	126
35	The Division of the Hand	137
36	Skin, Colour, Consistency and Flexibility of Hands	142
37	Fingers	145
38	The Thumb	160
39	The Nails	168
40	The Mounts on the Hand	171
	The Mount of Jupiter	174
41	The Mount of Saturn	179
42	The Mount of Apollo	183
43	The Mount of Mercury	186
44	The Mount of Mars	190
45	The Mount of Moon	194
46	The Mount of Venus	197
47	The Mounts of Uranus and Neptune	201
48	The Lines on the Hand	205
49	The Line of Life	217
50	The Line of Head	229
51	The Line of Fate	241
52	The Line of Heart	250
53	The Line of Apollo	256
54	The Line of Mercury	260
55	The Girdle of Venus	264
56	The Line of Marriage	266
57	The Lines of Children	270
58	The Line of Intuition	271
59	The Lines of Travel	272
60	The Line of Mars	275
61	The Line of Via Lasciva	277
62	The Bracelets	279
63	Useful Charts	281

Introduction

There are more things in heaven and earth, Horatio,
Than are dreamt of in your philosophy.
—Shakespeare

It is a matter of prolonged and bitter controversy whether subjects like numerology, palmistry, astrology, tarot and others are based on any scientific foundation. For thousands of years these subjects have been practised in all countries and at all times and even scientists and the educated people have been taking valuable tips from scholars of these subjects at critical moments in their lives. Even the topmost political leaders who mould the destiny of their nations, take advice from astrologers, palmists and mystics and enquire about their own destiny. It is a matter of great interest that during the Second World War, Hitler used to consult his astrologer on many occasions. However, when the astrologer found that after getting repeated success in battles, Hitler had started ignoring his hints, he stopped serving him. He then approached the then British Prime Minister Mr. Winston Churchill who consulted the astrologer till the end of the war. It is said that the great Emperor Napoleon Bonaparte used to spell his name as Napoleone Buonapart. But on the advice of a Numerologist he omitted the letters 'e' and 'u' from his name and heightened the power of his personality and became the Emperor. In spite of the liberal use of these mystic subjects (as they are called), in everyday life, they have never been acknowledged as scientific till today. They are therefore emperical sciences. Every experience is knowledge and therefore useful in day-to-day life. Even though these subjects do not fulfil the tests of science, a day may come when all such esoteric subjects will come within the purview of science. History shows that such subjects have played wonderful role in life and have given vast information which is still beyond the comprehension of modern science. It may please be remembered that in this atomic age, even trivialities contain immense power, the atom being equal to the whole in the importance of its existence. If, therefore, numerology, palmistry and other subjects be considered by the scientists too trivial for their attention, I would point out that many of the greatest truths the world has known, though once considered trifles, have become sources of tremendous force. I may cite an incident which proves the validity of the Chinese system of Tablets. Once some Russian monks wanted to meet the world-famous palmist 'Cheiro' who had disappeared and whose whereabouts were not known. The Chinese experts on the System of Tablets informed the Russian monks that they would find Cheiro in South America in a cave and that he would have a statue of Budha with him. After strenuous search at various places in South America, the Russian monks finally arrived at a cave which, they thought, could be the place where Cheiro was residing. They stood in front of the cave and enquired loudly whether there was anybody inside. An old man came out and asked what they wanted. In order to find out whether the old man was Cheiro himself, the monks just asked him whether he had a statue of Budha. Surprisingly enough, the old man answered in the affirmative. Convinced, the monks said "Then you must be Cheiro", and he was Cheiro.

How the System of Tablets could give such remarkable information is really a matter of surprise. Several such incidents and examples can be quoted. I will narrate one more example from my own experience. It was in 1980 that I was speaking to an audience of people who would not believe that such esoteric subjects could sometimes perform miracles. I wanted to prove to them that miracles do happen and, in fact, there must be some scientific laws and forces which might be working behind these miracles but that the present day science does not have sensitive instruments capable of discovering these forces. To prove my statement I showed them a pendulum and told them that with the help of that pendulum, I could answer any question put to me. I started my experiments and the first was to find out the number which was thought of by an individual sitting in the audience. The second experiment was to find out the message written in a note which was folded and kept before me. In the third experiment, I was given four x-ray photographs which were kept flat on the table ; with the help of the pendulum I had to spot out the defects shown by the x-rays. I was successful in all the three tests and naturally the audience was very much impressed ; it conceded that what I did was not a trick but a genuine miracle.

Mystery or miracle is correlated to explanation ; it means Something intelligible enough as a fact, but not accounted for, not reduced to any law, principle or reason. The ebb and flow of the tides, the motions of the planets, satellites and comets were understood as facts at all times, but they were regarded as mysteries until Newton brought them under the laws of motion and gravity. Such is the case with the study of numerology and palmistry. Though it has been considered as an occult study uptil now, the time is not far when science can prove that it does not have the occult symbol it carried with it, but can be studied and practised like any other science. Experience has been and will continue to be the great teacher in the technique of numerology and hand-reading. Experience is an effective teacher but we should be saved from the sad waste of needless experience. Palmistry and numerology have long felt the inadequacy of mere experience and are now reaching out for all the help that can be obtained from all growing sciences.

There is no doubt that prophecies are often falsified by subsequent events. The reason for this must be sought not in the unscientific nature of this study, but in our ignorance of the causes at work. The laws of biology are not always borne out by subsequent events, but no one would, on that ground, deny that biology is a science. The year of change in life can often be predicted farther in advance than the coming of a cyclone. Hence, the claim of numerology and palmistry to be regarded as a science cannot be denied on the ground that numerologists and palmists lack precision and prophetic power. The study of these subjects is just like the study of any other language. Once the grammar is digested, the language of numerology and palmistry is clear and understandable.

In this book I intend to describe how numerology and palmistry can help us to improve our prospects in life by understanding and realising our own selves by psycho-analysis. This book is divided into two parts; the first part deals with the study of numerology and the second part deals with the study of palmistry. I shall be dealing only with the salient features of the science of these subjects.

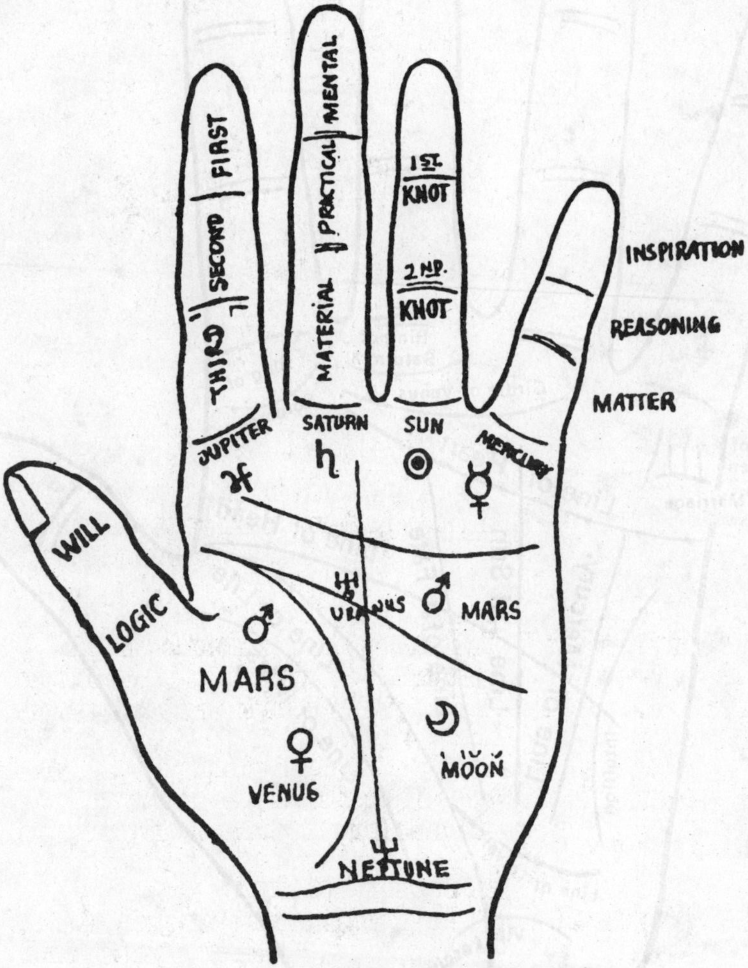

Fig 1 General Hand [Map of the Hand]
Mounts and their signs

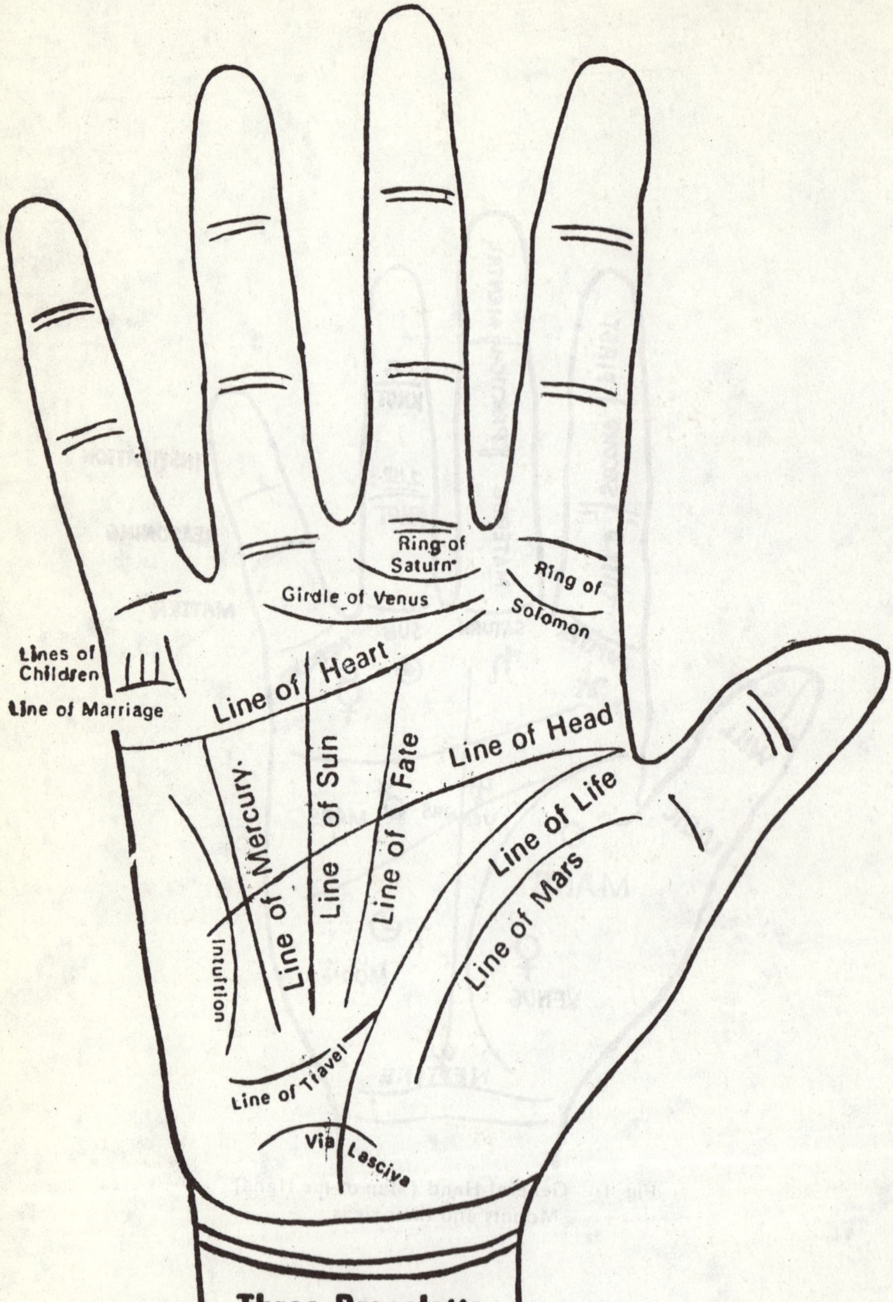
Ring of Saturn
Ring of Solomon
Girdle of Venus
Lines of Children
Line of Marriage
Line of Heart
Line of Head
Line of Mercury
Line of Sun
Line of Fate
Line of Life
Line of Mars
Intuition
Line of Travel
Via Lasciva
Three Braceletts

Fig. 2: Map of the Hand

CHAPTER 1

Part One : The Study of Numerology

History of Numerology

Man has landed on the Moon and scientists are busy getting control over the physical and mechanical planes. However, in doing so they have completely ignored the occult or the psychic side of the human being. For example, the mystery behind number seven or number nine has remained unsolved. The ancients considered number seven as a spiritual number and the number 142857 as the sacred number. But their methods and calculations have ever remained a mystery. The Hindus discovered that the precession of the Equinoxes takes place every 25827 years, but how or by what means they could arrive at such a calculation, has never been discovered.

We cannot rule out the idea that in bygone years the secrets were revealed to man by his more close connection with the God force. According to the Hindus, the Vedas which form the knowledge of human life and which describe several esoteric subjects, were revealed to man by God. In the Bible, we note certain ages when God walked with man. Even in the works of Greek philosophers we find an age described as one when the Gods talked with man and taught him the mysteries of creation. If we believe that there is a moment for birth and a moment for death, then as a logical sequence, we have to believe that there is a moment for each and every event in life from birth to death. That is why the ancient scholars had a foundation for ascribing to every human being his number in the universe. Not only this, but they believed that numbers have personalities, character and even sex.

The ancient people, such as the Hindus, the Egyptians and the Chaldeans, were masters of the occult significance of numbers but in the process of transmitting their knowledge to posterity, the key to the knowledge was lost. Thereafter this science fell into the hands of charlatans. For several centuries, the science of numerology has been taught to the students by their predecessors and has been practised in different countries. But the true origin and the fool-proof theories of these numbers have been lost to humanity for ever.

Apart from the question of mystical associations, the numbers themselves have a very ancient origin. We shall, however, never know the genius who actually invented the numbers. According to Prof. Max Muller, numbers were first invented by the Arabs. But it seems that the Arabs borrowed the knowledge from the Hindus who in their own turn (according to belief) acquired it from God.

The subject of numerology had absorbed the interest of the most profound thinkers of bygone days. We get references to figures and numbers in the Vedas and in the Upanishads. The Chinese considered odd numbers as denoting white, day, the Sun, heat and fire. They believed that even numbers indicated dark, night, the Moon, cold, water and earth. They incorporated into their culture the Phoenecian alphabets and its sounds and letters as well. Gematrica was the earliest form which revealed the hidden powers of numbers. It ascribed to every letter two values, one of sound and the other of number. The same system is followed even in the modern form of numerology.

The landmark in the history of numerology is Pythagoras. The discoveries of the Pythogoreans were numerous. They postulated the ten fundamental oppositions. 1) Odd and even 2) Limited and unlimited 3) One and many 4) Right and left 5) Male and female 6) Rest and motion 7) Straight and curved 8) Light and darkness 9) Good and evil 10) Square and oblong. It was their contention that the universe is the realisation of these opposites. Even numbers were considered soluble and consequently ephemeral, feminine and pertaining to the earth. Odd numbers were considered insoluble, masculine and of a celestial nature.

A whole science of number interpretation was developed by Pythagoras. He established a study centre at Crotona where this subject was taught and oaths of secrecy were taken. Later on, Plato accepted the qualities assigned to numbers by Pythagoras.

Theory of Numerology

It is based on the theory of vibrations and Cosmic Energy. In this Universe or the Cosmos, there are innumerable energies and forces which have their own vibrational force. If we can tune up our mind force to any of these forces, we can get tremendous energy. There are people who are gifted or have developed powers such as telepathy, clairaudience, clairvoyance etc., because they have the capacity to absorb the Cosmic Energy. One of the techniques of absorbing these energies is the use of the power of the numbers. Every individual is a constituent of the Universal Energy and emits waves and vibrations and radiates the mind force through numbers and colours of the planets he represents. The moment he is born, he is governed by a certain principal planet and a secondary planet and is governed by the numbers alloted to those planets. He thus starts radiating the vibrations of that number or the planet by which he is governed. His psychology, thinking, reason, emotions, ambition, likes, dislikes, health, career etc., are all dominated by the number he represents. If that number is in harmony with the number of any other person, he will experience a harmonious relationship with the other person. If on the contrary, his number is in opposition to that of his friend, the two can never live in harmony with each other. We can experience this theory of vibrations when we are travelling in a train or a bus coach. We may travel hundreds of miles through the train but we will never develop a friendship with a co-passenger if his number and rays emitted by him do not harmonise with our number and our waves. But sometimes we may experience the opposite. We may develop friendship with a passenger who is sitting at a distance from us and we enjoy our journey through discussions, talks and jokes with that person. If we try to analyse the facts, we will find that there was no apparant reason as to why we did not talk to or create companionship with the first type of passenger even though he was sitting next to us, and why we developed companionship with another passenger who was actually sitting a little away from us. But the answer lies in the theory of vibrations. Every individual is emitting vibrations which create either apathy or attraction towards another. This experience is sufficient to understand the unseen forces that govern all of us. The masters who studied these unknown forces and their results found out the answer in the existence of numbers which an individual is influenced by.

Utility of the study of Numerology

If by our study of numbers, we are able to find out the laws of nature that affect our lives, we shall be more happy, healthy and successful in life if we are in harmony and move with such laws. If we can increase the power of our number by constantly repeating it and making use of that number in each and every action, we can absorb the cosmic energy and benefit by that energy. It will add to our personality. We have several self-improvement goals, such as, improving our personality, improving our speech, improving our prospects in business, etc., similarly the study of numerology will improve our life and prosperity by increasing the vibrational force of our personality and lessening the intensity of our difficulties and obstructions.

I take the liberty to narrate one or two instances from my experience which will convince the readers of the practical utility of the study of Numerology.

A few years ago a businessman manufacturing electronic goods approached me and told me that he was trying for a collaboration with another big industry, but somehow, the actual documentation was being postponed and the contract could not be finalized. After working out his birth date and the name, I suggested to him to make a small change in his name and add one more 'a' to his name. In order that he should get quick results, he should go on writing his name with the new addition at least twenty to thirty thousand times. Surprisingly enough his long awaited contract was finalised within three weeks.

On another occasion, a relative of mine had complained about her two year old daughter who was extremely hot tempered and would go on crying for hours together. The daughter was a problem to the parents and they had to divert all their attention to her only. I studied the birth date and the name of the daughter and found that there was a disparity in the vibrations created by the birth date and the name. I suggested to change her name and repeat it at least twenty to thirty thousand times. After about five weeks, there was a remarkable change in the temper of the daughter and she showed considerable improvement in her behaviour.

One of my friends is governed by the number 4 and it is his experience that this number 4 is haunting him. He hardly escapes the influence of number 4 in the events in his life. He therefore decided to take full advantage of this number. Once he visited the place Las Vegas in America and found that a particular day was fully affected by number 4 and he decided to try his luck in gambling and tried the game cassino. He wanted to occupy chair number 4 and wanted to start the game at 4 pm. He played with his $ 40 and at the end he came out successfully with $ 4000.

On another occasion he wanted to prove his conviction to another of his friends and both of them decided to go to a cinema show. His friend purchased the tickets and the ticket numbers were 13 and 14. He purposely occupied the seat no. 14 (which makes a total of 5) and asked his friend to occupy the chair with no. 13 (making a 4). After about half an hour, a lady sitting behind requested my friend to exchange the seats if possible because the picture was not quite visible to her. He therefore exchanged the seats and occupied the chair no. 13 and his friend occupied the chair no. 14. Thus even against his wishes he was forced to occupy a chair the number of which was 4 when reduced to a single digit.

It is my experience that if the number 4 is dominant in the case of ladies, i.e. if they are born on 4th, 13th, 22nd and 31st of any month, they are of great will power, uneasy and very dominant. They are headstrong and sometimes even cruel. They always make others dance to their tunes. This is more so if they are born during the period of Mars and on the 22nd of the month such as 22nd March, 22nd April, 22nd October, 22nd November and even 22nd December. I request my readers to compare my experience with their own experience.

People have often come to me for suggesting to them a suitable name before they start an industry or print their letter heads. Several such instances can be quoted but the theory and the incidents quoted above are sufficient to understand the vibrational force of the numbers and their dominance in our life.

Alongwith the study of numerology, lucky colours and lucky stones are also recommended. The theory of vibration is equally applicable to colours or precious stones and therefore these aspects also have been dealt with in this book.

With this much introduction, I shall proceed with the interpretation of numbers, their importance and dominance and use in our life and how we can take the help of these numbers to improve our lot in life and achieve success, health and wealth.

Importance of Numbers

a) Basic facts about numbers

Voltaire has said "There is no such thing as chance. We have coined this word to express the known effect of every unknown cause." If then, chance does not explain the significant repetition of numbers, how shall we account for the mystical meanings which have also been attached to them from time immemorial ? We have to have faith in our ancestors that they had direct contact with God from whom they received the secrets of life. There is an old system of numerology known as the Kabala of Numbers. "Kabala" (Quaballah) means 'received from God'. As stated in the introduction, we cannot disregard the view that God walked with man and taught him the secrets of life.

i) Lucky and unlucky numbers : Quite often, a question is asked as to whether there are certain numbers which are considered lucky and certain others unlucky numbers. In the study of Numerology, there are no lucky or unlucky numbers as such. What is a lucky number for one person may be an unlucky number for another. It all depends upon what number one is governed by. Even then, in the past, some people have thought of certain numbers as unlucky. For instance, the Romans regarded even numbers as 'unlucky'. An independent importance is given to number 3. Most of the faiths of the world have recognised a trinity, for instance Brahma-Vishnu-Mahesh ; Horos-Isis-Osiris : Dharma-Artha -Kama. From earliest times sacrifices and vows have been repeated three times. There is a common superstition that events take place in threes and that the third time will be lucky. There is a story of Jesus. At the age of 12, Jesus was lost for 3 days. At 30 he took up his 3 years' mission. He accepted 12 apostles of whom one was to betray him for 30 pieces of silver and deny him 3 times. It is still the custom to bury the dead three days after the death. In the Church, the banns of marriage are read three times. Pythagoras and Aristotle based their philosophy on a triplet—Creation, Formation and Destruction.

Similarly, a separate importance is given to number 7. It is considered a mystic number. We have seven heavens, seven seas, seven wonders of the world, seven churches, seven thrones, seven days of the week etc.

ii) Odd and Even Numbers : As stated in the introduction, Pythagoras considered even numbers as soluble and consequently ephemeral, feminine and pertaining to the earth. Odd numbers were considered insoluble, masculine and of a celestial nature. The Chinese held similar views about odd and even numbers. They considered odd numbers as denoting white, day, the Sun, heat and fire which have masculine qualities.

They also believed that even numbers indicated dark, night, the Moon, cold, water and earth which have feminine characteristics. In the study of Numerology, there is a system of Pyramids, which I will deal with later on in these pages. According to the system of Pyramids, a question is asked spontaneously and instantaneously which is then expressed in numbers. These numbers are added and written in the shape of a Pyramid. Finally, there remains a single number. If that number is odd, it shows success ; if it is even, it shows failure. If the question is about a child, whether a woman would beget a son or a daughter, an even number foretells a daughter and an odd number indicates a son.

iii) Fear of number 13 : There are opposite views about the significance of this number. According to the West, this is not a lucky number. This is because this number is associated with the fact that 13 sat down to the Last Supper. The psychological impact of this occurrence is so much on the human mind that it is said that even in some of the hospitals in the west, a 13th bed is avoided but tactfully. However in the

East, this number has been singled out as an omen of good fortune. The opposition of the Church to occultism was one of the principal reasons why this number became taboo. It is stated that it would be unlucky if 13 were to eat together and that one of the 13 would die within the year. There is another cause why there is a fear of this number. The occult symbolism that stood for number 13 was represented by a mystic picture of "A skeleton with a scythe in its bony hands reaping down men." Nobody could understand its real significance and it was considered as an unlucky number. It can have an unlucky significance if the number 13 emerges by chance only and not purposefully.

iv) Significance of number 0 : '0' stands for infinity, the Infinite boundless being, the origin of all things, the Brahmanda or the egg of the universe, the solar system in its entirety. Therefore it signifies universality, cosmopolitanism. It also stands for negation and limitation. Thus, 0 means the infinitely great and the infinitely small. It means the circle of infinity and the point at the centre, the atom.

v) Special characteristics of numbers 4 and 8 : It has been observed in the study of numerology that those who are governed by these two numbers are always haunted by them. These two numbers go on establishing their dominance in the career of the individual and these numbers will always recur on several important occasions. For instance, supposing the man starts writing an important letter, he will find that the date on which he is writing the letter, is the 4th, 13th or 22nd or 31st of the month. In case he is dominated by number 8, the date will be 8th, 17th or 26th of the month. If such an individual enters into a contract or purchases a new car or a house, the date will usually be in the series of 4 or 8. As a general rule, numbers 4 and 8 indicate delays and difficulties in life though they have other positive and good qualities. If the individuals governed by 4 or 8 or both find it that the events that have taken place on these days have created hardship or obstacles in their progress, it is better to avoid these dates and numbers while deciding upon important moves. In that case, a person governed by number 4 should try to take his decisions on number 1 or 2 series and a person dominated by number 8 should take his actions on a 3 or 7 series.

I have observed that those who are born in April or August (4th and 8th month) and also have dates in the series of 4 and 8 have children who are dominated by either of the two numbers. At least one or two children out of the 4 are born in these series.

b) Affinity of Numbers

1) Numbers and their friends and planets : There are 9 planets and they are represented by 9 different numbers. In the birth date, there are only numbers, for instance, take a person born on 6–3–1956. These numbers indicate planetary influences. The planets as well as the numbers have harmonious vibrations with certain other planets and numbers. Following is the relation between planets and the numbers.

Number	*Planet*	*Friendly numbers*	*Unfriendly numbers*
1	Sun	1,3,4,5,7,9	2,6,8,
2	Moon	2,4,6,9	1,3,5,7,8
3	Jupiter	1,3,5,6,7,8,9	2,4
4	Uranus	1,2,4,5,7,8,9	3,6
5	Mercury	1,3,4,5,7,8	2,6,9
6	Venus	2,3,6,9	1,4,5,7,8
7	Neptune	1,3,4,5,7,8,9	2,6
8	Saturn	3,4,5,7,8	1,2,6,9
9	Mars	1,2,3,4,6,7,9	5,8

2) Months and their Planets : Each month has a dominance of a particular planet and the month has an affinity or attraction towards certain other months. These months and planets are as under.

Month	*Planet*	*Months of affinity*
January	Saturn	January, April, July, October.
February	Saturn	February, May, August, November.
March	Jupiter	March, June, September, December.
April	Mars	April, July. October, January.
May	Venus	May, August, November, February.
June	Mercury	June, September, December, March.
July	Moon	July, October, January, April.
August	Sun	August, November, February, May.
September	Mercury	September, December, March, June.

Month	*Planet*	*Moths of affinity*
October	Venus	October, January, April, July
November	Mars	November, February, May, August.
December	Jupiter	December, March, June, September.

3) *Square of Affinity* : From the above table of affinity, we observe that each month has an affinity towards every third month. Thus, the month January has an affinity towards the months of April, July, October and the month January itself. This forms a square which is represented as follows.

← January ←
April October
→ July →

4) *Rasis (Zodiacal Signs) and their periods* :

	Rasis	*Period*
1)	Aries (Mesh)	21st March to 20th April
2)	Taurus (Vṛishabha)	21st April to 20th May
3)	Gemini (Mithuna)	21st May to 20th June
4)	Cancer (Katak)	21st June to 20th July
5)	Leo (Simha)	21st July to 20th August
6)	Virgo (Kanya)	21st August to 20th September
7)	Libra (Tula)	21st September to 20th October
8)	Scorpio (Vrischika)	21st October to 20th November
9)	Sagittarius (Dhanu)	21st November to 20th December
10)	Capricorn (Makara)	21st December to 20th January
11)	Aquarius (Kumbha)	21st January to 20th February
12)	Pisces (Meena)	21st February to 20th March

5) *Division of the Rasis into four parts* : There are four elements, fire, earth, air and water. These elements (Tatwas) indicate their characteristics and the 12 Rasis are divided into these four elements. A person born under a particular Rasi is representative of the element and has his basic qualities according to the element. The elements also show the dangers the person is likely to undergo. For instance, a person governed by the element of fire, should be careful about electricity, stove, burning gas, heat etc. A person governed by the element water should be careful while swimming or crossing a river. A person with air element runs the danger of falling down from great heights or in air travels and finally a person with earth element has to be careful about snakes, horses and other

animals and accidents with vehicles. The periods covered by these elements are explained below.

a) *Fire* : 21st March to 20th April ; 21st July to 20th August ; 21st November to 20th December.

b) *Earth* : 21st April to 20th May ; 21st August to 20th September ; 21st December to 20th January.

c) *Air* : 21st May to 20th June ; 21st September to 20th October ; 21st January to 20th February.

d) *Water* : 21st June to 20th July ; 21st October to 20th November ; 21st February to 20th March.

c) The Ruling Number and the Fadic Number

There are two types of numbers in a birth date which play an important role in a person's life. As an example, we take a birth date such as 16–2–1948.

The Ruling Number : In the above birth date, 16 is the date of the month. We have to reduce this date to a single digit, 1 + 6 = 7. This number 7 is the ruling number of the person. It is also considered as the lucky number. All the dates of the month where the final digit comes to 7, such as 16 and 25 are lucky dates and the person should take all important actions on these dates. Supposing he wants to ask for a favour of his superiors, he should select one of these dates for the purpose. If he wants to write an important letter, he should put this date on the letter.

Similarly, all the years in life where the final total after reducing it to a single digit is 7 are the important years for that person and usually auspicious events take place in these years. In the present case, the years 7, 16, 25, 34, 43, 52, 61 etc., are significant years. In order to arrive at the same single digit we have to go on adding the number 9 to the earlier figure.

If the date of birth is 12, the ruling number is 3 (1+2=3) You go on adding 9 to the number 3 and you arrive at the same single digit. Such as 3+9=12 (i.e. 3). 12+9=21 (i.e. 3). 21+9=30 (i.e. 3) etc. All these dates 3, 12, 21, 30 are lucky dates and all the years in life making up 3 are lucky years.

The Fadic Number : This is also called the 'Fate Number' or the 'Number of Destiny'. In this case, a total of all the

HOW NUMBERS AND ZODIACS RULE HUMAN BODY

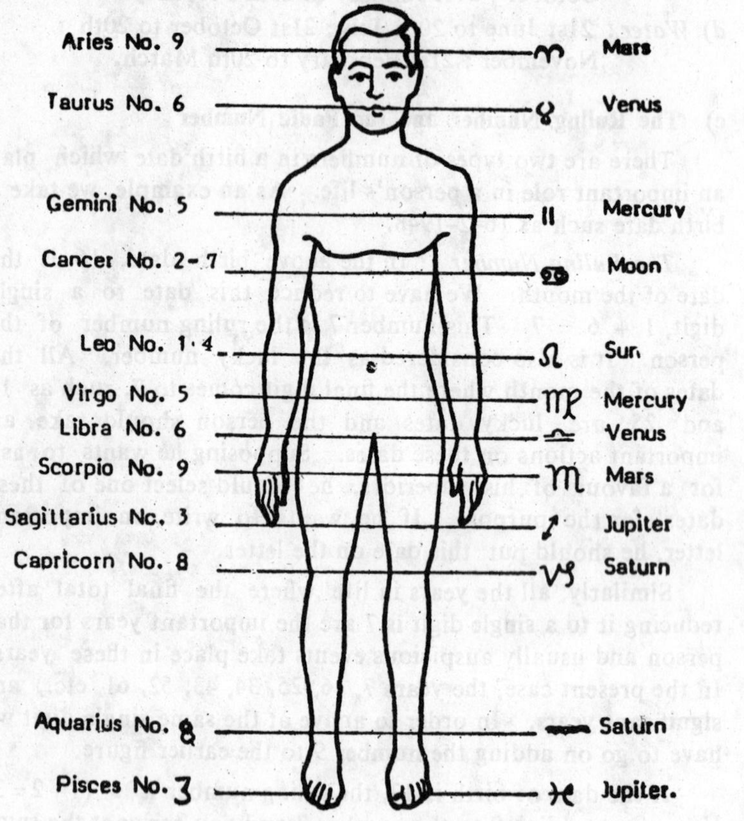

numbers in a birth date is to be taken. In the above illustration, the complete birth date is 16–2–1948. We have to add all the digits in the birth date, thus, $1+6+2+1+9+4+8=31$. Add $3+1=4$. This 4 is called the Fadic Number. The significance of this number is that it goes on repeating and recurring in the life of the person whether he desires it or not. The events that take place may be either good or bad but they are important and significant events and the person has no control over the number and the events.

Between the Ruling Number and the Fadic Number, the Ruling Number is more important, more lucky and more useful. One should take all important decisions and actions on the basis of one's ruling number only.

d) Influence of numbers and Rasis (Zodiacs) on the human body (See the figure on page 12).

Rasi	*No.*	*Planet*	*Part of the body dominated*
Aries	9	Mars	Head, brain
Taurus	6	Venus	Eyes, ears, nose, tongue, face
Gemini	5	Mercury	Hands, collar-bones, neck, respiratory track
Cancer	2	Moon	Heart, lungs, chest, blood
Leo	1	Sun	Heart, upper abdomen
Virgo	5	Mercury	Navel, bones, lower abdomen
Libra	6	Venus	Groins, semen, genitals,
Scorpio	9	Mars	Kidney, bladder
Sagittarius	3	Jupiter	Thighs and limbs
Capricorn	8	Saturn	Knees, bones and flesh
Acquarius	8	Saturn	Shanks and breathing
Pisces	3	Jupiter	Feet

For numbers 4 and 7 there are no separate Rasis but only the planets Uranus and Neptune are alloted to them.

CHAPTER 2

Significance of numbers from 1 to 9

How to find out the ruling number and the fadic number

In order to find out the significance of the **fadic** number in our life we can take into consideration our birth date. Supposing the birth date is 21–6–1948. We have now to total up all the numbers and in this case it works out as under: 2+1+6+1+9+4+8=31. We have again to add the numbers 3 and 1 whereby the final total is 4. In all cases we have to bring the total to a single digit. In the above example the total of all the numbers in the birth date is 4. This number is called the fadic number, that means many important events in our lives, whether good or bad will be governed by this number. This will be our **fadic** number. Suppose we have a failure in our college life or have won a gold medal, the date on which either of these events take place will be governed by the number 4 in which case either the total of all the numbers of that particular date will be 4 or the date of the month when the incident took place will be 4. To simplify the statement, let us suppose that the date of the incident is 9–12–1963. In this case the total comes to 31 and when reduced to a single digit it works out to 4. Alternately, the first date of the month of that incident may be either 4 or 13 or 22 or 31 which when reduced to a single digit makes 4.

Another method of finding out of the important and lucky number is to take only the date of the month. In the example taken above, the birth date is 21–6–1948 and the date of the month is 21, that is 3. This single number is considered as a lucky number. It means that number 3 and its multiple numbers are the lucky numbers and also the lucky years of the person born on 21st. He should make all his important moves and act on the date or dates which when converted into a single digit work out to 3, such as 3, 12, 21 and 30. This being his ruling number, he should do all his important correspondence on this date or its multiple. He should ask for a favour on this date or he should sign his important documents on this date and so forth. Similarly all the years in life which finally make 3, are the lucky and important years such as 3, 12, 21, 30, 39, 48, 57 etc.

After explaining how to find out our ruling number and the fadic number, I shall proceed further with the individual numbers from 1 to 9 and describe them from various angles.

CHAPTER 3

Number 1

All those born on the 1st, 10th, 19th and 28th of any month are governed by this number

Character

This number is governed by the planet Sun and shows originality, activity, energy, enthusiasm, art and brilliance. A person governed by this number is spontaneous, responds to nature and has the capacity to enjoy life. He is usually successful in life due to his active nature and capacity to mix in any society. He is an artist and has many talents but they are all spontaneous in nature. He has taste in everything and chooses always the beautiful. He is gifted with intuition and he hardly studies any subject by going deep into it. Even then he can influence others with his knowledge and flash. These characteristics make him a hero of the drawing room. He is changeable and is not constant in his friendship. He is honest and acknowledges his faults. He has a quick grasp of any subject and can participate spontaneously in conversation. He has a religious attitude but not in a fanatic or superstitious way. He also learns occult sciences and does wonders with his natural gift of intuition. By nature, he is cheerful, happy and bright and his outlook on life is very optimistic. A person born between 21st July and 20th August is also governed by number 1. He has strong will power and is independent in thought and action. On the one hand, he is practical, but on the other hand, he is idealistic. Sometimes he is obstinate and selfish. He is fond of inventions and has creative talents. He is a better judge of human nature than the average individual. He is born to lead, not to follow. A new idea is a greater thrill than money in the bank. He will always be young by reason of another new idea.

Finance

Number one person is a lucky person as far as his financial status is concerned. Even though he is extravagant due to his overenthusiastic personality, he also earns enough to maintain his ostentatious disposition in life. He may not amass wealth but his personality and behaviour will make others to believe that he is a rich person. He has a temptation for gambling and if not controlled in time, he may lose to a great extent.

Vocation

The main difficulty with a number 1 person is his attitude not to stick to any one profession or job for a long time. Usually, every three years there is a change in career. He is however suitable for advertising concerns, newspaper business, cinema industry and can also be successful in theatrical performances. He can show his art as an interior decorator. He being a good salesman, can choose his vocation which will have relations with foreign countries, such as an ambassadorship or a trade dealing in foreign commodities. He is a leader and can be the head of departments, a managing director etc. He can equally succeed as a surgeon, jeweller, electrician and in research projects.

Health

On the whole a number 1 person is a happy-go-lucky fellow and normally of good health. But he is also susceptible to certain health defects and has to be very particular about the following health troubles.

Heart trouble : With number 1 the heart trouble is a structural difficulty. This can be observed even in childhood.

Weak eye-sight : His another defect is poor eye-sight, sometimes even to the point of blindness.

Over-exertion : The most common trouble to be found with this number is over-exertion and he should always be on his guard and see that he is not exerting himself too much out of his over-enthusiasm. His straining too much is likely to make him susceptible to fevers.

Sun stroke : This is also a common weakness with him.

In addition to the above he is likely to suffer from bone fracture.

Marriage and Friends

Marriage : He has a natural attraction towards persons born in the period between 21st July and 20th August, between 21st November and 20th December and between 21st March and 20th April. It is therefore advisable that he selects his marriage partner from this period. He also has an affinity for those who are governed by numbers 1,3,4,5 and 7

Number 1 as husband: He is generous and desires his wife to shine in society. He wants his family members to dance to his tunes and will not tolerate disrespect. He has a kind and loving disposition and a noble heart.

Number 1 as wife : She is aristocratic by temperament and attracts people to her home and commands great respect. She needs a virile husband who can offer the romantic outlets that her passionate nature requires.

Number 1 person is always predisposed to marriage and he is fond of his helpmate provided his life partner is also of equal enthusiasm and has a love of beauty and of dress, at home and in public. It is however often seen that he hardly gets a companion of his choice, with the result that he is often disappointed in his married life.

Friends : His best friends are those who are governed by numbers 1, 3, 5, 7 and 9.

Fortunate Days

His lucky days are Sunday, Monday and Thursday.

Lucky Colours

He should use all shades of gold and yellow and also of orange and purple as his lucky colours.

Lucky Jewels and Stones

His lucky jewels are Ruby and Emerald and lucky stones are Moonstone and pale green stone.

Important Years in Life

His important years are 1, 19, 28, 37, 46, 55, 64, 73 etc.

His good qualities and drawbacks are as under

Good qualities	*Drawbacks*
Aspiration	Aloofness
Attack	Domination
Authority	Impertinence
Confidence	Inflexibility
Determination	Pride
Research	Showmanship
Vigour	Spendthrift nature

Special characteristics of those born on 10th, 19th and 28th of any month

Born on the 10th of the month: He is very impressive with a magnetic personality and is respected for his knowledge and intelligence. He gets financial benefits from relatives such as father, father-in-law, wife, mother etc. He gets success after his 46th year. He gets good position in service and succeeds in business also. He has broad shoulders and a manly figure. He loves truthfulness. This number shows honour and self-confidence. The person can get fame or notoriety depending upon his will-power and character. He usually has good health and quickly recovers from sickness. He likes to help others but hardly gets a response from them. This is particularly so in the case of relatives.

Born on the 19th of the month: He is very active, energetic and enthusiastic. He has research aptitude and likes to handle subjects in systematic and methodical ways. He takes quick decisions and always likes to keep himself busy in some concrete project. Sports is his hobby and he is interested in several games such as horse riding, shooting, and other athletic games. He is hasty and impetuous in love affairs which end in quarrels. He is courageous and has force of character. He likes to help others even going out of the way. He can maintain the secrets of others and others can confide in him. This number promises success, honour and happiness. It is very difficult for others to understand him. He is always in company but at heart feels lonely. He is obstinate and finds it difficult to extend co-operation. He is prudent and notices even a trivial thing. He is not an excellent speaker but can explain himself best in writing. He can be a good writer.

Born on the 28th of the month : He is very generous and spends on charitable works such as schools, institutions. hospitals etc. He is not as lucky as numbers 1, 10 and 19 and has to undergo difficulties in public and private life. He should select his marriage partner carefully. He has to provide carefully for the future as he is likely to lose through trust in others. He is also likely to make many changes in his career. He hardly reveals his emotions and therefore appears cold. He has an unyielding will power and does not hesitate to carry out his plans.

The study of numbers is nothing else but psycho-analysis. The deep rooted feelings, sentiments, emotions, ambitions and abilities are best represented by numbers. If one can know oneself through one's number, life will be easy and successful.

Please also refer to the individual month you are born in. Combine your characteristics, lucky days, colour and jewels shown by your number and also by the month you are born in and then find out the common factors and arrive at the final conclusion.

CHAPTER 4

Number 2

All those born on the 2nd, 11th, 20th and 29th of any month are governed by this number.

Character

This number is governed by the planet Moon. It shows high imagination, idealism and a dreamy nature. The person has fantasies and lacks a practical approach. He revels in his own dreams and therefore shuns society. He does not like to enjoy the company of others as he finds them too ordinary for his imaginary world.

He loves natural and beautiful things in life such as the sea, flowers, scenery and the vastness of the sky. He takes pleasure in spending hours in the company of the high tides of the sea or in rivetting his eyes to the galaxy of the stars in the sky.

He is very unsteady, fickle-minded and a lover of change. He therefore has a fancy for travel, especially long travels which would satisfy his urge for the life of the imagination. Such travels keep his imagination engaged and he will go on building castles in the air.

Persons born between 20th June and 20th July are also governed by number 2.

Finance

A person governed by this number is a lethargic fellow and is not capable of doing any hard work. He also does not have the physical capacity to stand the strain of everyday life. The outcome therefore is mediocre financial status. He however can improve his financial condition, provided he is able to create art out of his imagination. He may be a good author or a painter who can create novels and weird paintings and earn a good livelihood. However his unstable mind often drags him away from routine work and this creates uncertain sources of income. This person therefore is not stable as far as finance is concerned.

Vocation

The high imaginative power possessed by the number 2 person will help him to be a good composer of music or a writer of fiction or romance. He can as well be a good artist and can create works of ever-lasting value. Immortal paintings, dramas and splendid poems will be the outcome of a prominent and influential number 2. He has a great vocabulary and linguistic capacities among all numbers and can be successful as a teacher or a professor of various languages. He can also be a good translator or an editor.

Health

His main health problem is his poor blood circulation. He is susceptible to all sicknesses arising out of poor blood circulation such as anaemia and a weak heart.

Since the Moon is the ruling planet of number 2, the uneasiness which is a prominent characteristic, creates mental worries and sleeplessness. He is also susceptible to diabetes and asthmatic trouble

Marriage and Friends

Marriage : He has a natural attraction towards persons born in the period between 21st October and 20th November and between 19th February and 20th March. It is therefore advisable that he finds his marriage partner from this period. He also has an affinity for those who are governed by numbers 2, 4 and 6

Number 2 as husband: He has a natural love and attraction for home than any other type. There are two types of husbands belonging to this number, the one is dominating and exacting. He is fault-finding and nothing satisfies him. The other type is passive, lazy and indulgent. He will marry for the sake of money so that he may ultimately get comforts.

Number 2 as wife : She is sympathetic, affectionate and devoted. She is satisfied with anything her husband provides her with. However she is moody, changeable and sensitive.

A Number 2 person is cold and does not have the fire of passion. Sometimes he may select a partner who is either far older or younger than himself.

Friends : His best friends are those who are governed by numbers 2, 4, 6 and 9.

Fortunate Days

His lucky days are Mondays, Tuesdays and Fridays

Lucky Colours

A Number 2 person should use all shades of white, cream or blue as his lucky colours.

Lucky Jewels and Stones

His lucky jewels are pearls and diamonds and lucky stones are Moonstones and Agate.

Important Years in Life

His important years are 2, 11, 20, 29, 38, 47, 56, 65, 74 etc.

His good qualities and drawbacks are as under

Good qualities	*Drawbacks*
Emotionality	Coldness
Fellowship	Envy
Honesty	Haste
Imagination	Introvert
Simplicity	Shyness
	Whimsicality

Special characteristics of those born on the 11th, the 20th and the 29th of any month

Born on the 11th of the month : He is usually successful in life and in love and gets honour, position and authority. He is loyal to his friends and is of a royal disposition. He should guard himself from secret enemies. He has interest in mysticism, philosophy and science. He can expect travels, favours and honours in life.

Born on the 20th of the month : He has many friends and benefits through wealthy women. He has a flair for writing and can be known as an author or a novelist. His prosperity lies near water, river or the sea. This number has a peculiar significance. It shows new plans, and new resolutions for the betterment of people at large. If this number is used in connection with future events, it indicates delays.

Born on the 29th of the month : This person is moody and changing and therefore uncertain about his action. He is courageous and bold but takes risks in life and does not stick to anything till the end. He is intelligent and also a deep thinker but there is a tendency to carry everything to extremes. He is not very lucky in his married life. His interest is in his business.

As stated earlier, the study of numbers is nothing else but psycho-analysis. The deep-rooted feelings, sentiments, emotions, ambitions and abilities are best represented by numbers. If one can know oneself through one's number, life will be easy and successful.

Please also refer to the individual month you are born in. Combine your characteristics, lucky days, colours and jewels shown by your number and also by the month you are born in and then find out the common factors and arrive at the final conclusion.

CHAPTER 5

Number 3

All those born on the 3rd, 12th, 21st and 30th of any month and those between 19th February and 20th March and between 21st November and 20th December are governed by this number.

Character

This number is governed by the planet Jupiter. It stands for morality, pure love and justice with mercy and is known as the greatest beneficiary and the uplifter. The vibrations emitted by this number are essentially harmonious and they lead to sympathy and untiring effort to do good to all, devout piety and true dignity. The abuse of the same vibrations causes the stimulation of Jupiterian virtues leading to hypocrisy, especially in religious matters. The good nature is marred by excess in many directions.

He is usually lucky in life. Vibrations radiating through him attract all that is good to him and his affairs prosper as a consequence. The judge who gives sane decisions and merciful sentences, the physician and the church dignitary, the world's teachers and philosophers are all mostly governed by the number 3.

This is a good number. The person is confident about his ability. He is self-reliant and takes his own decisions. He has a habit of talking loudly. He is fond of show and likes to observe form, order and law. He is jovial in spirit and cordial in manner. His passions are healthy, spontaneous and without inhibitions. He is free in his expressions.

He takes an active interest in sports and outdoor activities from his earliest youth. He has tremendous enthusiasm and is not self-centered. His intellect is of a very high quality. He has a kind of vision that understands the world and loves it for what it is and not for what it ought to be. He is a broad-minded person, tolerant, humorous and truthful. He is open-hearted with good understanding and entirely lacking in malice or petty jealousies.

The main characteristics of number 3 person are, ambition, leadership, religion, pride, honour, love for nature, enthusiasm, generosity, respect and reverence.

Finance

He is a lucky type and somehow manages to earn enough for his livelihood. He also gets opportunities for higher grade positions in life and thereby earns quite a lot. His ambition, leadership and enthusiasm always push him forward and usually he gets all the comforts in life. The number 3 person is early out of puberty and poverty.

Vocation

His love for position and command makes him a politician. I have observed certain persons of this number occupying very high posts such as ministers, ambassadors, judges and secretaries. He is gifted for public life, statesmanship, high offices etc., it may be in the army or in the church. He is a good teacher as well as a preacher. Professions of doctors, bankers, advertisers and actors are also suitable for him.

Health

The number 3 has chief influence over the blood and the arterial system. It also governs the sense of smell. This person is liable to suffer from chest and lung disorders, throat afflictions, gout and apoplexy and sudden fevers. He may also suffer from sore throat, diphtheria, adenoids, pneumonia, pleurisy and tuberculosis of the lungs.

Marriage and Friends

Marriage : He has a natural attraction towards those born in the period from 21st June to 20th July and from 21st October to 20th November. It is therefore advisable that he finds his marriage partner from this period. He also has an affinity for those who are governed by numbers 3,6,7 and 9 .

Number 3 as husband: As a general rule, he attains puberty at an early age and marries early. However as he is ambitious, his ambitions also make him expect too many things from his wife and thus he becomes disappointed. He desires to have a wife of whom he should be proud. She should have an attractive personality, a commanding presence, charming manners and intelligence. It is always better for him to choose a number 3 person or a number 6 person as his life partner. He is most loving, thoughtful and considerate. His passions are adventurous and demand immediate satisfaction.

Number 3 as wife : She is the best companion to her husband. She is not an intruder but takes active interest in the business of her husband. She is efficient in house-keeping and has a sympathetic and balanced outlook on her children. Her passions are healthy and joyous and her approach to physical love is highly refined and inspiring.

Friends : His best friends are those who are governed by numbers 1, 3, 5, 6, 7, 8, 9.

Fortunate Days

His lucky days are Tuesdays, Thursdays and Fridays.

Lucky Colours

He should use all shades of yellow, violet, purple and green as his lucky colours.

Lucky Jewels and Stones

His lucky jewel is topaz and lucky stones are amethyst and cat's eye.

Important Years in Life

His important years are 3, 12, 21, 30, 39, 48, 57, 66, 75 etc.

His good qualities and drawbacks are as under

Good qualities	*Drawbacks*
Ambition	Cruelty
Dignity	Dictatorship
Individuality	Hypocrisy
Philosophy	Spendthrift nature
Prestige	Vanity

Special characteristics of those born on the 12th, the 21st and the 30th of any month

Born on the 12th of the month : Authority and honours are the significant aspects of this person. He has vanity and is proud, ambitious and aspiring. He is fond of pleasures and is attracted to the opposite sex. However sometimes he prefers loneliness. He likes to sacrifice for others but becomes a victim of others' plans or intrigues. His relations with others are smooth and harmonious. He is quick to notice trifles. He has lofty ideals.

Born on the 21st of the month : He is kind, generous and a loving father. He achieves fame, reputation and honours at a very late age. He is cheerful and fond of travel. He has a strong feeling of self respect. Surprisingly, he has a suspicious nature.

Born on the 30th of the month : He is fortunate, generous and optimistic. He has a noble and religious mind. He likes to travel and visit places of pilgrimage. He can be successful as a teacher, educationist or in administration. He appears gentle and sincere, but has a hidden characteristic. He may be active but is restless. When faced with difficulties, he is strong enough to overcome them.

Numbers help us to know ourselves. They guide us in knowing ourselves and various shades of our sentiments, emotions, ambition and abilities. We should try to understand the number ruling us and follow its indication.

By doing so we can overcome several of our difficulties and pitfalls and finally lead a healthy and successful life.

Please also refer to the individual month you are born in. Combine your characteristics, lucky days, colours, jewels shown by your number and also by the month you are born in and then find out the common factor and arrive at the final conclusion.

CHAPTER 6

Number 4

All those born on the 4th, 13th, 22nd and 31st of any month and those born between 21st June and 20th July and between 21st July and 20th August are governed by this number.

Character

This number is governed by the planet Uranus and shows energy, force and advancement. It shows revolution and unexpected happenings in life. Usually the changes that take place are for the better. This number represents the higher faculties of the mind. It shows activity and intelligence engaged in the reconstruction or the betterment of human life. The peculiar nature of this person is that he constantly aims at changes in life and society and is after the liberation of the mind from the bondage of environment and society. He dislikes hypocrisy and loves art and music. He has an attractive personality.

This number is considered as the negative part of number 1. It has the same characteristics as that of number 1, but these characteristics are in a dormant condition. It means that a number 4 person is required to be pushed forward so that he can show his abilities.

Because of his peculiar nature to oppose the views of others or to advance arguments, he is often misunderstood and makes a great number of secret enemies who constantly work against him.

Finance

As regards finance and monetary status, he is usually well settled in life though he experiences delays and difficulties in his undertaking. He may not amass wealth but can maintain the show of wealth. He is a spendthrift and his home is well decorated. His financial prosperity usually starts after the age of 40.

Vocation

He will be successful in trades such as transport, electricity and all sorts of machinery. He will equally be successful as an engineer, building contractor, scientist and industrialist. He is also attracted towards mystic subjects such as palmistry and astrology and can do well in these subjects also.

Health

His respiratory system is usually weak and he suffers from breathlessness. His knees, shanks and feet are also affected. Sometimes he suffers from urinary infection.

Marriage and Friends

Marriage : He has a natural attraction towards persons born in the period between 19th February and 20th March and between 21st October and 20th November. It is therefore advisable that he selects his marriage partner from this period. He also has an affinity for those who are governed by numbers 1, 2, 4, 7 and 8.

Number 4 as husband : He is shrewd and intelligent and expects his wife to share his views. He is dominating and wants all affairs of the house to be run as per his desire. He is generous and has a kind and loving heart.

Number 4 as wife : She is smart and attractive. She has the art of dressing and has a strong will-power. She aims at several things but hardly succeeds in getting mastery over one. She loves interior decoration but does not have the capacity to work hard for it and she will get it done through others. She is many-times dictatorial and moody and spoils her day due to her own whimsical nature. She loves her home but is not attached to it very much. She is often uneasy and it is better for her to find a friend governed by number one or two.

Friends : He is fond of friends and company but hardly gets a close friend because of his unsteady, changing and moody nature. He will get his close friends who are influenced by numbers 1, 2, 4, 5, 7, 8, 9.

Fortunate Days

His lucky days are Sundays, Mondays and Saturdays.

Lucky Colours

His lucky colours are electric blue, electric grey, white and maroon.

Lucky Jewels and Stones

Lucky jewels are Diamond, Coral and Pearl.

Important Years in Life

His important years are 4, 13, 22, 31, 40, 49, 58, 67, 76 etc.

His good qualities and drawbacks are as under

Good qualities	*Drawbacks*
Activity	Changeablity
Endurance	Domination
Energy	Stubbornness
Realiability	Vindictiveness
Method and System	Zealousness

Special characteristics of those born on the13th, the 22nd and the 31st of any month

Born on the 13th of the month : He is an intelligent person, of tall stature and good complexion. He is considerate and benevolent. He likes literature and scientific books. He likes to remain active though in a peaceful way. He occupies positions of high responsibilities and gets riches. His success and career start after his 31st year. Though outwardly he looks mild, inwardly, he is obstinate. He is faithful and sympathetic but has difficulty in expressing his love. He has all the qualities of number 4 but in an exaggerated form.

Born on the 22nd of the month : He is also tall, with good eyes. Usually he occupies good positions but without much responsibility. He is rather easygoing, unsteady in nature. Sometimes his actions are spasmodic. On the whole he is lucky in his affairs and benefits from the opposite sex. He is happy with his family life but is also fond of a companion. He is faithful and dedicated to others. Sometimes, he feels very lonely. His social field is limited and he has few friends. He does not care for disputes. He has too much economy of sentiments.

Born on the 31st of the month : This date shows ambition, pride and austerity. He is interested in honourable occupations such as working with charitable institutions, institutions for the deaf and dumb, the physically handicapped etc. He gets success after his 40th year but he expects quick results and early reputation. He is lucky in financial matters. He is realistic and of strong will power. He has a strong attraction for the opposite sex. He loves travelling.

The study of numbers is nothing else but psycho-analysis. The deep-rooted feelings, sentiments, emotions, ambitions, abilities are best represented by numbers. If one can know oneself through one's number, life will be easy and successful.

Please also refer to the individual month you are born in. Combine your characteristics, lucky days, colours and jewels shown by your number and also by the month you are born in and then find out the common factors and arrive at the final conclusion.

CHAPTER 7

Number 5

All those born on 5th, 14th and 23rd of any month and those born between 21st May and 20th June and between 21st August and 20th September are governed by the number 5.

Character

This number is governed by the planet Mercury and it shows shrewdness, quickness, scientific pursuits, business ability, industry, intuition and diplomacy. A person governed by this number is active and quick and this does not pertain to physical agility only but to the mental side as well. He is very skilful and has an intuitive faculty. He is equally proficient in games where he uses his hands as well as his brain. He has the capacity to judge the ability of his opponents in games and knows very well how to take advantage of the weak points of his opponents. He is fond of oratory and eloquence in expressing himself. He has the capacity to pursue his objectives and knows very well how to plan for achieving his ends. He is deeply interested in occult subjects and has a fancy to master all the intricacies of such abstruse subjects.

He is a nervous person. He is therefore restless. He has an intuitive perception and has the capacity to be either good or bad. On the good side, he is a shrewd person and not vicious or criminal. He is fond of family life and loves children. His pleasure are mainly mental and he evaluates everything in terms of business.

Finance

Since number 5 is a business number, the person can expect opulence. With his shrewd characteristics, he is capable of developing his industry, carrying out his plans systematically with the result that he gets good returns for the efforts he has put in. He is lucky as far as his financial position is concerned.

Vocation

He is adaptable to the role he has to play in the drama of life. With his adaptability he comes in contact with various classes of people and becomes successful in whatever he accepts in business. Banking is a good business for him. The planet Mercury also shows ability for medicine or surgery. His capacity to argue his points can make him a good lawyer.

Health

His basic health defect is his biliousness and nervousness. However his biliousness has close relation with his psychological disturbance. Experience shows that his biliousness increases with the increase in tension and the same is reduced or disappears when his nervous trouble is under control.

Number 5 rules over nerves, neck, arms, ears and the respiratory system.

Marriage and Friends

Marriage : He has a natural attraction towards persons born in the period between 21st September and 20th October and between 21st January and 20th February. It is therefore advisable that he finds his marriage partner from this period. He also has an affinity for those who are governed by numbers 1,5,7 and 8

Number 5 as husband : He is lucky and successful in his married life. His selection is good and usually he selects a person of his own type. He loves his partner. He expects neatness and cleanliness from his partner and also desires that his partner should share with him the enjoyment of life. He is proud of his wife and likes to see her well-dressed. In return, he proves himself to be a good husband. He loves his children and is fond of home. Even if he travels long, he is very much attracted towards home and is eager to return early and be amongst the members of his family. He is liberal in spending on clothing and other wants of the members of his family and furnishes his house with good taste.

Number 5 as wife : She has interest at home as well as outside. She has many activities and manages them well. She likes tidiness and, though she seldom does her own work, she gets it done through her commanding personality.

Friends : His best friends are those who are governed by numbers 1, 3, 4, 5, 7 and 8.

Fortunate Days

His lucky days are Wednesdays, Fridays and Saturdays.

Lucky Colours

His lucky colours are white and green. He should not use red colour.

Lucky Jewels and Stones

His lucky jewels are Emerald and Diamond. He may use Sapphire also.

Important Years in Life

His important years are 5, 14, 23, 32, 41, 50, 59, 68, 77 etc.

His good qualities and drawbacks are as under :

Good qualities	*Drawbacks*
Co-operation	Lack of perseverance
Practicality	Scepticism
Shrewdness	Unreliability
Vigilance	

Special characteristics of those born on the 14th, the 23rd of any month

Born on 14th of the month : This person has an attractive personality and is liked by all. His nature is co-operative and he does not like to provoke others. He usually occupies a good position in life and is successful in his business. He is not talkative but slightly reserved. This is an intelligent and shrewd number. In women, it indicates good marriage but they should take care in child bearing. A number 14 man is inconsistant in love and experiences some romantic and impulsive attachment in early years. He is fortunate in money matters.

Born on the 23rd of the month : He is usually popular amongst women. His fortune is near the water. He is successful in life and enjoys honour and wealth. He may get money through inheritance. He keeps himself busy in his own way. He gets help from superiors and gets protection from them. He is a lucky person.

The study of numbers is nothing but psycho-analysis. The deep-rooted feelings, sentiments, emotions, ambition and abilities are best represented by numbers. If one can know oneself through one's number, life will be easy and successful.

Please also refer to the individual month you are born in. Combine your characteristics, lucky days, colour and jewels shown by your number and also by the month you are born in and then find out the common factors and arrive at the final conclusion.

CHAPTER 8

Number 6

All those born on the 6th, 15th, and 24th of any month and those born between the period 21st April to 20th May and 21st September to 20th October are governed by this number.

Character

This number is governed by the planet Venus which stands for love, sympathy and adoration. A person governed by this number is a born artist and love for art and beauty in life have an attraction for him. He is a pleasant personality to meet. It is always charming to be with him. His company is full of enthusiasm, energy and charm. His talk is interesting and lively. We may sometimes be required to put aside our ideas of morality and social conduct in understanding and appreciating his feelings and discussions. Number 6 stands for beauty, health, vitality, warmth, attraction and above all love. A person of this number is fond of music, dancing and poetry. He loves to have a life full of ease and luxuries, money and happiness. He prefers spending to saving. He will have rich clothes, jewellery, perfumes and all sorts of beautiful things.

He is necessarily a loving type and he has a feeling of kinship and humanity. He will therefore not desert his friends and always likes to understand the grievances and difficulties of others with a considerate approach. He prefers joy to gloom and has the capacity to carry others along with him to participate in the moments of enjoyment. His outlook is bright and vivacious.

Finance

He is not attracted towards money and accumulation of wealth is not his aim in life. All his interest is directed towards attaining pleasures and gratifying his desires. He therefore spends his earnings on whatever attracts him. He also never repents having spent his money on his art which may not ultimately give him monetary rewards. Opulence therefore is a rarity with him but he somehow has the knack to make both ends meet and have the minimum comforts he wants. He may sometimes be lucky in having windfalls.

Vocation

He will shine as an interior decorator, architect, jeweller, musician, hotel manager or a confectioner. He can be equally successful as a broker, estate broker or as a commission agent.

Health

On the whole he is a healthy person and bad health does not trouble him. However he is susceptible to epidemic fever and influenza. Occassionally, he is prone to nervousness but not in a chronic way.

Marriage and Friends

Marriage : This person has a natural attraction towards persons born in the period between 21st August and 20th September and between December 21st and January 20th. It is therefore advisable that he should choose his wife from this period. He has an affinity for those who are governed by the numbers 2,3,6 and 9

Number 6 as husband : He is attracted to marriage and usually marries early in life. He expects his partner to be neat and have charm and grace. His is usually a large family with many children. He loves his children and home. He is very kind, generous and devoted. Though he creates a lively atmosphere in the house, he somehow finds it difficult to meet all the necessities of the members of his family. This may sometimes create unpleasantness and make him unhappy in his married life. Art is everything to him and he remains impractical in not understanding the material values of a successful life.

Number 6 as wife : She never resorts to divorce and endures extreme hardship rather than desert her mate. She is a devoted mother and loving wife, satisfied with her husband's efforts in her behalf. She loves domestic life and is a perfect housewife.

Friends : His best friends are those who are governed by numbers 2, 3, 6 and 9.

Fortunate Days

His lucky days are Mondays, Tuesdays, Thursdays and Fridays.

Lucky Colours

He should use all shades of blue, rose and pink. It is better he avoids yellow.

Lucky Jewels and Stones

He can use Turquoise, Emerald, Pearl and Diamond.

Important Years in Life

His important years are 6, 15, 24, 33, 42, 51, 60, 69, 78 etc.

His good qualities and drawbacks are as under :

Good qualities	*Drawbacks*
Harmony	Absence of foresight
Love	Interference
Peace	Moodiness
Strong memory	Timidity

Special characteristics of those born on the 15th and the 24th of any month

Born on the 15th of the month : This person has good intelligence and good memory. He is fit for responsible positions and can be an ambassador, consul, governor etc. He is very ambitious and boastful but hasty and proud by nature.. He is interested in lower type of occultism. He also has interest in art and music. He appears to be gentle but has very strong convictions. He has a habit of worrying inwardly and leading a melancholy life. His fate is to make sacrifices for others.

Born on the 24th of the month : He is fortunate in getting assistance from people of high rank. He benefits through the opposite sex. His prosperity is after marriage and he marries a rich girl. He succeeds in speculation and enjoys good monetary status. He strictly defines the line between personal and social matters. He is methodical in his ideas. He possesses a strong ego and sometimes tries to force his opinions on others.

The study of numbers is nothing else but psycho-analysis. The deep-rooted feelings, sentiments, emotions, ambition and abilities are best represented by numbers. If one can know oneself through one's number, life will be easy and successful.

Please also refer to the individual month you are born in. Combine your characteristics, lucky days, colour and jewels shown by your number and also by the month you are born in and then find out the common factors and arrive at the final conclusion.

CHAPTER 9

Number 7

All those born on the 7th, 16th and 25th of any month and those born between 21st June and 20th July are governed by number 7.

Character

This number is governed by the planet Neptune and has the same qualities as those of number 2 which is governed by the planet Moon. This man has individuality and is original and independent. He is restless by nature and is fond of change. He likes to visit foreign countries and becomes interested in far off lands. He has peculiar ideas about religion and dislikes following the beaten track.

This is a spiritual number and Supreme Consciousness is developed in this individual. He is like a free bird and likes to break the traditional bondage and restrictions. It is possible that the greatest of the prophets and spiritualists may have the planet Neptune dominating them. His behaviour is a mystery to others and he is many times absent-minded. He thinks out logically and achieves great aims. He is stubborn and disregards the opinions of others. He has a good talent to earn money. In general, he is somewhat indifferent and cares little for materialistic things. He desires the best or none at all. He is sensittve and hides his real feelings by apparent indifference. He dislikes mingling with common people. He prefers to spend his hour with his favourite book. When his opinion is solicited, he speaks with authority. He knows his ground.

Finance

Usually, there are number of changes in the life of number 7 person and as such, it is difficult for him to amass wealth. However, this being a mystic number, the person can be well placed in life provided he finds a job of his choice. In that case he can be a wealthy person with all amenities and comforts.

Vocation

His love of sea travel and interest in foreign countries can make him a successful merchant, exporter or importer. He can as well deal in dairy products, fishery, chemical industry and other products such as soap etc. He can also study medicine and surgery.

Health

His main trouble is his nervous constitution and all his illness will be due to his nervousness. He is liable to suffer from faulty blood circulation, stomach disorder and fever.

Marriage and Friends

Marriage : A number 7 person has natural attraction towards persons born in the period from 20th October to 20th November and from 19th February to 20th March. It is therefore advisable that he finds his marriage partner from this period. He also has an affinity for those who are governed by numbers 1,3,4,5,7 and 8

Number 7 as husband : He is very emotional and understands the feelings of his wife. He is very considerate and will never try to impose his ideas on the wife. He is liberal, fond of picnics, travels and cinema theatres. He is a spendthrift and likes to live lavishly. His family is moderate in size and has all comforts in life.

Number 7 as wife : She is very moody and her behaviour is unpredictable. She is very uneasy and gets disturbed over small matters. She is good at entertaining friends and she likes to invite people for parties or dinner. She expects her husband to look after her all the time.

Friends : His best friends are those who are governed by numbers 1, 3, 4, 5, 7, 8 and 9.

Fortunate Days

His lucky days are Sundays, Mondays, Wednesdays and Thursdays. He should take his decisions and act on these days especially when the date is also 7th or 16th or 25th of the month.

Lucky Colours

He should use all shades of green and yellow.

Lucky Jewels and Stones

His lucky jewels are Topaz and Emerald and lucky stones are Moon Stone and Cat's Eye.

Important Years in Life

His important years are 7, 16, 25, 34, 43, 52, 61, 70, 79 etc.

His good qualities and drawbacks are as under:

Good qualities	*Drawbacks*
Austerity	Despondency
Peace	Diffidence
Reflection	Restlessness
Serenity	Whimsicality
Tolerance	

Special characteristics of those born on the 16th and the 25th of any month

Born on the 16th of the month : He is rather easygoing and does not like to work hard. He is good-humoured and generous. He is very sensitive and emotional. He soon gets up set and is soon pleased. He is frequently indisposed. He is fortunate in getting good and successful children. However there is some sort of sorrow in married life. He appears to be calm but his mind is always in turmoil and is sometimes short-tempered. He will not disclose his nervousness and is slow in taking decisions. He does not like interference.

Born on the 25th of the month : He is a jack of all trades but master of none. He is interested in several subjects but does not have the capacity to go into details. His knowledge therefore is very shallow. He likes to travel and has connections with foreign countries. He is honest, faithful and good-natured. But he is fickle-minded and inconsistent. His memory is good and he is a good orator or teacher.

The study of numbers is nothing else but psycho-analysis. The deep-rooted feelings, sentiments, emotions, ambitions and abilities are best represented by numbers. If one can know oneself through one's number, life will be easy and successful.

Please also refer to the individual month you are born in. Combine your characteristics, lucky days, colours and jewels shown by your number and also by the month you are born in and then find out the common factors and arrive at the final conclusion.

CHAPTER 10

Number 8

All those born on the 8th, 17th, and 26th of any month and those born between 21st December and 20th February are governed by this number.

Character

This number is governed by the planet Saturn and shows an extreme sense of discipline, steadfastness, constancy and dutifulness. The person is a sober and solitary type. He is a lover of classical music but mostly of a melancholy type. In arts he loves landscapes, natural scenery and flowers. Number 8 is considered to be a balance wheel to character. He is a pessimist. He prefers solitude to company. He shuns society rather than courts it. He is cautious about the future and he takes decisions very carefully on matters which pertain to mundane affairs. He is a prudent person, wise and sober amongst all the numbers. He is never overenthusiastic and is more or less gloomy and melancholy. He is also ambitious and persevering. He is capable of enormous efforts for the attainment of desired objects. He is sceptical and analytical. He is creative, productive and dominating. He is likely to be misunderstood. He usually feels lonely at heart. He understands the weak and the oppressed and treats them in a warm-hearted manner. He is a born manager who can keep others busy. He admires fair play and is willing to pay a fair compensation. He has a good memory for names and faces.

Finance

The peculiarity of number 8 is the delay in life in all matters. Naturally in financial matters also there is delay and stability is achieved at a very late age. This person has to work hard and he rarely succeeds in getting opulence. He has therefore to avoid number 8 playing a part in his life and instead he can choose number 3 or 7 for all his important actions and moves in life. However, if his experience shows that 8 is a lucky number for him, he can insist on that number only, in which case wealth and prosperity is not difficult for him. If 8 is found to be a lucky number in one's life, one can try lottery and luck in horse racing. But usually this number is connected with delays and hard work and a person has to be verv cautious in financial matters.

Vocation

Subjects suitable for him are occult sciences, chemistry, physics, medicine and also higher mathematics. He can be successful in industries dealing with coal mines, timber, etc. and in construction companies. He can be a good accountant and also a good administrator. However, as stated earlier, he has to strive hard in his career and can get fruits of his hard work only in the later years of his life.

Health

His main health defects are nervousness, irritation, trouble with legs, teeth and ears, paralysis and rheumatism. He is a bilious type and many times suffers from chronic melancholia. It is very interesting to note that the delaying characteristic in his life is also observed in his sickness. The ailments he suffers from also take a long time to cure. Varicose veins and haemorrhoids are a common tendency of a strong 8 personality.

Marriage and Friends

Marriage : He has a natural attraction towards persons born in the period 21st April and 20th May and between 21st August and 20th September. It is therefore advisable that he selects his marriage partner from this period. He also has an affinity for those who are governed by numbers 4, 5, 7 and 8

Number 8 as husband : Basically, a number 8 person does not have a desire to get married. He prefers loneliness and likes to be left to himself. He has less attraction for the opposite sex. Usually he tries to postpone his marriage with the result that if at all he marries, it is at a very late age. He also finds it difficult to choose his wife. As he prefers seclusion to gathering, he often makes his married life miserable. He is very orthodox in his views and does not allow his wife to adopt modern ideas in dress at home or in public places. The natural result is disappointment on the part of his wife and hatred for her husband. If however he has a desire to be successful in married life, he should prefer a person who is also interested in deep and serious studies and likes to devote herself to philosophy and occult subjects.

Number 8 as wife : She has a masculine personality. She is capable and systematic. She enjoys her family life and likes to make sacrifices for her children and for the ambition of her husband. Her fault is that she lacks feminine warmth, sentiment and delicacy.

Friends : His best friends are those who are governed by numbers 3, 4, 5, 7 and 8.

Fortunate Days

His lucky days are Wednesdays, Thursdays and Saturdays.

Lucky Colours

He should use dark grey, dark blue, purple and black.

Lucky Jewels and Stones

His lucky jewels are Sapphire, black Pearl, black Diamond. His lucky stones are Cat's Eye and Amethyst.

Important Years in Life

His important years are 8, 17, 26, 35, 44, 53, 62, 71 etc.

His good qualities and drawbacks are as under :

Good qualities	*Drawbacks*
Authority	Cynicism
Methodical	Delay
Practical	Vindictiveness
Steady	Nervousness
Systematic	Laziness

Special characteristics of those born on the 17th and the 26th of any month

Born on the 17th of the month : He is a good organizer and a good thinker. He has a creative and constructive mind. He is a lover of peace and a philanthropist. He is attracted towards occultism and mysticism. He is courageous and proud. He has strong individualism. He is highly intelligent and clever. As regards emotions, he is calm. At times he is generous to a fault and at times very stingy. He is interested in research and seeks knowledge. He is conservative and dominating.

Born on the 26th of the month : He wants to enjoy life without doing anything. He is sluggish and lethargic. He revels in wine and women and is fickle-minded. He is careless about the number of children. He is lucky in money matters and gets easy money. He is smart but lacks positiveness. He likes to put up a good appearance but has a worrying nature. He has problems in his love affairs.

Numbers help us to know ourselves. They guide us in knowing ourselves and various shades of our sentiments, emotions, ambition and abilities. We should try to understand the number ruling us and follow its indications. By doing so, we can overcome several of our difficulties and pitfalls and finally lead a healthy and successful life.

Please also refer to the individual month you are born in. Combine your characteristics, lucky days, colours and jewels shown by your number and also by the month you are born in and then find out the common factors and arrive at the final conclusion.

An interesting experience of delay shown by the number 8

Once a retired person called on me and informed me that he had retired three years back but still he had not got his pension and his case was not finalised even after three years. In fact, he was working as an officer in the same department where pension matters were settled. He had visited his office several times during the last three years and every time his juniors in that office promised to settle the case within a week's time. He then asked me as to when his case would be settled and he would get his pension. In Numerology there is a system with the help of which we can solve such questions. I just asked him to write down his question and after his doing so, the question was solved in the numerical way and the final digit arrived at was 8. I immediately informed him that the number indicates delay and he would have to wait for sometime more to get his pension but how long could not be predicted.

For the next two years he used to visit me and the delay shown by the number 8 was really trying his patience. After about a year thereafter he called on me with a packet of sweets and gave me the happy news of his receiving the pension. But till the last moment number 8 played the delaying game and the old man had to go to Bombay to take his pension when he was informed that it had been sent to Poona by money order only two days earlier. After returning to Poona, he was told that the money order had been returned to Bombay office. This is really an extraordinary case I ever met.

CHAPTER 11

Number 9

All those born on 9th, 18th and 27th of any month and also those born between 21st March and 20th April and between 21st October and 20th November are governed by this number.

Character

This number is governed by the planet Mars and shows aggression, resistance, courage, dash and quickness. A Martian is considered as a fighter. He is always aggressive in all his acts and will not stop till he achieves his end. He has the capacity to fight even against all adverse elements and circumstances. A Martian does not know defeat and if we had an army of Martians, there would not be anything like defeat for them. It would be either victory or death. It is said that the great Emperor Napoleon Bonaparte was a believer in this science and he had a battalion of soldiers who were pure Martians. A Number 9 person is not very tactful or delicate in his talk but his intention is good and his vigorous manner should not be misunderstood as rough behaviour.

He is fiery and dashing and does not have sickly sentiments. He has audacity and vigour from start to finish. He is also fond of games and vigorous exercise. When the date of the month is 9 and the total of all the birth date is also 9, he is governed by a strong number 9 and his Mars is very powerful. In such a case, he has strong sexual passions and he is attracted towards the opposite sex. He is prepared to go through any ordeal to gratify his desire.

He is a brave person to whom conflict does not bring the thought of danger. He is exceedingly devoted to his friends and will fight for them. He has sympathy and consideration for the weak. He loves children and animals. He takes delight in showing mercy to others. He likes the healing profession. He is backed by self-control, moral courage and the power of forgiveness. His psychological aptitude is remarkable and under all circumstances he proves his strength of will and exhibits courage.

Finance

He is lucky in his monetary affairs and earns far more than an average person. He is also very liberal while spending, especially for his sweetheart. He enjoys all the comforts that money can bring.

Vocation

A Number 9 person is found in all walks of life but he will be more suitable for the army and professions where there is full scope for his aggression and courage. In the army he will rise to high positions, in politics he will be eminent and in business he will exhibit his dashing and pushing nature. He can be a good doctor, or a chemist or a businessman dealing in iron and steel.

Health

His main health defect arises from heat and he is susceptible to troubles such as piles, fevers, small pox etc. He is also likely to suffer from kidney or bladder stone. Throat trouble, bronchitis, laryingitis also trouble him.

Marriage and Friends

He has a natural attraction towards persons born in the period between 21st July and 20th August and between 21st November and 20th December. It is therefore advisable that he selects his partner from this period. He also has an affinity for those who are governed by numbers : 3,6 and 9

Number 9 as husband: He has robust health and has strong circulation of blood which makes him more passionate and enthusiastic about married life. He is fond of a beautiful wife and likes her to be submissive and passive to his sexual desires. He is fond of family and children and likes to have a good house. He usually leads a good married life in spite of his hot-tempered nature and eccentricities. He has a romantic mental picture of what he wants in his wife. This mental picture demands perfection. The most difficult thing in the married life of a number 9 person is to satisfy his romantic conception of physical love. He has a voracious appetite and his wife with her devotion should harmonise with him physically. Usually, we find him suspicious about his wife.

Number 9 as wife : She will make a wonderful wife for an ambitious man. She is a witty and clever conversationalist with a wonderful social presence. She will assist her husband in his business. She may also start her own activity and add to the family income. She will be happy if married to a passionate and possessive man.

Friends : His best friends are those who are governed by numbers 1, 2, 3, 4, 6, 7 and 9.

Fortunate Days

Lucky days are Mondays, Tuesdays, Thursdays and Fridays.

Lucky Colours

He should use all shades of red, white and yellow.

Lucky Jewels and Stones

His lucky jewels are Topaz, Pearl and Ruby and lucky stones are Blood stones and Garnet.

Important Years in Life

His important years are 9, 18, 27, 36, 45, 54, 63, 72 etc.

His good qualities and drawbacks are as under :

Good qualities	*Drawbacks*
Activity	Destructive
Courage	Eratic
Dash	Hot-tempered
Energy	Impatient
Enthusiasm	Quarrelsome

Special characteristics of those born on 18th and 27th of any month

Born on 18th of the month : This person has tenacity and

will-power which will overcome any difficulty. He is not that much dashing as that of number 9, but he is fearless and courageous. His strong health makes him passionate. He inherits property from his father. He has a disciplined mind and likes to help others. He is painstaking with good judgement, and wise.

Born on 27th of the month : On the whole he is a conflicting personality. He is confident and likes to do something for those whose life is miserable or are handicapped. He can develop a spiritual personality and can practise spiritual healing. On the other side he is fond of women and can develop illicit contacts and create scandal. Sometimes he creates unhappiness in his married life. He is very sensitive and moody and his actions and moves are unpredictable.

Numbers help us to know ourselves. They guide us in knowing ourselves and various shades of our sentiments emotions, ambitions and abilities. We should try to understand the number ruling us and follow its indications. By doing so we can overcome several of our difficulties and avoid pitfalls and lead a healthy and successful life.

Please also refer to the individual month you are born in. Combine your characteristics, lucky days, colours and jewels shown by your number and also by the month you are born in and then find out the common factor and arrive at the final conclusion.

After discussing all the numbers from 1 to 9 and their compound numbers, it would be helpful if I summarise the conclusions in a nutshell by way of a ready-reckoner. I therefore give here a chart showing the picture at a glance.

Summary Chart of Numbers

No.	Characteristics	Finance	Vocation	Health Defects
1	Originality, activity, energy, brilliance	Good luck	Ambassador Surgeon Head of dept.	Sun stroke Eye sight Heart trouble
2	Unsteady, fickle-minded, high imagination. love of travel.	Mediocre luck	Author, Painter, Clerk.	Poor blood-circulation
3	Confidence, dignity, prestige, honour.	Good luck	Minister, Judge, Administrator.	Chest and lungs disorder.
4	Energy, force, Revolution	Good	Transport, Electricity, Machinery	Knees, feet, Urinary infection
5	Shrewdness, intuition, diplomacy, eloquence.	Good	Banking, Business, Lawyer.	Biliousness Nervousness Respiration
6	Love, sympathy, adoration.	Mediocre	Decorator, Architect, Jeweller, Musician.	Nil
7	Originality, Independence, Restlessness	Doubtful	Merchant, Exporter, Dairy, Fishery, Medicine.	Nervousness Boils Fevers
8	Dutiful, constant, steadfast, gloomy, Melancholia.	Success by hard work	Science, Chemistry, Medicine, Accounts.	Legs, teeth, ear, rheumatism.
9	Dash, aggression, courage, resistance	Good	Army, doctor, Iron-steel.	Piles, fever, Kidney, •Layrngitis.

Marriage partner *Born between*	Friends	Lucky Days	Lucky Colours	Lucky Jewels	Important Years
21st July to 20th Aug. 21st Nov. to 20th Dec. *Nos.* : 1,3,4,5,7 .	1,3,4,5 7, 9	Sunday Monday Thursday	Gold, Yellow, Orange, Purple.	Ruby, Emerald, Moon-stone Pale green stone	1, 10, 19, 28, 37, 46, 55, 64, 73.
21st Oct. to 20th Nov. 19th Feb. to 20th Mar. *Nos.* : 2,4,6	2, 4, 6, 9	Monday Tuesday Friday	White, Cream, Blue.	Pearl, Diamond, Moon-stone, Agate.	2, 11, 20, 29, 38, 47, 56, 65, 74.
21st June to 20th July. 21st Oct. to 20th Nov. *Nos.* : 3,6,7,9	1, 3, 5, 6, 7, 8, 9	Tuesday Thursday Friday	Yellow, Violet, Purple, Green.	Topaz, Amethyst, Cat's eye.	3, 12, 21, 30, 39, 48, 57, 66, 75.
19th Feb. to 20th Mar. 21st Oct. to 20th Nov. *Nos.* : 1,2,4,7,8	1, 2, 4, 5, 7 , 8, 9	Sunday Monday Saturday	Elect. blue, Elect. gray, White, Maroon.	Diamond, Coral, Pearl.	4, 13, 22, 31, 40, 49, 58, 67, 76.
21st Sept. to 20th Oct. 21st Jan. to 20th Feb. *Nos.* : 1,5,7,8	1, 3, 4, 5, 7, 8	Wednesday Friday Saturday	Green, White.	Emerald, Diamond.	5, 14, 23, 32, 41, 50, 59, 68, 77.
21st Aug. to 20th Sept. 21st Dec. to 20th Jan. *Nos.* : 2,3,6,9	2, 3, 6, 9	Monday Tuesday Thursday Friday	Blue, Rose, Pink.	Turquoise, Emerald, Pearl, Diamond.	6, 15, 24, 33, 42, 51, 60, 69, 78.
20th Oct. to 20th Nov. 19th Feb. to 20 Mar. *Nos.* : 1,3,4,5,7,8	1, 3, 4, 5, 7, 8, 9	Sunday Monday Wednesday Thursday	Green, Yellow.	Topaz, Emerald, Moon-stone, Cat's eye.	7, 16, 25, 34, 43, 52, 61, 70, 79.
21st April to 20th May 21st Aug. to 20th Sept. *Nos.* : 4,5,7,8	3, 4, 5, 7, 8	Wednesday Thursday Saturday	Dark Gray, Dark Blue, Purple, Black.	Sapphire, Black Pearl, Black-Diamond, Cat's eye.	8, 17, 26, 35, 44, 53, 62, 71, 80.
21st Nov. to 20th Dec. 21st July to 20th Aug. *Nos.* : 3,6,9	1, 2, 3, 4, 6, 7, 9	Monday Tuesday Thursday Friday	Red, White, Yellow.	Topaz, Pearl, Ruby, Garnet.	9, 18, 27, 36, 45, 54, 63, 72, 81.

CHAPTER 12

The Month You are Born In

After the date of the month, the next thing to be considered is the month you are born in. Every month is influenced and dominated by a particular planet and the person born in a particular month represents the characteristics of that particular planet and is the symbol of that planet. You are therefore influenced by the planet shown by the individual date of the month and also by the planet represented by the month. Before arriving at the final conclusion, you have to combine the aspects shown by both the planets and then find out your friends, marriage partners, lucky jewels, stones etc.

Born in January

The month of January is dominated by the planet Saturn and the person is governed by Saturn.

Character

He is sceptical and does not believe in anything unless he is convinced about the facts. He does not take quick decisions unless he is sure of the result. He is very cautious and does not like to speculate. His mind is analytical and philosophic and he thinks deeply. He has energy and ambition and develops perseverance. He is very studious and methodical but takes everything seriously. He has few friends and feels lonely in life. He is generally misunderstood. He is independent in thought and action and does not like to be dominated by others. He always desires leadership in his enterprise, otherwise he loses interest in the work. His ideas about duty and social behaviour are strange and therefore he does not get on easily with the neighbour. He is attracted towards intelligent and clever people but never interferes with their affairs. He is usually disturbed by his home and family affairs and has to look after distressed or invalid relatives.

Health

Varicose veins and haemorrhoids are common problems with the person born in January. In addition, nervousness, melancholia, irritation, rheumatism and biliousness also trouble him.

Marriage and Friends

His best friends and marriage partners are those who are born between 20th December and 20th January, between 20th April and 20th May and between 20th August and 20th September. It is therefore advisable that he selects his marriage partner from this period. He also has a natural affinity towards those born on 8th, 17th and 26th of any month.

A January husband : He is considerate and treats his wife and family members with the same courtesy that he accords to strangers. He is kind and generous and gives without thought of return or reward. He accepts marriage as a part of the domestic scheme and succeeds in it because of his attitude which contributes a great deal toward harmony at home. His drawback is his impersonality which his wife feels as lack of interest in domestic life.

A January wife : She is a fine companion, capable, intelligent, adaptable and talented. Her home is a social centre on account of her social and friendly manners. Her interests are wide and she does not like to watch how her husband spends his spare time. Though basically she is unconventional, she is kind and would rather suffer herself than create a situation which would make others unhappy. As she is intelligent, she would be appreciated as a good wife by an intelligent husband who could use her abilities for his own self.

Lucky Days

His fortunate days are Wednesdays, Thursdays and Fridays. He should try to act on these days for all his important moves.

Lucky Colours

He will be happy and cheerful if he uses grey, violet, purple or black colours for his clothes.

Lucky Jewels and Stones

He should wear either pearls, garnets, sapphire or Moonstone on his finger.

CHAPTER 13

Born in February

The month of February is dominated by the planet Saturn and the person is governed by Saturnian characteristics.

Character

A person born in this month values honour, prestige and dignity. He is oversensitive and is easily hurt in his feelings. In spite of his large contacts in society, he has a feeling of loneliness in life. He has strong intuition and can read people instinctively. He has the capacity to keep the secrets of others and relieve their distress. He has the capacity to give excellent advice to others and be in a place of trust. He requires some opportunity to show his qualities but when he gets one, he surprises everyone by the hidden powers and abilities he possesses. He will use his energies and abilities for the good of others and usually leaves a name behind by service to humanity or by some great invention that has brought unusual benefit to the world at large. He will have great power over excitable people or those who are hysterical or insane and he will find himself thrown among such types in his journey through life. He has an attraction for the mysterious and the unknown and is devoted to studies of the occult and of esoteric subjects. He is attached to his family and loves his wife.

Health

Poor blood circulation, anaemia, palpitation and weakness of the heart, disorder of the bladder and kidneys, are the main health defects of this person. He is also liable to suffer from sore throat and difficulty with the respiratory tract. He will be inclined to buy any quack medicine.

Marriage and Friends

His best friends and marriage partners are those who are born between 20th January and 19th February, between 20th May and 20th June and between 20th September and 20th October. It is therefore advisable that he selects his marriage partner and friends from this period. He also has a natural affinity towards those born on 8th, 17th and 26th of any month.

A February husband : He is a loving, considerate, thoughtful and attentive husband. He loves his home and spends much of his time at home only. He is emotional and of a dreamy nature. His notions are more real to him than the facts of life. He therefore finds it difficult to cope with the realities and difficulties of life. He lacks stability, strength and realism in his career. He is very sensual and can be dangerously perverted by self-indulgence. Sexual satisfaction is very important to him and he seeks it persistently all his life.

A February wife : She is remarkably adapted to family life. She likes a luxurious life and desires her house to be a heaven. She is a devoted, kind and sympathetic type of wife.

Lucky Days

His lucky days are Wednesdays, Thursdays and Saturdays and he should plan all his important actions on these days.

Lucky Colours

He should always use violet or purple or gray colours in his clothes or paint his rooms with these colours. All shades of blue are also favourable to him.

Lucky Jewels and Stones

His most lucky jewels are Amethyst, Diamond or Topaz. He may also wear cat's eye.

Before selecting your lucky jewels, colours and days please refer to your individual number in the second chapter and find out the common description and select the final jewel or the colour.

CHAPTER 14

Born in March

Jupiter is the ruling planet of those who are born in the month of March. Naturally, such a man is governed by Jupiterian qualities.

Character

A person born in this month is courteous, generous and broad-minded. He has a natural understanding and intuition. He is ambitious and feels that he must know his subject well. He is loyal to his friends and generally succeeds in all positions of responsibility. He is strict about law and order. He is very easygoing and surrounded by false friends. He has a dual personality and his action depends upon which personality dominates him at a particular moment. He has a mystical side as well as a practical side. He likes to search for the unknown and the esoteric. Although he is generous, he is anxious about money matters and worries about his future monetary position. Artists, musicians and literary people are born in this month.

Health

His sickness is mainly psychological and he usually suffers from mental depression, insomnia, nervousness etc. He also suffers from rheumatic trouble, intestinal disturbance and pain in the feet. His overanxiety often causes faulty digestion and poor blood circulation is the result.

Marriage and Friends

His best friends are those who are born between 19th February and 20th March, between 20th June and 20th July and between 20th October and 20th November. It is therefore advisable that he selects his marriage partner and friends from this period. He also has a natural attraction towards those born on 3rd, 12th, 21st and 30th of any month.

A March husband: He is highly emotional and sensitive. He desires that everything should be given to him without his asking for it. He never thinks that he should contribute something of his own for getting enjoyment. His passions are animal-like, strong and quick. He enjoys the company of his children and is one with them in many ways.

A March wife : She has a great sense of comfort and decorates her home in a luxurious way. She is beautiful and talented but spends her time in an idle way, seeking entertainment. When she is of good or robust health, she makes a devoted, charming and sympathetic wife.

Lucky Days

His lucky days are Tuesdays, Thursdays and Fridays. He should therefore plan all his important actions on these days.

Lucky Colours

He should try to wear clothes of yellow, violet, purple or green colours. He may also use these colours for his drawing room or the bed room.

Lucky Jewels and Stones

His lucky jewels are Topaz, Sapphire and Emeralds.

Before selecting your lucky jewels, colours and days please refer to your individual number in the second chapter and find out the common factor and select the final jewel or the colour.

CHAPTER 15

Born in April

The month of April is dominated by the planet Mars and the person is governed by Martian characteristics.

Character

A person born in this month is dominating, energetic, active, hot-tempered and enthusiastic and a fighter. He has a capacity to organise an industry or business. He is an independent worker and can do his job when left to himself. He does not like any interference in his work, but if subjected to interference, he will step out and let the other fellow take his place. If he keeps his head cool, he can reach any heights and achieve great success in life, but his arrogance and obstinacy are the factors which often create enemies and thus spoil his career. He is endowed with strong will-power and determination and he always has new and original schemes. However, he is hasty in decision and action. Sometimes he goes to extremes and creates enemies due to his frank and outspoken nature. He is usually lucky in life and amasses good money. He is gifted with intuition and can know what is likely to happen in the future. He is a warrior and will fight all obstacles experiencing many dangers and changes in life.

Health

Though he is of a strong constitution and energetic, he is susceptible to mild fevers and inflammation. In his emotional state he is likely to take alcohol which he should avoid because he needs control and not stimulation. Since he is governed by the planet Mars, his head and face are more affected than any other part of the body. Pain in the teeth, ears or eyes, rushing of blood to the head, headaches and danger of apoplexy are his health weaknesses. He seldom escapes wound to the head. He is also liable to suffer from liver, bladder and stomach troubles.

Marriage and Friends

His most harmonious relationship is with those born between 20th March and 20th April, between 20th July and 20th August and between 20th November and 20th December. He should therefore select his friends and marriage partner from this period. He also has a natural affinity towards those born on 9th, 18th and 27th of any month.

An April husband: He is romantic and wants his wife to be beautiful, good and clever. He has a voracious appetite for sex and his wife has to understand how to satisfy his romantic conception of physical love. He is very dashing and courageous and looks well after his wife and children.

An April wife : She is very energetic and enthusiastic and likes to help her husband either in his work or business or would like to start her own activity. She is a good conversationalist and witty. She is efficient and a good companion. She is proud of her appearance and of her family and makes others jealous of her by her behaviour. She needs a passionate and possessive husband who would allow her to spend lavishly. Her attitude towards her children is generous but not sympathetic. She is irritable and impatient and not willing to see their problems from their point of view.

Lucky Days

His lucky days are Mondays, Tuesdays, Thursdays and Fridays and he should try to take important decisions on these days.

Lucky Colours

His lucky colours are rose, crimson or pink. He should try to make use of these colours in his clothes or his house.

Lucky Jewels and Stones

His favourable jewels are Coral, Pearls or Garnets.

Before selecting your lucky jewels, colours and days, please refer to your individual number in the second chapter and find out the common factor and select the final jewel etc.

CHAPTER 16

Born in May

The month of May is governed by the planet Venus and the person is dominated by Venus's characteristics.

Character

He has great power of endurance, both physically and mentally, and can stand great strain. He is very social and loves society, theatres, cinema houses, picnics, travels etc. He is artistic and likes to decorate his house well and also to dress well. Others take him to be richer than he usually is. In love, he is generous and will make sacrifices to any extent. He is emotional and sentimental. He is a good host and has a taste for good food. He can be a good nurse, healer, public servant, or head of the department by virtue of his faithfulness and loyal friendship. He will also get success in art and music because of his sense of harmony and rhythm. He is lucky in money matters and gains through association, partnership or through marriage.

Health

On the whole his health is good but he should always avoid wine, strong drinks and rich food. He is liable to suffer from complaints of the respiratory track and kidneys and self-indulgence.

Marriage and Friends

His most harmonious relationship is with those who are born between 20th April and 20th May, between 20th August and 20th September and between 20th December and 20th January. He also has attraction for those born between for 20th October and 20th November. He should therefore try to select his friends and his wife from this period as far as possible. He also has a natural attraction towards those born on 6th, 15th and 24th of any month.

A May husband: As a husband, he is very generous, devoted and faithful. He cares for his home inspite of any outside interest. He tries his best to provide good education and clothes to his children. He often marries a person of a higher economic status. He is attracted to beauty and usually he gets a good-looking wife. He finds his married life enjoyable and it is never tiresome to him.

A May wife : She is a devoted and affectionate wife. She has the capacity to endure hardships and to adapt herself to circumstances. She is calm and reserved but at the same time social and everybody's friend. She makes herself dependent although she can rely on herself if necessary. She is of an easy-going type and enjoys picnics, theatres and the company of friends.

Lucky Days

His lucky days are Mondays, Tuesdays, Thursdays and Fridays. He should therefore make use of these days for a successful future.

Lucky Colours

The successful colours for him are blue, rose and pink.

Lucky Jewels and Stones

He can wear Emerald, Pearl or Diamond as his lucky jewels or stones.

Before selecting your lucky jewels, colours and days, please refer to your individual number in the second chapter and find out the common factor.

CHAPTER 17

Born in June

The month of June is dominated by the planet Mercury and the person is governed by the characteristics of Mercury.

Character

The Mercurian Rasi for this month is Gemini which has the symbol of Twins. The main characteristic of the person is duality and he plays a double role in life. It is very difficult to understand him. Sometimes he looks hot-headed and sometimes he appears very cool. He may like a particular thing but at the same time he may criticize it. He is sharp, brilliant and quick and can win over his rivals. He is ambitious but hardly knows what he wants to achieve. His company is enjoyable, but only when he is in the right mood, otherwise his behaviour is uncertain. One cannot expect him to be constant in his ideas or plans. He is usually restless and wants what he does not have. He can be successful as an actor or a lawyer or in any other occupation where he is required to change his role quite often. However, he will hardly admit his dual personality unless he is in a self-analytical mood. Owing to his changing moods, he can hardly go in for a project where much time is required for thought and decision. He is therefore not reliable in his plans which will often be postponed until he is forced by circumstances to carry them out. He is very sensitive and finds it difficult to bear any strain of worry or disturbance and experiences brain exhaustion and nervousness. Even though there are many ups and downs in his life, he is not much affected by them.

Health

He is not robust in health. His main health problems are due to mental activity and uneasiness of mind. He therefore suffer from nervous trouble and unless he gets good sleep and change of atmosphere, his nervousness will grow. He is also liable to suffer from blood disorders, weakness of the respiratory system, throat infection and sometimes skin disease.

Marriage and Friends

He has a natural attraction towards people born between 20th May and 20th June, between 20th September and 20th October and between 20th January to 20th February. It is therefore better that he selects his partner and friends from these periods. He also has a natural affinity towards those born on 5th, 14th and 23rd of any month.

A June husband : As a husband, he is good. He is intelligent, talented and social. He should get a wife who will understand his interests and who is not tied to household affairs. Though he has a lot of interest in women, he is not flirtatious. If he can give a direction to his activities, he will be successful.

A June wife : She is an intelligent companion to her husband. She is always busy and likes to take an active part in social life. She is not much absorbed in her home affairs, and she likes to make use of her energy and be active. She is, of course, a practical type and expects returns for her service. She adores discipline and tidiness and commands obedience. Though she has conversational abilities and a romantic personality, she will never sacrifice her home and husband for her romantic life. She makes a good wife to a doctor, or lawyer, or industrialist or any one who spends most of his time among his clients and social contacts.

Lucky Days

His lucky days are Tuesdays, Thursdays and Fridays. He should plan all his important moves on these days.

Lucky Colours

Yellow, violet, purple and green are his lucky colours. He should try to use these colours in his clothes or at home.

Lucky Jewels and Stones

His lucky jewels are Sapphire and Emerald.

Before selecting your lucky jewels, colours and days, please refer to your individual number in the second chapter and find out the common factor and select finally the jewel or the colour.

CHAPTER 18

Born in July

The month of July is governed by the Rasi Cancer and the planet Moon. Naturally the person is dominated by the characteristics of the Moon.

Character

He has a good memory and love for his own people. He is industrious but is inclined to speculate and desires quick money. He is very sensitive, instinctive and impressionable. He has attraction for the past. He has exaggerated ideas about his abilities. He has sympathy for those who suffer. He has the capacity to persuade people to donate generously to funds in aid of hospitals or in aid of the handicapped. Generally the organizations managed by him have good funds and are financially sound. His main characteristic is restlessness. He is over-anxious about his financial matters but once he is well-placed in life, he retains his position. His another peculiarity is his contradictory behaviour. He is moody, timid and uncertain. However his strong imagination helps him to be a good musician, artist or a writer. Being sensitive, he is quickly hurt and depressed. He is usually successful in his mission in life but experiences trouble at home.

Health

In order to maintain good health, he has to be very particular about his diet. Because of his disturbed stomach, he suffers from gastric trouble, rheumatism, gout and sometimes trouble of the respiratory tract.

Marriage and Friends

His natural attraction is for those who are born between

20th June and 20th July, between 20th October and 20th November and between 20th February and 20th March. He should therefore choose his wife from this period. He also has a natural affinity towards those born on 2nd, 11th, 20th and 29th of any month.

A Ji..y husband : He is on the whole good-natured. He is devoted to his family and children. He likes to spend most of his time at home. However there are two types of July husbands. One is the dominating type and the other is the easy-going type. The first type likes others to dance to his tunes. He is very exacting and tries to find fault in everything. He is critical about everything and that creates tension in the mind of the family members. Nothing satisfies him. He is constantly demanding and interfering in family routine. He is very sensual and seeks constant erotic stimulation.

The other type of July husband is passive, lazy and self-indulgent and marries for money and comfort. Since he is submissive he often gets what he wants in life.

A July wife : She is devoted, sympathetic, adaptable and satisfied with her work, position and status. She is a good mother and loves her children and family. Her presence is sanctifying and she is loved and respected by others. She has intuitive faculties and sometimes can guide her husband in his business with wonderful accuracy. However a July wife may have the other side also when she is very moody, whimsical and changing. This creates trouble for her as well as for others. In that case she is very possessive and demanding.

Lucky Days

His lucky days are Sundays, Mondays, Wednesdays and Thursdays. He should take advantage of these days when taking important decisions and actions in life.

Lucky Colours

His lucky colours are green and yellow and he should try to adopt these colours either in his clothes or while painting walls at home.

Lucky Jewels and Stones

He should use Pearl or Diamond in his ring. That would help him to get confidence and achieve success in life.

Before selecting your lucky jewels, colours and days, please refer to your individual number in the second chapter and find out the common factor and select the final jewel or the colour or the day.

CHAPTER 19

Born in August

The month of August is governed by the planet Sun, also called Apollo. A person born in August therefore has Apollonian characteristics.

Character

He has originality, dignity, prestige and honour. He has a majestic personality which commands respect. His assistants adore him and work willingly. He is generous and has a good understanding of human problems. In his career, he succeeds and achieves the highest position. He is fond of theatres, shows and picnics. He is fresh in his outlook and responds to nature and can enjoy life. He is usually popular due to his active nature and his ability to mix in any society. His mission is to give life, energy and enthusiasm to the world at large. He has many talents but they are of a spontaneous nature. He has a style and a grace which influence others and attract people to him with his natural brilliance and versatility.

Health

Even though he is a happy-go-lucky fellow and normally enjoys good health, he is also susceptible to certain health problems and has to be very particular about the following diseases.

Heart trouble : With him, heart trouble is a structural deformity and this can be observed even in childhood.

Weak eye-sight : He has magnetic eyes but they can be weak in sight.

Over-exertion : The most common trouble with him is over-exertion. He should always be on his guard and not exert himself too much.

Sun stroke : He is also susceptible to this sickness.

Marriage and Friends

He is attracted to those born between 20th July and 20th August, between 20th November and 20th December and between 20th March and 20th April. His attraction is also towards those born on the 1st, 10th, 19th and 28th of any month. He should therefore select his partner and friends from this period.

An August husband: He is generous and desires his wife to shine in society. He has a kind and loving disposition and a great heart. He is proud of his family and gives them the best of everything. His love is deep and romantic. He expects his family members to dance to his tunes and will not tolerate disrespect. His opinions are fixed; he has fixed ideas as to what he should get from his wife and children. He may have a romantic affair outside but will not tolerate such behaviour on the part of his wife. In this matter he is very suspicious of her.

An August wife: She is a lovable person and by her grace, dignity and social nature she attracts many people. She can manage her house very efficiently and she is the right wife for an energetic and enthusiastic husband. She is patient and makes sacrifices. She pays every attention to the welfare of her husband and children. Only she knows what sacrifice she makes for them, but others hardly understand her devotion. She is very passionate and needs a virile and masculine husband to satisfy her romantic nature.

Lucky Days

Sundays, Mondays and Thursdays are the lucky days for a person born in the month of August.

Lucky Colours

His luckiest colours are gold, yellow, orange and purple. It is always better that he makes use of these colours either in his clothes or at home.

Lucky Jewels and Stones

He should use Ruby, Topaz or Amber for improving his personality.

Before selecting your lucky jewels, colours and days, please refer to your individual number in the second chapter and find out the common factor and select the final jewel or colour.

CHAPTER 20

Born in September

The month of September is dominated by the planet Mercury and a person born in this month is governed by the characteristics of Mercury.

Character

He is very active and quick. This is true not only of his physical agility but also of his mind. He is very skilful and has intuition. He is proficient in games where he uses his hands as well as his brain. He has the capacity to judge the ability of his opponents in games and knows very well how to take advantage of the weak points of his opponents. He is fond of oratory and eloquence in expressing himself. He is energetic and constantly working; he is adroit and crafty and a constant schemer. He has the capacity to pursue his objectives and knows very well how to plan to achieve his ends. He hardly loses any opportunity and puts every hour to use. He is deeply interested in occult subjects and has a fancy to master all the intricacies of such abstruse subjects. He is a lover of nature and is fond of animals like horses and dogs. He is also interested in reading books, but not of romances : his subjects are likely to be scientific.

Health

His basic health defect is biliousness and nervousness. His biliousness is closely related to his psychological disturbances. Experience shows that his biliousness increases with increase in tension and is reduced or disappears when his nervous trouble is under control. If he suffers from nervous trouble, he may get paralytic trouble, mostly in his arms or upper portion. He may also experience stammering or impediments in speech.

Marriage and Friends

His most harmonious relationship is with those who are born between 20th August and 20th September, between 20th December and 20th January and between 20th April and 20th May. He also has a natural attraction towards people born on the 5th, 14th and 23rd of any month.

A September husband: He is a lucky and successful husband. His selection is good and usually he selects a person of his own type. He loves his partner. He expects neatness and cleanliness from his wife and also desires that she should share with him the joys of life. He wants her to be stylish and full of fire and life. He loves his children and loves home life.

A September wife: She has interests at home as well as outside. She has many activities and manages them well. She likes tidiness and though she seldom does her own work, she gets it done, by her commanding personality.

Lucky Days

Wednesdays, Fridays and Saturdays are the lucky days for the September person.

Lucky Colours

His lucky colours are green and white. He should try to wear clothes of these colours and paint his house also in these colours.

Lucky Jewels and Stones

The most lucky jewels for him are Sapphire, Emerald and Diamond. He should wear them in a ring and on his little finger.

Before selecting your lucky jewels, colours and days, please refer to your individual number in the second chapter and find out the common factor and make the final selection.

CHAPTER 21

Born in October

The month of October is ruled by the Rasi Tula meaning a scale or a balance and by the planet Venus. A person born in the month of October is therefore governed by the qualities of Venus.

Character

He has a pleasant personality. His presence radiates enthusiasm, energy and charm. We may sometimes be required to put aside our ideas of morality and social conduct in understanding and appreciating his feelings and views. He is gifted with health, vitality and warmth. He has a great attraction for beauty and love. He desires a life full of ease, luxury, money and happiness. He prefers spending to saving. It is true that he has vigour and warmth of passions but that does not necessarily mean that he is fond of sex. He is a born artist, and art and beauty in life have an attraction for him. Therefore his love for nature and beauty should not be misunderstood. He tries to understand the grievances and difficulties of others through a considerate approach. He prefers joy to gloom and has the capacity to carry others along with him to moments of enjoyment. His outlook is bright and vivacious. He likes to remain honest and truthful in love and friendship.

Health

On the whole this person has good health. However, he is susceptible to fever and impurities of blood, and nervousness. He may also suffer from pain in the back and severe headache and peculiar maladies of the skin.

Marriage and Friends

He will find lasting union and friendship with persons born

between 20th September and 20th October, between 20th January and 20th February and between 20th May and 20th June. He also has a natural attraction for those who are born on the 6th, 15th and 24th of any month.

An October husband: He likes marriage and usually marries early in life. He expects his partner to be neat and have charm and grace. His is usually a large family. He is very kind, generous and devoted and loves his children and home. Though he creates a lively atmosphere in the house, he somehow finds it difficult to provide all the necessities of the members of his family. This may sometimes create unpleasantness in the family and make him a little unhappy.

An October wife : She is a devoted mother and loving wife, satisfied with her husband's efforts in her behalf. She loves domestic life and is a perfect house-maker. She never resorts to divorce and endures extreme hardship rather than desert her husband. She has the tact to get along with people and attracts an interesting social circle. At the same time she never neglects her home duties. Though she is attractive and has a group of admirers seeking her favour, she is sober and never encourages indiscriminate flirtation.

Lucky Days

His lucky days are Mondays, Tuesdays, Thursdays and Fridays.

Lucky Colours

He should wear blue, rose or pink colours or use these colours for painting the walls of the house.

Lucky Jewels and Stones

Opal and Pearl are lucky for him and he should wear either of these jewels in his ring.

Before selecting your lucky jewels, colours and days please refer to your individual number in the second chapter and find out the common factor and select the final jewel or the colour.

CHAPTER 22

Born in November

The planet Mars rules the month of November and therefore a person born in this month is governed by Martian qualities.

Character

He is a fighter and a soldier. He is aggressive and will not stop till he achieves his end. He has the capacity to fight even against adverse elements and circumstances. He is also a fighter in his mental world. He is very active. brisk and energetic. He cannot be tactful or delicate in his talk but his intention is good. His vigorous manner should not be misconstrued as rough behaviour. He is fiery and dashing and does not have sickly sentiments. He is a brave person to whom conflict does not bring the thought of danger. He is exceedingly devoted to his friends and will fight for them. He is very generous and magnanimous. He has sympathy and consideration for the weak. He loves children and animals. His main characteristics are aggression, resistance, courage, coolness and quickness.

Health

His main health defect arises from heat and he is susceptible to troubles such as piles, fevers, small-pox etc. He is also likely to suffer from kidney trouble or bladder stone. Throat trouble, bronchitis and laryngitis also often pester him.

Marriage and Friends

He will find lasting union or friendship with those born between 20th October and 20th November, between 20th February and 20th March and between 20th June and 20th July.

He also has a natural attraction towards persons born on the 9th, 18th and 27th of any month. He should therefore find his wife from this period.

A November husband : He has vigour and strength and is very passionate and enthusiastic about married life. He is fond of a beautiful wife and likes her to be submissive and passive to his sexual desires. He is fond of his family and children and likes to have a good house. He usually leads a good married life in spite of his hot-tempered nature and eccentricities. He has a romantic mental picture of what he wants in his wife. This mental picture demands perfection. He desires a clever and very good wife. The most difficult thing for his wife is to satisfy his romantic conception of physical love.

A November wife : She makes a wonderful wife for an ambitious man. She is a witty and clever conversationalist with a wonderful social presence. She can assist her husband in his business. She may also start her own activity and add to the family income. She will be happy if married to a passionate and possessive man. Though she likes her children she is not very much attached to them and likes them to develop on their own. She must always keep herself busy, otherwise her moodiness will disturb her family life. It is advisable that she has a friend in whom she can confide.

Lucky Days

Mondays, Tuesdays, Thursdays and Fridays are his lucky days.

Lucky Colours

Red, white and yellow are his lucky colours and he should try to use these colours in his clothes or in the house.

Lucky Jewels and Stones

His lucky jewels are Coral or Pearl, and he should use one of these in his ring.

Before selecting your lucky jewels, colours and days, please refer to your individual number in the second chapter and find out the common factor and select the final jewel or the colour.

CHAPTER 23

Born in December

The month of December is governed by the Rasi Sagittarius and the planet Jupiter. They are therfore mainly dominated by the characteristics of Jupiter.

Character

Jupiter stands for morality, pure love and justice and is known as the greatest benefactor. A person born in this month is devotional, religious and a man of dignity. He is generally lucky and is prosperous. He is confident and self-reliant and takes his own decisions. He is fond of show and likes to observe form, order and law. He is jovial in spirit and cordial in manner. His passions are healthy, spontaneous and without inhibitions. He is free in his expressions. He takes an active interst in sports and out-door activities from his earliest youth. He has tremendous enthusiasm in life. He is not at all self-centred. His intellect is of a very high order, his nature far-sighted and practical. He has a kind of vision that understands the world and loves it for what it is and not for what it ought to be. He is a broad-minded person, tolerant, humorous and truthful. He is open-hearted with good understanding and is entirely lacking in malice or petty jealousies.

If he possesses in excess the qualities of Jupiter, he has arrogance, boastfulness, vindictiveness, criminal jealousy, tyranny and superstition. He is also egoistic, selfish and shrewd.

The basic characteristics of a person born in the month of December are ambition, leadership, religion, pride, honour, love for nature and enthusiasm.

Health

His main health defects relate to blood circulation, the arterial system and the liver. He is likely to suffer from chest and lung disorders, throat afflictions, gout and sudden fevers, He may also suffer from tonsilitis, sore throat, diphtheria, adenoids, pneumonia and pleurisy. He is also likely to suffer from skin diseases.

Marriage and Friends

His most harmonious relationship is with those who are born between 20th November and 20th December, between 20th March and 20th April and between 20th July and 20th August. He also has attraction towards those who are born on the 3rd, 12th, 21st and 30th of any month. He should therefore select his wife and friends from these periods.

A December Husband : As a general rule he attains puberty at an early age and marries early. However, as he is ambitious, his ambition makes him expect too many things from his wife and so he becomes disappointed. He desires to have a wife of whom he can be proud. She should have an attractive personality, commanding presence, charming manners and intelligence. He is most loving, thoughtful and considerate. His passions are adventurous and demand immediate satisfaction.

A December Wife : She is the best companion of her husband. She is not an intruder but takes active interest in the business of her husband. She is efficient in house-keeping and has a sympathetic and balanced attitude towards her children. Her passions are healthy and joyous and her approach to physical love is highly refined and inspiring.

Lucky Days

Tuesdays, Thursdays and Fridays are his lucky days.

Lucky Colours

His lucky colours are yellow, violet, purple and green. He should use these colours either in his clothes or at home.

Lucky Jewels

Topaz and Amethyst are the lucky jewels for him.

Before selecting your lucky jewels, colours and days, please refer to your individual number in the second chapter and find out the common factor and select the final jewel or the colour.

Summary Chart of Months

Month	Characteristics	Health Problems	Marriage Partner and Friends *Born Between*	Lucky Days	Lucky Colours	Lucky Jewels
January	Sceptic, slow, decisive, cautious, analytical, methodical.	Nervousness, Melancholia, Rheumatism, Biliousness.	20th Dec. to 20th Jan. 20th April to 20th May 20th Aug. to 20th Sept. *Nos.* : 8, 17, 26.	Wednesday, Thursday, Friday.	Gray, Violet, Purple, Black.	Pearl, Moon-stone, Garnet, Supphire.
February	Honour, Prestige, Dignity, Sensitivity, Good advisor.	Poor blood-circulation, Heart, Bladder, Kidney.	20th Jan. to 20th Feb. 20th May to 20th June 20th Sept. to 20th Oct. *Nos.* : 8, 17, 26.	Wednesday, Thursday, Saturdy.	Gray, Violet, Purple.	Topaz, Amethyst, Diamond.
March	Courageous, Generous, Dual personality.	Depression, Insomnia, Rheumatism.	20th Feb. to 20th March 20th June to 20th July 20th Oct. to 20th Nov. *Nos.* : 3, 12, 21, 30.	Tuesday, Thursday, Friday.	Yellow, Violet, Purple, Green.	Topaz, Emerald, Sapphire.
April	Dominating, Energetic, Hot-tempered, Active, Organisor, Obstinate.	Fever, Inflammation, Teeth, Ears, Eyes.	20th March to 20th April 20th July to 20th August 20th Nov. to 20th Dec. *Nos.* : 9, 18, 27.	Monday, Tuesday, Thursday, Friday.	Rose, Crimson, Pink.	Pearl, Garnet, Coral.
May	Generosity, Sacrifice, Endurance, Love of travel and picnic	Respiratory track, Kidney.	20th April to 20th May 20th August to 20th Sept. 20th Dec. to 20th Jan. *Nos* : 6, 15, 24.	Monday, Tuesday, Thursday, Friday.	Blue, Rose, Pink.	Emerald, Pearl, Diamond.
June	Sharp, Brilliant, Quick, Moody.	Psychological, Nervousness, Blood-disorder.	20th May to 20th June 20th Sept. to 20th Oct. 20th Jan. to 20th Feb. *Nos.* : 5, 14, 23.	Tuesday, Thursday, Friday.	Yellow, Violet, Purple, Green.	Sapphire, Emerald.

Month	Characteristics	Health Problems	Marriage Partner and Friends *Born Between*	Lucky Days	Lucky Colours	Lucky Jewels
July	Industrious, Speculative, Sensitive, Moody, Musician.	Gastric trouble, Rheumatism, Respiratary track.	20th June to 20th July 20th Oct. to 20th Nov. 20th Feb. to 20th March *Nos.* : 2, 11, 20, 29.	Sunday, Monday, Wednesday, Thursday,	Green, Yellow,	Pearl, Diamond.
August	Originality, Dignity, Talents, Style, Grace.	Heart, Eye sight, Over-exertion.	20th July to 20th August 20th Nov. to 20th Dec. 20th March to 20th April *Nos.* : 1, 10, 19, 28.	Sunday, Monday, Thursday,	Gold, Yellow, Orange, Purple.	Topaz, Amber.
September	Activity, Quickness, Skill, Intuition, Oratory.	Biliousness, Nervousness.	20th Aug. to 20th Sept. 20th Dec. to 20th Jan. 20th April to 20th May *Nos.* : 5, 14, 23.	Wednesday, Friday, Saturday,	Green, White.	Emerald, Diamond. Sapphire.
October	Enthusiasm, Energy, Charm, Spendthrift.	Fever, Impurities of blood, Skin.	20th Sept. to 20th Oct. 20th Jan. to 20th Feb. 20th May to 20th June *Nos.* 6, 15, 24.	Monday, Tuesday, Thursday,	Blue, Rose, Pink.	Opal, Pearl.
November	Fighter, Active, Brisk, Dashing, Courageous.	Fever, Piles, Kidney, Bladder, Throat.	20th Oct. to 20th Nov. 20th Feb. to 20th March 20th June to 20th July *Nos.* : 9, 18, 27.	Monday, Tuesday, Thursday, Friday,	Red, White, Yellow.	Coral, Pearl.
December	Religion, Morality, Love, Justice.	Poor blood circulation, Arterial system, Liver.	20th Nov. to 20th Dec. 20th March to 20th April 20th July to 20th August *Nos.* : 3, 12, 21, 30.	Tuesday, Thursday, Friday,	Yellow, Violet, Purple, Green.	Topaz, Amethyst.

CHAPTER 24

What does your Birth Date Indicate?

After discussing the date of the month and the month of birth, I shall elucidate further details about the birth date as a whole.

Let us suppose that the complete date of birth of an individual is 7th May 1961. This birth date has been selected just at random. In any birth date we have to take three factors into consideration. First is the date of the month which, in this case, is the 7th. Second is the month, which, is May and the third is the total of all the numbers in the birth date which, in the present case, is $7+5+1+9+6+1=29=2$.

The Date of the Month

We have already discussed and studied the significance of this date[1] earlier. The date of birth is the individual seal depicting the basic characteristics of the individual. This date also shows the important years in one's life and helps one to improve one's personality by repeating its frequency in day to day action. A person born on the 7th of the month has originality, individuality and independence. He loves to travel and is a free bird. This is a spiritual number and Supreme Consciousness is developed in this individual. His behaviour is a mystery to others and he is often absent-minded. His important and lucky years in life are 7, 16, 25, 34, 43, 52, 61, 70 etc.

The Month of Birth

The month of birth shows the social circle of the individual. It shows his childhood and also the social status of the family he is born in. It also indicates the influence of brothers, sisters and playmates. It shows his attraction towards friends and relatives who are governed by the characteristics shown by the number of the month. In the present case, the month is May, *i.e.* the fifth month. Therefore the social circle of the person is dominated by number five. He is therefore attracted towards those who are intelligent, industrious and have quickness, scientific pursuits, business abilities and intuition. He selects friends who are well read and can impart their knowledge. A person born in May does not like to talk about ordinary things in life and dislikes kitchen discussions.

The Total of the Birth Date

The gross total indicates the number of destiny. In the present case, it is two. It shows his personality in a general way. Since the number two is governed by the Moon, the person is unsteady in life, whimsical and changing. His individual date is seven which is governed by the planet Neptune which also has similar characteristics. Therefore this person is more dominated by the Moon and his ideas, behaviour, likes, dislikes etc. are heightened. His important years in life will be 2, 11, 20, 29, 38, 47, 56, 65 etc., where the total of the digits comes to two. This destiny number is not necessarily a lucky number and it shows both good and bad events in life. Thus there is a difference between the date of the month and the destiny number.

Numerical Horoscope

We can arrange the date of birth in the form of a horoscope. From this horoscope we can know the level of the person's thoughts, whether he thinks on an idealistic plane or on a material plane or on a lower plane. We can present it in the form of Dharma, Artha and Kama; or Satwa, Rajas and Tamas. Let us suppose that the birth date of a person is 12–6–1953.

I shall give below a standard form of the numerical horoscope.

3	1	9	Dharma
6	7	5	Artha
2	8	4	Kama

We have now to place the numbers in the given birth date in the appropriate squares alloted to each number in the standard horoscope. Our birth date is 12-6-1953. While placing the numbers we have not to consider the number of the century. The year of birth is 1953. Here we have to omit 19 and consider only the year 53. The horoscope of the birth date 12-6-53 will be as under.

3	1		Dharma
6		5	Artha
2			Kama

On the mental level he is dominated by number 3 and 1. The number 3 is governed by the planet Jupiter and the number 1 is ruled by the Sun. It means that the mental thinking of the person is dominated by the characteristics of Jupiter and the Sun and the person is ambitious, religious and dignified. The Sun gives him originality, oratory and activity.

On the material level he has the qualities of Venus and Mercury. Mercury is a business planet and Venus shows art. The combination produces a person who will use his creative art or talent to earn money.

On the lower plane the person is governed by the imaginative faculty of the Moon. But his imagination will be on the level of Kama only and he may utilise his success for indulging in lower vices only. We can summarize the character of the person and say that he has art and creativity shown by the number 6 and the planet Venus ; he has originality and activity shown by the number 1 and the planet Sun ; he also has ambition shown by number 3 and the planet Jupiter and he will utilise all these qualities to make money and get success in practical life as shown by the number 5 and the planet Mercury. The Moon indicates that he may indulge in low vices.

If in a birth date a number is repeated a second time or a third time, that number gets double or triple power. If in the above birth date, the month is January instead of June, in the horoscope number 1 will be repeated a second time. If the year of birth is 51 instead of 53, the number one will be repeated for the third time (12–1–1951). If the birth date is 16–6–1953, the number 6 is repeated two times; that means the influence of Venus is doubled. In such a case we have to add a line to the number to show its double power, add two lines to show the triple power. Thus, the birth date 12–1–1951 will have the following horoscope.

	1″	
		5
2		

In the above case, the triple power of the number 1 is indicated by the additional two lines.

Missing Numbers

After preparing the necessary horoscope from any known birth date, we may notice that certain numbers are missing in the horoscope. According to an age-old theory, the missing numbers indicate the effect of our Karma (action) in our previous birth. Due to certain acts of ours in our previous birth, we have to suffer the disadvantages of the missing numbers. We will not get the benefits of the planets which are missing in the horoscope. For instance, the number 3 is missing, that means that the person does not have characteristics such as ambition, love of religion, prestige, honour, dignity etc. which are indicated by the planet Jupiter. Supposing the number 8 represented by the planet Saturn is missing the person lacks a practical outlook and materialistic philosophy shown by the planet Saturn. In short, the missing numbers indicate a lack of power represented by the missing numbers. It is therefore advisable that the person should understand his virtues as well as his drawbacks and limitations and try to develop the qualities of the missing numbers which would help him to overcome the obstacles in life and lead a successful life.

By casting the horoscope from the birth date, we can immediately know the dominating characteristics of the person as well as his weaknesses shown by the missing numbers. We can also know the level of thought he is governed by. This study is useful for a detailed psycho-analysis of the person.

CHAPTER 25

What is in a Name?

A) Uptil now we have studied how the individual numbers in a given birth date radiate vibrations and how these vibrations heighten one's personality or help one to improve one's lot in life by repeating the lucky number indicated by the date of the month. Now I shall explain how even the name emits certain vibrations and how we can change the vibrations of our name by making a slight change. It is necessary that our birth date vibrations and those of the name should be in harmony in order to have a smooth sailing in life. People have often come to me complaining that there is always a delay in their life or they do not get the desired or expected results. After studying their cases, I have found that many a time the vibrations thrown out from their birth date and those emitted by their names are not in harmony and therefore the total vibrations of their personality are not powerful. In that case, I have to make a suitable change in the name so that its radiations are in unison with those of the birth date. It is my experience that the desired results are acquired by making a slight change in the name.

Once a friend of mine, who is running an electronic industry, complained that a big company had promised to purchase all the products of his electronic industry, but somehow even after three years the actual contract could not be finalized. After my suggession to add one more letter to his name and to repeat that name several thousand times, he took a paper and a pencil and went on writing his altered name for five to ten minutes everyday. After about three weeks he informed me that he got the result of his repeated vibrations and the agreement was finally signed. I shall describe this theory in brief.

B) Each letter is given a number and it is as follows: A–1, B–2, C–3, D–4, E–5, F–8, G–3, H–5, I–1, J–1. K–2, L–3, M–4, N–5, O–7, P–8, Q–1, R–2, S–3, T–4, U–6. V–6, W–6, X–5, Y–1, Z–7. The prefixes, Mr. Mrs. Shri, Smt, etc. are not to be taken into consideration. Let us suppose that the name of an individual is Ramesh Vishnu Tiwari. The numerical vibrations are *214535 613556 416121*

The Total is 20 26 15

Single digit: 2 + 8 + 6 = 16 = 1 + 6 = 7

If the individual always writes his complete name as above, his final vibrations, when reduced to a single digit, are of number 7. If this number 7 is a friend of the number indicated by the date of the month in his birth date, (as shown earlier while dealing with the number seven) he can continue signing his full name. He can also use his full name, on his letter heads and on his name plate. On the whole he will have smooth sailing in life and his objects will be achieved.

Supposing the full name does not harmonise with the person's birth date, we have then to see whether any other formation of the name is suitable to make the necessary harmony. For instance let us try the following names.

1) Ramesh V. Tiwari
2) R. V. Tiwari
3) R. Tiwari or 4) Ramesh Tiwari.

We should work out numerical values of each of the above combinations and see which is most suitable for the birth date. In case none of these is suitable or matches the birth date, we can add one or two letters to the name and alter the spelling. For example, in the first name we can add one more 'm' and write 'Rammesh', or one more 'a' and write 'Ramesha'. If this is also not suitable, we should try the spelling of the word 'Tiwari' as 'Tiwaari'. Instead of the letter 'i' at the end we can also spell as 'y'. But the numerical values of 'i' and 'y' are the same, that is one. Therefore using 'y' instead of 'i' would not make any difference. This is how we have to try various combinations in the name and create new vibrations which would finally harmonise with the birth date vibrations and improve the personality of the individual. Once we set right the name vibrations, it is necessary to repeat those vibrations several thousand times every day by writing the name on a paper for some five to ten minutes. I assure my readers that such changes do help the individual to make his life healthy and smooth. I have tried this method hundreds of times in my study.

Mental Vibrations and Material Vibrations

I shall go slightly deeper into our theory of vibrations. In the name vibrations, we can have two parts, one mental vibrations and the other material vibrations. The number values of all the vowels in a name are written on the top and the number values of the remaining letters (consonants) are written at the bottom. By doing so we shall know the mental as well as the material picture of the thoughts of an individual. For clarification, we shall take the same name which we have discussed above, Ramesh Vishnu Tiwari. In this name we have to separate the vowels and the consonants. In the name Ramesh we have two vowels, 'a' and 'e'. So we write the numerical values of these letters at the top and those of the consonants at the bottom. Thus for Ramesh : $\frac{1+5}{2+4+3+5} = \frac{6}{14}$ In the name Ramesh the mental vibrations are 6 that means those of Venus. The material vibrations are 14 *i.e.* 5 which means Mercury. In short, on the mental plane, Ramesh is governed by Venus. He loves beauty, nature, art, decency and such things which are the characteristics of the planet Venus and number 6.

On the material plane the name Ramesh represents number 5 and the planet Mercury. He is shrewd, clever and has a business aptitude. He loves science, research and intellectual work. We can similarly work out the mental and material vibrations from the complete name and find out the total personality.

If a man wishes to start a business we can suggest to him a suitable name for his enterprise. An auspicious name can be suggested for a house or for a building. An appropriate name can be given to a newly born baby. and so on. It is said that Emperor Napolean made a slight change in his name and he became the Emperor.

CHAPTER 26

The Day for a Move

As we refer to an almanac for a muhurath or an auspicious day, numerology can help us to know what day is good for a specific act. We are interested in knowing whether a day is good or not for a particular act, for instance, we want to ask for a favour, or we want to enter into a contract, or we want to embark on a journey, or we want to start a new course of study. In numerology there is a system whereby we can find out a lucky day for a certain step.

We have to take only the date and the month in our birth date and add them to the total of the digits of the date of a particular day. Supposing the date of birth is 16–1–1965 and today is 13–12–1985. We have to work out as under.

The first date	16
Add the month January	1
Add todays' date	13
Add present month	12
Add the year	1985
Total	2027 = 11 = 2

Number 2 is auspicious for certain acts of ours and so also other numbers from 1 to 9. I shall give below the significance of these numbers and we should choose the right day for our step. Supposing we want to take legal advice, number 3 is auspicious for that act. According to the above working, today is the day of number 2. Therefore for taking legal advice we should select the next day. Every day is favourable to certain kinds of activity and we should take our action on the proper day.

Significance of numbers from one to nine

No. 1 Vibrations emitted by number 1 are favourable for :

1) Planning ambitious projects

2) Expressing novel ideas
3) Starting some original work
4) Enrolling for a language course
5) Developing a new friendship
6) Interview with a new boss
7) Participation in music and atristic activities
8) Purchasing machinery and equipment
9) Trying for a competition or election
10) Going on a journey

*

No. 2 Vibrations emitted by number 2 are favouroble for :

1) Improving financial status
2) Selecting a life partner
3) Trying to get cooperation from others
4) Entering into a contract
5) Gaining others' confidence
6) Diplomatic talk and discrimination.

*

No. 3 Vibrations emitted by number 3 are favourable for :

1) Furthering your ambition
2) Going in for presentation articles
3) Taking legal advice
4) Making new investments
5) Trying for a favour or assistance
6) Presenting credentials
7) Studying a new subject
8) Developing contacts with editors.

*

No. 4 Vibrations emitted by number 4 are favourable for :

1) Providing educational facilities to children
2) Entering into a contract
3) Fixing securities
4) Arranging home affairs
5) Consulting a doctor
6) Dealing with agriculture.

*

No. 5 Vibrations emitted by number 5 are favourable for :

1) Playing with children
2) Participating in a garden party

3) Attending to correspondence
4) Making new acquaintances or friendships
5) Giving talk on the radio
6) Arranging a short trip.

*

No. 6 Vibrations emitted by number 6 are favourable for :

1) Making yourself attractive and charming
2) Developing love contacts
3) Visiting a beauty parlour
4) Proposing marriage
5) Patching up old quarrels
6) Taking rest and reading books
7) Attending a conference.

*

No. 7 Vibrations emitted by number 7 are favourable for

1) Controlling unwanted talk
2) Taking care about diet
3) Peace and meditation
4) Developing psychic studies
5) Taking decisions about family matters
6) Adopting a child
7) Consulting a Guru or a spiritual authority.

*

No. 8 Vibrations emitted by number 8 are favourable for :

1) Studying mysticism
2) Acquiring power of intuition
3) Developing spiritual healing
4) Making love
5) Trying one's luck in a race or a lottery
6) Donations to charitable institutions
7) Contesting an election
8) Looking after financial matters.

*

No. 9 Vibrations emitted by number 9 are favourable for :

1) Visiting charitable institutions
2) Dealing with confidential documents
3) Practising spiritual healing
4) Earning fame and reputation
5) Rectifying old mistakes

6) Trying for a journey or a picnic
7) Doing original work
8) Visiting musical concerts

*

A few years back a big officer from the army called on me one Sunday and informed me that he was expecting orders from the Head Quarters at Delhi for his transfer to Nagaland. He had been stationed in Poona for six or seven years and naturally had arranged for the education of his two daughters in Poona upto the tenth standard. His immediate transfer would disturb his family life and so he was very uneasy about his transfer. I worked out the next three or four days according to the formula we have studied above. The next day fell under the vibrations of number 3. I advised him to contact his Head Quarters on the trunk telephone and ask as a favour to get his transfer postponed by a few months till the examinations of his daughters were over. I also worked out the day next to that which came under the vibrations of number 4 which favours 'arranging home affairs' or 'providing educational facilities for the children'. I therefore predicted that most probably he would get his orders under number 4. He returned to me after about 6 days and told me that he got the orders on the day predicted and that he was proceeding to Nagaland in a day or two.

In addition to the favourable day, if our lucky number also falls on that day, it will achieve positive results for the action taken on that day.

I request my readers to try this method when taking decisions on different matters and to keep a regular note and see the results for themselves. I am sure that they will achieve success.

CHAPTER 27

Day of the Week from the Birth Date

It is an interesting calculation to find out the day of the week from the complete date of birth. It is equally interesting to know that a numerologist, during his discussions with his client, can astonish his client by telling him his day of birth. He can do so by secretly doing certain calculations from the complete date of birth of his client. This secret formula is as under.

There are certain numbers alloted to each month and to centuries. Numbers alloted to centuries are as under :

No. 4 to the 18th Century. No. 2 to the 19th Century.

No. 0 to the 20th Century and no. 6 to the 21st Century.

The numbers allotted to individual months are as under.

No. 1 to January. No. 4 to February and March. No. 0 to April.

No. 2 to May. No. 5 to June. No. 0 to July. No. 3 to August.

No. 6 to September. No. 1 to October. No. 4 to November and

No. 6 to December. In leap years, numbers to January and February are 0 and 3.

Let us take a birth date, 16–8–1960.

1) We have to divide the last two digits of the century by 4.
   Thus $60 \div 4 = 15$.
2) Add this figure of 15 to the year of birth *i.e.* 60.
   Thus $60 + 15 = 75$
3) Add the date of birth to the above figure of 75.
   $16 + 75 = 91$.
4) Add the number allotted to the month of birth.
   $3 + 91 = 94$.
5) Add the number allotted to the 20th century which is 0.

Now divide this figure of 94 by 7 and find out the remainder. The remainder is 3 and therefore the day is Tuesday. The relation between the remainder and the day of the week is as under :

If the remainder is 0, it is Saturday.
If the remainder is 1, it is Sunday.
If the remainder is 2, it is Monday.
If the remainder is 3, it is Tuesday.
If the remainder is 4, it is Wednesday.
If the remainder is 5, it is Thursday.
If the remainder is 6, it is Friday.

In the above birth date, 16–8–1960, we notice that it is a leap year and if the month of birth is January or February instead of August, the month number will be 0 or 3.

The day of the week also has its ruling planet which also affects the behaviour of the person.

CHAPTER 28

Tracing Things Lost

Theory: Everyone has a conscious mind and a sub-conscious mind. Modern science is investigating the function of the sub-conscious. It has discovered that this has a tremendous potential and a power which can often show wonderful results. Every brain, while functioning, creates definite vibrations or waves in the ethereal atmosphere. These waves impinge upon the brains of others and cause a perception of personality so that the individuals affected will immediately create a mental image of the person whose thought is projected and whose presence is shortly made apparent to the senses. However, in this process the transmitter is wholly unaware of the fact that his thought waves have an effect on the sub-conscious of the other person. This process takes place on the level of the sub-conscious of the two persons. A conclusion, based upon a close study of this familiar but little understood phenomenon, is that the sub-conscious of the projector is not only aware of the presence of other minds, but is capable of projecting itself into immediate relations with them. This projection is received by the sub-conscious of the other person and later on received by the conscious mind. Extremely sensitive persons not only receive the waves but also a vision.

This sub-conscious mind has an ability to peep into the future and can register future events well in advance on its surface. Based on this theory and assumption, it is inferred that the mind can give out certain numbers which can be interpreted to locate the place where a lost article can be found.

A person who has lost his article is asked to utter any 9 numbers one after another. The numbers should come spontaneously. These nine numbers are totalled up and 3 is added to the total. The total is referred to the nature of the question.

Example : The nine numbers given at random are set as under. 967487942 = 56 + 3 = 59

The interpretation of number 59 is then referred to the chart. The answer is "It is in a flour or powder required for cooking purpose." The meaning of various numbers is as follows. If the resultant is

1—The article may be in the living room near a white curtain. A smart child may know it.
2—It is near some utensil and a servant may be helpful.
3—Among books or papers or in a passage.
4—It is actually misplaced and not lost.
5—Try for it under a cloak or garment or on a hanging hook.
6—Near the footwear.
7—A female member of the family has kept it while arranging clothes.
8—On the top of a cupboard or a shelf. Take the help of an assistant.
9—In the robes or clothing of young ones.
10—It is in the drawing room, you will get it back.
11—It is near a water place, but not in the house but at some distance. Think of a picnic spot you recently visited.
12—The article is safe. Search for it at your working place.
13—Search for it in your cloak room or on the hanger.
14—You may not recover the article. Anyway search the cleaning place.
15—Somewhere near where the animals (cows, horses, dogs) are kept. Enquire of your spouse.
16—You can get it. Contact your cook.
17—Near the important securities and on the shelf.
18—It is in the house only and hidden in clothes.
19—In a small passage or lane slightly away from the house.
20—It is only misplaced. Search near water or the carpet.
21—It is in a trunk, suit-case or a box.
22—It is at a height within the house. May be on a shelf.
23—It is in the wardrobe or among washing clothes.
24—It is safe and will be found in due course.
25—Be quick to search for it among your articles.
26—It might be in a very safe place. Contact elder members.
27—Ask the car driver or search for it in the garage.
28—Forget about getting back the article. It is totally lost.

29—It has been given to someone. It will be returned to you.
30—It was lost during the play of children. Contact them.
31—Don't worry. It is near the bath room or washing place.
32—It is in the passage or a corridor or a closed place.
33—It is hidden in your clothes.
34—You may get it near the cooking gas or a fire-place.
35—It may be near the attached bath.
36—You will get it through your servant.
37—It is lying on the floor in your room.
38—It is near the swimming tank.
39—It is on a shelf
40—By chance it has been wrapped in your clothes.
41—Near the footwear.
42—It is near water or in the premises of the servant.
43—Search for it near the garage.
44—It is near the oil containers.
45—It is on the cupboard or a shelf.
46—Ask your partner.
47—One of your servants has committed the theft.
48—It is near the drinking water.
49—You will not get it.
50—It is in a box, suitcase or a trunk.
51—It is near your place of bath.
52—Enquire with the mistress of the house or her relatives. It has changed hands.
53—A person who is in possession of the article will return it.
54—Search where the children play.
55—It is near a water draining place.
56—It is where you last halted.
57—It may be in your playing kit.
58—It is very difficult to get it back. Two persons have got hold of it.
59—It is in flour or powder required for cooking. Ask the senior servant.
60—You can forget about it. It is lost for ever.
61—It is near a wall.
62—It is very difficult to trace it.
63—It may be in the lumber room.
64—It is not lost. Search for it in dark corners.
65—Chances of getting it back are poor.

66—It has been stolen by two servants who have conspired. A slightly handicapped servant may be questioned. But little possibility of recovery.
67—A boy in the family will assist you in the matter.
68—Ask someone to collect it from the top of the house.
69—It may be at the entrance of the house of your relative or at a place you last visited.
70—It is near a water place.
71—Search for it on the floor near your feet.
72—It is near a water reservoir.
73—You will have to lodge a regular complaint about the theft.
74—It will be found by a careful servant.
75—Youngsters have taken it and it will be returned in a damaged condition.
76—It is near some food.
77—A servant in the house will fetch it for you.
78—Very difficult to recover.
79—Search near the iron cupboard.
80—It is in a box, trunk or a case.
81—You will be lucky to find it in your clothes.
82—You will get it in the kitchen.
83—A young girl will recover it from a water tank.
84—It is in a box or case.

CHAPTER 29

The Pyramid System

The Pyramid system in the field of numerology is another wonder of the psychic phenomenon. As stated in the earlier chapter, man is gifted with psychic powers which are of various kinds and we must know how to tap those powers. In the study of numerology, there is a vast scope for the use of these psychic powers in daily life. With the help of the Pyramid System, any question can be solved with great accuracy. However the questioner must be sincere, his difficulty should be real, and the same question is not to be repeated again. If we try to play mischief with this system, the answers and results will be wrong. In nature there are symbols which have their own laws and functions but which are wholly unintelligible to the modern world. Our ancient scholars were masters of occult powers and they discovered the hidden meaning of these symbols in nature. The Pyramid System is also the outcome of their discoveries.

Taking it for granted that the person who approaches us for consultation is sincere about his difficulty, and his difficulty is genuine, he should be requested to ask his question in a spontaneous manner. The words should come naturally, without much thought.

Such a question being put, the number of the words is counted and set down. This figure is followed by the number of letters in each of the words, and the line is completed. The figures in this line are then successively added together, the first with the second, the second with the third, the third with the fourth, and so on until they have been paired and added. This addition is reduced to a single digit if it exceeds 9, and then written in the second line and in between the two numbers which have been added. These are then treated in the same manner by successive pairing and addition and a third line is produced. Each successive line being one figure less than the one above it, it follows that the process eventually tapers to a single figure. It is this figure that is referred to its planetary equivalent and the interpretation made thence in accordance with the nature of the question. Let us take an example.

A person asks "Shall I go abroad?"

There are 4 words in this sentence, so the figure 4 is set down. "Shall" contains 5 letters, "I" 1, "go" 2, "abroad" 6. Then the first line stands thus : 4 5 1 2 6. The Pyramid when completed will be as follows :—

4 5 1 2 6
9 6 3 8
6 9 2
6 2
8

The resultant figure is 8 which is the number of Saturn which shows delays, difficulties and probable disappointment. If the resultant number is 1, it would mean success in the enterprises or efforts and the person will undertake foreign travels.

If the resultant is 2, it is dominated by the planet Moon and this would indicate love for travel and therefore success.

If the resultant is 3, it is governed by the planet Jupiter which shows ambition, prestige and honour and the answer would be 'Yes'. If the resultant is 4, it is dominated by Harshal (Uranus) which shows revolutions and uncertainties and therefore the answer is "Doubtful".

In the same manner we have to interpret the significance of the resultant number in accordance with the question.

In the Pyramid System, the interpretation also should be spontaneous. It should come out immediately. However, in order to get a correct interpretation of the number, it is necessary to be conversant with all the qualities of that number.

Sometimes it is also useful to note whether the resultant number is odd or even. As stated in the introduction, according to the Chinese system and also the Pythagorean system, odd numbers are positive, energetic, manly, showing heat and fire, whereas even numbers denote a female, darkness, coldness and are of ephemeral value. Supposing a woman expecting a child shortly asks whether she will have a son or a daughter, and the resultant number is odd, the answer is a son and if the number is even, the answer is a daughter. Thus we have to use this Pyramid System very intelligently and our intuition has to play a part in it.

CHAPTER 30

Horse Racing

It is difficult to find an individual who is not interested in getting a windfall or getting rich in one night. Everybody is interested in lottery, horse racing, cassino and such other sports or games whereby he would get rich without effort. Horse racing is one of the avenues which has been an attraction to millions of people all over the world.

There are various systems or methods with the help of which a winner in the horse race is worked out. People take into consideration the age of the horse, his previous record, the handicap he has got, his weight, the length of the race, the jockey who is to ride him and so on and so forth. Numerology is one of the simplest methods to work out the horse which will achieve success and bring money. The method of finding out one's lucky horse is as under.

1) The person should always try his lucky number only. If he is born on the 1st, 10th, 19th or 28th of any month, his lucky number is 1 and he is governed by the planet Sun. Number 4 is the counterpart of number 1 and therefore this person should always try those horses whose serial numbers are 1 and 4.

2) Every number has its lucky colours. The jockeys wear caps of different colours and the person should find out a jockey who is wearing a cap of his lucky colour.

We have now to combine the number of the horse and the lucky colour. The lucky colours of number 1 person are yellow, orange and gold. If the jockey is wearing a cap having one of these colours, well and good. If the colours are different but of those of number 4, the person can try horse number 1 because number 4 is equally lucky for him.

If the colour of the cap is not in harmony with the lucky number, the person should see whether the horse is a favourite or a fluke. If the horse is a favourite and the colour is lucky, it is advisable to try on that horse.

3) We should work out the mental vibrations (vowels) of the name of the horse and the name of the jockey. If these vibrations are in harmony with our name vibrations we try that horse or that jocky which is favourable to us. It is also useful if their vibrations and those indicated by numbers favourable for marriage are in harmony.

From the above, it is clear that before we select the horse we have to think of (a) our lucky number (b) lucky colour (c) name of the horse (d) name of the jockey (e) the colour of jockey's cap (f) our lucky number for marriage (g) whether the horse is a fluke or favourite. After taking all these factors, and their combinations into consideration, we have to make the final selection of the winning horse.

CHAPTER 31

Epilogue

Nature gives us warning of coming dangers. We have to understand that it is a warning and try to avoid the danger. I know a person who got up one fine morning and decided to take a jolly trip to a neighbouring village. He asked his wife to go with him. But due to some other commitments, the wife was reluctant to join him. This was the first warning not to take the trip. Thereafter, he went to his garage and found that one of the wheels of his car had burst. This was the second warning but he did not take notice of it. He replaced the wheel and took out the car. Since his wife was not willing to accompany him, he wanted to contact a friend for a happy ride. On his way to his friend, the fuel in the car gave out and he had to leave the car on the road and go to collect the petrol. This was the third warning. Finally he got his friend to join him and soon found himself on the highway. Within half an hour, the replaced wheel burst all of a sudden and he lost control over his car which finally left the road and went into a ditch. There were a few fractures in his legs and the back and he had to spend some three months in the hospital. This is how we ignore the warning given to us by nature. According to Hindu shastras, 'Lakshana' (omen) gives us an indication of what is going to happen.

I may quote another incident such as occurs in everybody's life. It may happen that we get up in the morning and we find that we are either out of sorts or have a headache. This is also a lakshana of a bad day ahead. On such occasions we should try to avoid responsible work and postpone any important work. That will save us from mistakes and calamities.

Numbers help us to understand ourselves, our family members, our boss and subordinates. By knowing their numbers, we can know their psychology, likes, dislikes and moods. This will help us in developing our approach towards them.

After the study of numerology for the last several years, I have found that numbers 1, 4, and 8 have some specialities of their own. Persons governed by number 1 tend to make changes and every three to four years there is a change in their career. Number 4 women are dominant and dictatorial and also very uneasy. This is particularly true of women who are born on 22nd of March, or November or December. Number 8 always shows delay in life. The delay may be in any field. It also indicates hardships and difficulties.

Everybody is interested in winning a lottery or money in a horse race. Such people should always try their ruling number. If the lucky number is 1, the person should purchase a lottery ticket where the total of all the numbers comes to the single digit of 1, or he should purchase a ticket where the last number is 1. He should also work out the day on which he should purchase the ticket.

In chapter 2, we have studied the Importance of numbers according to the date of the month in our birth date. In chapter 3 we have studied the same aspects of the month of our birth date. Between the date of birth and the month of birth, we have to give importance to the date of birth. It is true that millions of people are governed by each number or each month and one may wonder how all these millions of people can have the same thinking, behaviour and characteristics. But experience proves that people governed by a particular number have many common points and their likes, dislikes, ambition, health etc., are quite similar.

This self-evaluation is necessary if we desire to prosper in life. We can also improve our personality by repeating our number in all our actions and also by using our lucky colours and lucky jewels. Experience shows that sometimes a radical change in life can take place and an ordinary life can have a turning point. An ordinary person can reach heights undreamt of.

Numerology as explained in these chapters is equally helpful in selecting a marriage partner. In normal course, the horoscopes of the two are compared in order to find out their compatibility. But interpreting horoscopes is a matter of deep study and its place can be taken by the study of numerology. I have prepared charts for the date as well as for the months which indicate our friends and our affinities. These charts will be helpful in selecting a partner in life so as to ensure a happy married life.

I have explained the science of Numerology in simple language and only that portion which will be useful in our day-to-day life. Please refer to the ready-made charts given for quick reference, for your guidance and also for the guidance of your friends and relatives.

Part Two: Study Course in Palmistry

After the publication of my exhaustive book "Brighten your Future Through Palm Reading" in March 1985, published by IBH Prakashana—Bangalore, I received innumerable letters from several parts of India, suggesting that I should write an elementary course for the study of palmistry so that a layman could pick up this subject and the study could be propagated on a large scale for the benefit of humanity in getting success and happiness in life. It has also been my long-felt desire to enlighten the public on this subject and present palmistry on a scientific basis so that an educated man would not look at it as mere superstition but would consider it on a rational basis and use the study for practical purpose in day to day life. The letters I received encouraged me and prompted me to take up this work. I hope I shall be able to explain to the public in simple language how the study of palmistry can be made use of in practical life. Even though this book is primarily meant for a beginner, the study course developed herein is sufficient for any one to practise Palmistry independently as a profession and earn fame, popularity and money.

This book is primarily meant for a beginner and all the basic ideas of the study of palmistry have been explained including the several objections raised against this study which a student of palmistry has to face in daily life. This is probably the first book written in the form of a study course, though there are several institutions which conduct correspondence courses. *If, as luck many have it, this book is recognised as a standard text book for the primary study of palmistry, justice will have been done to my efforts to spread the knowledge of palmistry to a large and wide class of people and help them to improve their life and career to a great extent.*

Every student of occultism has to his credit a large number of interesting cases and I am not an exception to it. Therefore before proceeding with the study, I would like to narrate a few of my experiences in this field which could prove the utility of the subject in daily life.

1) Once a lady with her newly married daughter visited me asked whether her daughter had any chances of visiting foreign countries. After scanning her hand, I found that her Line of Life had ended on the mount of Moon (Fig. 3–a). Besides this marking there were no other signs showing foreign travels, such as a line of voyage. On the strength of the course of the Line of Life covering a greater portion of the mount of Moon, I predicted that, not only she would visit foreign countries, but she would spend most of her later life in foreign countries only. In a short time thereafter, her husband secured a job and was posted to the U.K ; she has been staying there for about 20 years.

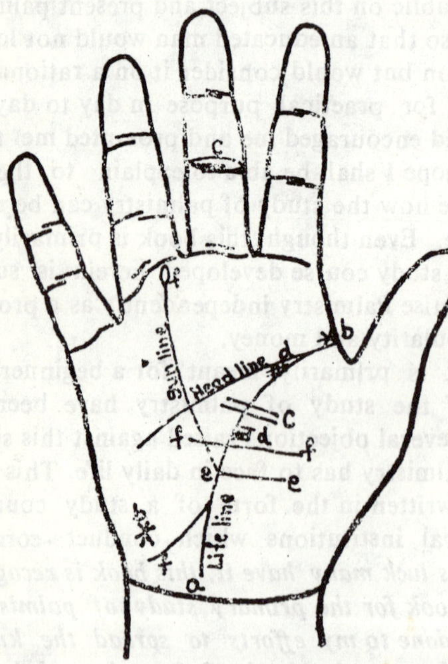

Fig. 3

2) Sometimes a fun-fair or an exhibition is organised by social institutions, such as the Lions' Club, the Rotary Club, Womens' Councils etc. in aid of the poor, the blind

handicapped children etc. Many a time I was offered a stall in such functions and I had an opportunity to see the hands of a greater variety of people who visited my stall for fun. The contribution collected was naturally donated to that institution in whose aid the function was arranged. Only two questions were allowed and only five minutes were alloted to every individual. On one such occasion, people were visiting me one after another. It was really a test for me and most of the visitors wanted to test my knowledge and also ridicule the study of palmistry. Many of them had got their promotions very recently but even then they asked me when they would get the promotion. Many of them had visited foreign countries, but they would ask whether they had any chance of foreign travel. Many of them were married but would ask when they would marry. Fortunately, I could stand their tests and could succeed in my examination. It so happened that once a girl about 23 years old came in and after putting her palm before me asked me what I knew about her mother. The question was critical and the reply still more difficult. However, I found a star at the edge of the mount of Jupiter and touching the Life Line which indicated loss of mother. A star on the lower mount of Moon showed mystery in life. I told her, point blank, that her mother was dead and she had a mysterious death (Fig. 3–b). She was extremely surprised and felt very shy and apologized for testing my knowledge.

3) On another occasion a man of forty entered the stall and talked to me about his losses in business and asked when he would overcome the financial crisis. I observed two parallel lines from the mount of Uranus and cutting the Line of Life which indicated auspicious events and a sign of yova on the second joint of the Saturn finger which meant unexpected luck in lottery (Fig. 3–c). I also calculated his lucky number as 4 and asked him to try this number in a lottery or gambling. As luck would have it, he got an opportunity to visit the United States of America for his business and one fine morning he remembered my prophecy and decided to try his luck. The date was 4, *i.e.*, his lucky number. He decided to go to Las Vegas, the well known place in America for gamblers. He started playing the game of Cassino exactly at 4 p.m. He occupied the fourth chair and staked 40 dollars. Surprisingly,

his luck was very powerful on that day and after repeating the number 4 all times, he came out successfully with 4,000 dollars. In his business also he banked on number 4 wherever he went and made a fruitful trip.

4) Once a man about thirty-five years of age was complaining about his bad relations with his wife and unhappiness in married life. He also had difficulty in getting a divorce. After looking at his hand, I saw a grill on the Head Line and another grill on the mount of Venus, both touching the Life Line (Fig. 3-d), which indicated change of religion. I advised him accordingly and he succeeded in getting the divorce after his changing his religion.

5) One day a couple approached me for consultations. The wife was well educated and was a great social worker as well as an author. Somehow, her efforts and work in the social field did not get any recognition. Her hands also did not show any reputation in that direction. I therefore looked at the hands of her husband which showed the joining of the Sun Line to the Life Line and at the same time a line from the Mount of Venus joining the Sun Line on the Life Line (Fig. 3–e). This marking shows reputation and honour to the wife. In a short period thereafter, the State Government appreciated the social work of the lady and conferred on her the title of "Dalit Mitra" (Friend of the poor).

6) I will narrate just one more interesting experience.

Once I was travelling by train and was reading a book on palmistry. A fellow-passanger sitting on the opposite seat in front of me was clothed in a saffron shirt and had a white beard. Some of the persons surrounding him were addressing him as 'Gurujee'. From his talk I could guess that he had a number of disciples. He looked brilliant with sharp eyes and his talk was very intelligent showing his vast study in philosophy and mysticism. After my keeping aside the book from my hand, he suddenly bent forward and asked me whether I would solve his difficulty from his hand. He stretched his hands and questioned me whether he had any chances of settling down in foreign countries. I noticed a curious and an unusual marking on his hand. A cross line from the mount of Venus was cutting the Line of Sun and the Sun Line ended in an island. It meant loss of reputation, scandal and disgrace. He also had

a powerful line of voyage falling out of the Life Line and going to the Mount of Moon (Fig. 3–f). I said to him that his hands showed foreign travels but he would leave the country in a suspicious and disgraceful way and he should guard himself against any scandal. After a few years, as fate would have it, the public raised objections to his activities and he was forced to leave India for ever.

CHAPTER 32

Introduction

The study of palmistry is as old as history and various systems of palm-reading have been evolved in different countries from time immemorial. Even though the study has a long history, it is still a matter of prolonged and bitter controversy whether palmistry is a science. In this small book I propose to give some facts and explanations which prove that palmistry is a natural science based on experience.

Causes of Discredit

It is necessary for every student of palmistry to know why this subject has never been accepted as a worthwhile study. Many causes have contributed to the degeneration of palmistry. There is intrusion of a prejudice of the majority of the educated public who regard palmistry as mere superstition and condemn it on the ground that modern scientists reject it. But they should note that in this atomic age, what they considered trivial has been discovered to contain immense power, the atom having gained immeasurable importance. If, therefore, palmistry be considered by them too trivial for their attention, I would remind them that many of the greatest truths the world has known, though once considered trivialities, have become sources of tremendous force. Another reason for the degeneration of this science is that though numerous treatises have been written on it, unfortunately the tradition and dicta of old writers, whose modus operandi in building up the science was anything but scientific, have been retained by modern authors. This together with ignorant persons practising the cheiromantic art, has brought palmistry into discredit. Thirdly, science has vigorously ignored the study of the hand regardless of the fact that occultism formed the basis of scientific discovery, that astronomy was developed from astrology, that chemistry was developed from alchemy and that it was through occultism that the path of thought was first opened leading to the development of philosophy and psychology. The taboo, which impelled scientists to exclude cheirology from their researches, has caused the study to fall almost entirely into the hands of charlatans.

The study of palmistry is receiving attention in the medical world and the science known as dermatoglyphics is developing. But the prophetic aspect of hand-reading has still not been explored by modern science and it has still remained a matter of experience. There is no doubt that prophecies are often falsified by subsequent events. The reason for this must be sought not in the unscientific nature of this study but in our ignorance of the causes at work. The laws of biology are not always borne out by subsequent events, but no one would, on that ground, deny that biology is a science. The year of change in life can often be predicted much longer in advance than the coming of a cyclone. Hence, the claim of palmistry to be regarded as a science cannot be denied on the ground that palmists lack precision and prophetic power. Palmistry is a grammar and it is to be studied just like any other grammar. Once the nouns, pronouns, verbs, etc., are digested, the language of the hand is clear and lucid.

Wise men are ignorant of many things, which later every common student will come to know. Everyday sciences such as the science of the hand are establishing themselves more and more firmly as concrete and exact. Once upon a time the study of the hand was regarded as esoteric and mystical. 'Mystery' says Bain, 'is correlated to explanation; it means something intelligible enough as a fact, but not accounted for, not reduced to any law, principle or reason'. The ebb and flow of the tides, the motions of the planets, satellites and comets were understood as facts at all times, but they were regarded as mysteries until Newton brought them under the laws of motion and gravity. Such is the case with the science of palm-reading. Though it was regarded as an occult study uptil now, scientific research has proved that it does not have the occult symbol it carried with it, but it can be studied and practised as any other science.

Origin and History of the Science

From the earliest times, importance has been given to the hand by teachers in their writings, by priests in their ceremonies and by the common man in his superstition. This is because of the importance of the hand in our daily life when we notice that there exists scarcely a single event in our lives in which the hand is not the prime agent, the apparatus whereby we live, move and have our being.

The Hindus, the Egyptians and the Chinese are the oldest races whose philosophy and wisdom are every day being more and more revived. Long before Rome or Greece or Israel was even heard of, the monuments of India point back to an era of learning beyond and still beyond.

In the Indian tradition, eight methods have been suggested for foreknowledge of good and evil. They are, 1) Anga (Limbs), 2) Swapna (Dreams), 3) Swara (Sound), 4) Bhoomi (Attitude), 5) Vyanjana (Marks on the body), 6) Lakshana (Omens), 7) Utpatha (Phenomena like earth-quakes, volcano) and 8) Anthriksha (Sky—appearance of comet, circle around the Moon or the Sun, dropping down of satellites etc).

The ancient Indian sages gave out the knowledge of the hand which they gathered through three means *viz.* 1) Seeing (Darshan), 2) Touching (Sparshan) and 3) Analysing (Vimarshan). The knowledge thus gained, threw light on all the aspects of life.

According to the Indian tradition, Anga Vidya was first invented by the Sea God 'Samudra'. It was thereafter developed and handed down to humanity by sages like Narada and Gargya. Lord Skanda is held to be the patron deity of this science. Since God Samudra is the originator of the science, the study is called the Samudrika Shastra (The Science of Samudra).

We find further that this study of the hand spread in different countries and grew, flourished and found favour in the sight of those whose names are as 'Stars' of honour in the firmament of knowledge. We find it sanctioned by such men as Aristotle, the Emperor Augustus and many others of repute.

It is said that the Roman Emperor Caesar was so well versed in the study of the hand that on one occasion, when a foreign Prince presented his credentials, Caesar asked him to show his hands. After examining them he denounced the Prince as an imposter as he could not find any sign of royalty or royal descent on his hands. Several such illustrations can be quoted from India and other countries. One such example from Indian stories can be cited. When King Dushyanta forgot his wife Shakuntala, she approached him on a later occasion when she was with child. But King Dushyanta, due to the curse of Durwas Rishi, could not remember her. At that time the Prime Minister of the King told Shakuntala that according to the horoscope of the King, he would first have a son and the palm of the son would indicate all signs of a World Conqueror (Chakravarti). If therefore, Shakuntala begot a male child with signs on his hand showing royal birth and the potentiality of a World Conqueror, the King would accept her as his wife. This is an extraordinary example showing how the palm played an important role in giving a verdict.

We find references in the Bible in its seventh Verse of the 37th Chapter of Job where it is stated that "God placed signs and marks in the hands of all the sons of men, so that all men might know their works."

Queen Elizabeth, the daughter of the King Henry VIII, encouraged such studies and used to consult Dr. John Dee, her favourite palmist and astrologer.

All this goes to prove that the study in question is not only one of the most ancient in the world, but one that has occupied the serious attention of the most exalted minds in history.

Utility of the Study

The above discussion should prove to any rational-minded person that the study of the hand has its basis and foundation. Religion explains that the lines foretell the future, civilisation proves that Palmistry played an important part on many occasions, medicine gives recognition showing that the hand is related to the brain, which rules the character of a man and so his future too. Napoleon said, "Perhaps the face can decieve but never the Hand." Hitler had a band of occultists. All these go to prove the stability of the science and its utility in everyday life. Though it is not a perfect science, as no branch of human knowledge is, its investigations are none the less important. It does help humanity to a great extent. A palmist is a guide and his function is to show people the periods of ups and downs in their lives. They have to take hints and go forward. "Forewarned is forearmed." When we can tell our sons and daughters what sphere in life they are best fitted for and what studies they can best master, we shall have largely reduced the failures of young men and women. When we can prevent the marriages of people whose temperaments make it absolutely impossible that they should live together harmoniously, we shall have largely brought down the number of divorces and wrecked lives. If the hint is taken, life is easy; if people ignore it, they dig their own graves.

The hand is a valuable indicator of the health of the person. The shape of the hand, the mounts on the hand, the lines on the hand and the most important, the papillary ridges found all over the hand and the whorls and loops formed by them are all very important to diagnose the disease of the person. Many times remote causes of the diseases are located on these ridges.

The psychological aspect of the hand is also of great utility. Children can be coached for particular studies. The delinquent child can be found out by the study of his palm, and different treatments can be given to him to overcome his delinquency. Criminal psychology will play an important part in the detection of the criminals and research is possible to collect statistical data to establish signs of criminal traits on the palm.

To be brief, the study of the hand is useful to doctors in locating the disease, to educationists in choosing the proper career for the student, to psychiatrists in locating mental deficiencies, to criminologists in detecting the criminal, to the law courts in deciding doubtful parentage and to the common man in building up his career. I am not over-estimating this science by giving undue praise to it, but I am stating the exact value of the study and what it can do for humanity.

Palmistry is a treasure island. Valuable and tremendous information can be gathered from the hand. The only thing we must posses is the knowledge that the hand is a cave like that of the forty thieves and we must know the key word 'Open Sesame'. If we have the art to unfold the hand, if we have an insight into the working of the mounts and lines on the hand, it is easy to delineate the life of persons clearly.

Some of the standard objections and arguments raised against this science

Every student of palmistry is confronted with the following questions put to him by a so-called educated public.

1) *Is Palmistry a Science ?* : Modern science has not yet found the approach by which it can bring the study of palmistry in the rigid framework of the word "Science". Science has its own limitations. There are several experiences which have proved the sound basis of palmistry and it is always the experience in a particular field that paves the way to further research and make that experience an exact science. However, in spite of the great development of modern science in various fields, it has failed to produce appliances and means which can prove palmistry as a science. In Indian literature, there are some books available which explain how to cast a horoscope from the hand. If an exact chart of planets can be prepared from the palm which shows the existence of planetary position at the time of birth, what more proof is required to establish the fact that the planets influence the destiny of man and that their prominence can be located on the palm ?

2) *Do the lines on the hand change ?* : Yes, the lines on the hand do change. But the change takes place in the off-shoots or the rising and falling lines from the main lines. The formation and the course of main lines do not change. Therefore the main lines indicate the path of life whereas the small lines, either appearing or vanishing, indicate the events that have to take place shortly. The lines have a psychological significance and the mind produces, controls or alters the lines on the palm. The main lines indicate what the natural course of the life is, new lines just beginning to form show emotions and ideas just developing within the person. Experiments are going on to catch the thought waves of man in order to understand his mind, and scientists are spending years in the search for a key with which they can unlock the secrets of the human mind. One key is the hand, a perfect mirror giving insight into the working of the human mind. People can easily change their faces but not so easily their minds. The hand reveals the

man as he is, not as he may pretend to be. Sometimes, even small shades of the mind are seen on the hand. Hereditary and natural tendencies and those which have created profound impressions upon his mind can all be seen on the hand.

3) *If everything is predestined, what is the use of knowing one's Fate in advance ?*: According to Indian philosophy, there is always a struggle going on between Free Will and Predestination. The role of Predestination is to induce a thought in a particular direction. Whether to act on that thought or not is left to the Free Will. A thought to commit a murder or a crime is according to the principle of Predestination, but whether to act upon that thought or not is in the field of Free Will. The palm shows what is likely to happen in the future, but we can avoid the danger by exerting our Free Will. The lines on the hand also indicate the opportunities and also the lossess and scandals we have to go through. We can take advantage of the opportunities and avoid losses by taking care, well in time.

4) *What is the role of Intuition in predicting events ?*: Events are already shown on the palm. However, sometimes one sign can have several interpretations and it becomes a matter of combinations of other signs and lines on the palm so as to arrive at a definite conclusion regarding the meaning of that particular sign or line. Intuition helps to combine different possible interpretations and arrive at a conclusion. This type of intuition is required in each and every profession. For instance, even a doctor needs the help of his intuition to come to a decision based on his observations of his patient. Therefore we can say that Intuition is an additional aid to a palmist but not a necessity.

5) *Which palm of ladies is to be studied, the left or right?*: There is an age-old theory that the right hand of the man and left hand of the woman should be studied. The reason is the ancient palmists considered the right hand as the active hand and the left as the passive hand. Since the man plays an important role in family life and does most of his work with his right hand, it was the practice to study his right hand only. On the contrary, ladies remain at home and do the household duties. They are by nature submissive and passive. They have

to depend entirely on their husbands or the man of the family. As such, the left hand of ladies used to be observed.

According to the Indian system, indications of marriage of a man are to be read on the left hand and that of a woman on the right hand. Also it mentions that the left hands of children upto 14 years should be studied.

The above theory was improved upon and developed later. It is now accepted that the left hand indicates a man's inner sentiments and desires and the right hand shows the possibility of the fulfilment of his desires. The right hand is connected with the left hemisphere of the brain which is the centre of the conscious mind, whereas the left hand is connected with the right hemisphere of the brain indicating the subconscious mind. Therefore the right hand shows the conscious behaviour whereas the left hand shows the subconscious behaviour of the person.

Students are requested to learn this introductory chapter by heart so that they will be able to face any argument made by a pseudo-scientist.

CHAPTER 33

Preliminaries

Importance of Hand-Prints

Before we start hand-reading, it is obligatory to take a handprint of the person whose hands are under examination. Many students of palmistry are under the impression that naked hands are clearer than the hand impressions. But if they start taking the handprints and make it a rule to do so, in a short time they will find from a large collection of hand-prints they will have in their collection that the handprints are not only of great use to them but that they can notice a number of lines which are not readily visible to the naked eye, even with the use of a magnifying glass. There are a number of advantages in taking handprints and some of them can be stated as under.

a) The map of the hand is more clear and we know the starting point, the course and the end of each and every line.

b) The study of Mounts, which forms the core of the subject of palmistry, is difficult without a hand-impression. The development of any mount is easier to judge. We can know the position of the apex of the papillary ridges on the mount from which we know whether the mount is properly developed or it is displaced or inclined to another mount.

c) We can calculate a period of an event to a marked degree of accuracy, if we have the hand-print before us.

d) Jotting down our observations as regards signs on the hand, such as breaks, crosses, islands etc. can be done easily.

e) Lastly, the hand-print taken remains with us as a permanent record. It may happen that the same customer comes to us after a long time and if we have on record his previous hand-print, it will be possible for us to compare his new hand-print with the old one.

How to Take the Hand-Prints ?

There are various methods of taking hand-prints, but the simple and easy method is with the stamp-pad and the roller. It is better to use black ink for the stamp-pad and use a rubber roller which is usually available in a shop selling photographic appliances.

The students should please note that it is necessary to take hand-prints of both the hands.

Chart of the Study of Palmistry

The study of palmistry is known as Chirosophy. The science of Chirosophy is divided into two parts. The first part is known as Chirognomy which deals with the shape of the hand, the shape of the fingers, the development of the hand and the fingers, and with the shape and development of the nails. The second part is known as Chiromancy or Chirology or Palmistry and is concerned with the lines on the hand and their interpretation. This division is explained in the following chart.

Chirosophy

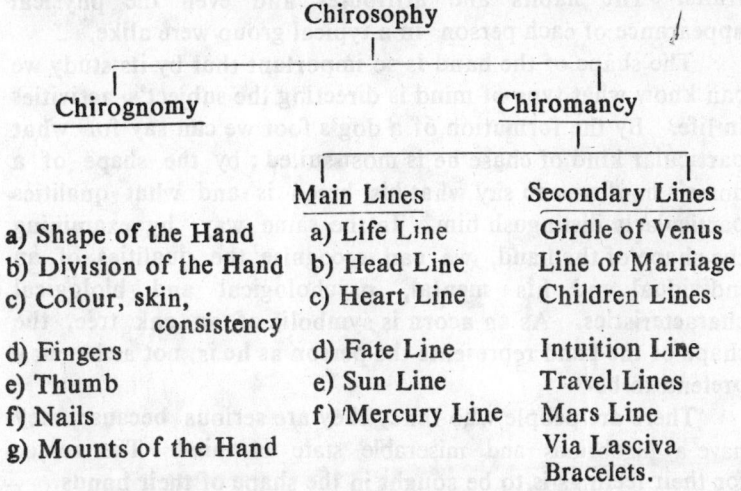

Chirognomy	Chiromancy	
	Main Lines	Secondary Lines
a) Shape of the Hand	a) Life Line	Girdle of Venus
b) Division of the Hand	b) Head Line	Line of Marriage
c) Colour, skin, consistency	c) Heart Line	Children Lines
d) Fingers	d) Fate Line	Intuition Line
e) Thumb	e) Sun Line	Travel Lines
f) Nails	f) Mercury Line	Mars Line
g) Mounts of the Hand		Via Lasciva
		Bracelets.

In this book I shall explain the salient features of each of the above factors so that the student will be equipped with the basic material of the study of palmistry. With the help of this information, any student will be in a position to read the palm of his friends or relatives with good success.

CHAPTER 34

The Shape of the Hand

1) Introduction, 2) Large and small Hands, 3) Broad and short, and long and narrow Hands, 4) Seven types of Hands: a) The Elementary, b) The Square, c) The Spatulate, d) The Conic, e) The Psychic, f) The Philosophic and g) The Mixed type of Hand.

Introduction

A careful study of this chapter will enable the students to start practice of hand-reading. There is an age-old theory that in the beginning all humanity was divided into seven types and each type was made up of individuals endowed with certain traits. The habits and attributes and even the physical appearance of each person in a typical group were alike.

The shape of the hand is so important that by its study we can know what type of mind is directing the subject's activities in life. By the formation of a dog's foot we can say for what particular kind of chase he is most suited; by the shape of a horse's hoof we can say what his breed is and what qualities particularly distingush him. In the same way, by examining the shape of the hand, we can recognise the qualities of an individual and his mental, psychological and biological characteristics. As an acorn is symbolic of an oak tree, the shape of the hand represents the person as he is, not as he may pretend to be.

There are people who fancy they are serious because they have a lugubrious and miserable state of mind. The reason for their feelings is to be sought in the shape of their hands.

Large and Small Hands

The first thing to be noted about the shape of the hand is whether the hand is large or small. There is no exact measurement which would give us a correct idea about the largeness or smallness of the hand. But the very appearance of the hand gives the impression that it is a large hand in comparision with the normal size of the hand. This is purely a matter of observation, experience and judgement. However, there should arise no difficulty in distinguishing a large hand or a small hand from a normal one.

Large Hands

It is surprising that persons with large hands have a love for small things with minute details. Normally, we expect that large hands should go in for large things and small hands for small things. But the fact is just the opposite. It has been observed that jewellers, watchmakers, engravers and persons who are engaged in trades, where every minute detail is to be observed, invariably have large hands. Their love for details is remarkable. Such persons are, therefore, fit for research work, where patience is required. They always like to go to the root of a a thing and from the root to the fruit they will examine each part carefully and gain perfect knowledge of the subject.

Small Hands

Small hands display the characteristics which are incompatible with those of large hands. Thus, such persons prefer to carry out large ideas and as a rule, make plans far too large for their power of execution. They love to manage large concerns and govern communities, and, speaking generally, even the writing of small hands is large and bold. Small hands display a warm heart and delicacy of the mind. Small-handed persons not only go in for large attempts but for too large a thing. It is towards the dwarf that the giant is irresistibly attracted and in like manner it is by the gaint that the dwarf is invariably fascinated. The Pyramids and the temples of Upper Egypt and of India seem to have been built by people whose hands were small, narrow, spatulate and smooth.

Broad and Short and Long and Narrow Hands

The hand proper, that is, the palm excluding the fingers, is either broad and short or long and narrow. A broad hand indicates the following characteristics : a) Breadth of vision, b) Common sense, c) Activity, d) Versatility.

The long and narrow hands have the following characteristics : a) A dreamy nature, b) Lack of concentration, c) Interest in many things but success in none, d) Strong selfish motives.

Seven Types of the Hand

There are seven types of hands. They are as follows : i) the elementary, ii) the square, iii) the spatulate, iv) the conic, v) the psychic, vi) the philosophic and vii) the mixed.

These seven types are sufficiently distinct from one another in their peculiarities to be clearly and distinctly described.

i) The Elementary Hand (fig. 4)

a) *Characteristics*

In appearance, the elementary hand is coarse and clumsy. The palm is large, thick and heavy. The fingers are short and the nails are also short. There are very few lines on the palm.

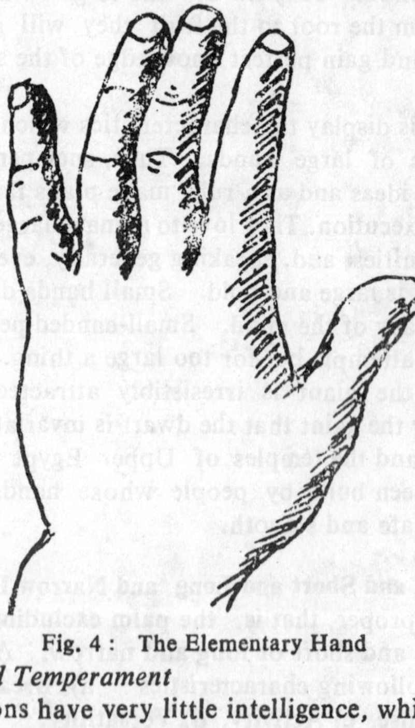

Fig. 4 : The Elementary Hand

b) *Nature and Temperament*

1) Such persons have very little intelligence, which leans more to the order of the brute.

2) They have little or no control over their passions.

3) The thumb being short and the first phalange of the same being more pronounced, they are violent in temper but not courageous.
4) They have no aspirations and they simply eat, drink, sleep and die.
5) They are dull and sluggish.
6) They are more troubled by phantoms and spectres.
7) They have no thirst for knowledge and they even despise wisdom and knowledge.

*

ii) The Square Hand (fig. 5)

a) *Characteristics*

A square hand means the palm proper square at the wrist, square at the base of fingers and the fingers themselves square.

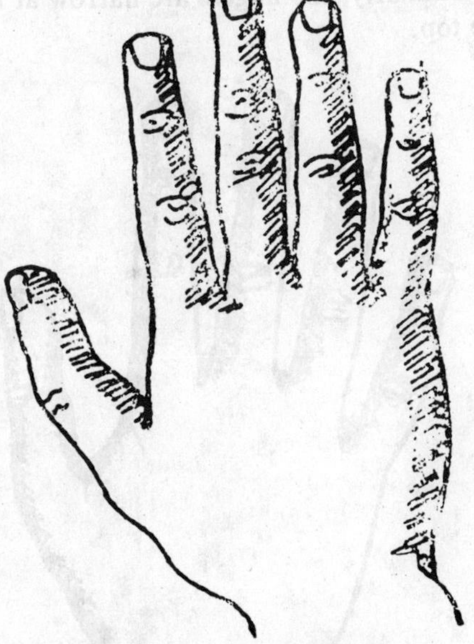

Fig. 5 : The Square Hand

b) *Nature and Temperament*

1) Such persons are punctual, orderly and precise in manner.
2) They love tradition and have a practical out-look.
3) Conventionality, perseverance and foresight are the main characteristics of the square hand.

4) They are too materialistic.
5) They have good common sense and discipline.

c) *Defects of the type*

1) Their greatest fault is that they are inclined to reason by a twelve-inch rod and disbelieve all they cannot understand.
2) Hypocrisy and conceit, coldness, stiffness of manner, harshness in punctuality are the other main defects.

*

iii) The Spatulate Hand (Fig. 6)

a) *Characteristics*

This type is so called because of its formation like the spatula of the chemist. In this case, the shape at the wrist of the hand is very narrow, and the sides of the hand rise upward separating the distance between them. The figure will give a good idea. Similarly, the fingers are narrow at the bottom and broad at the top.

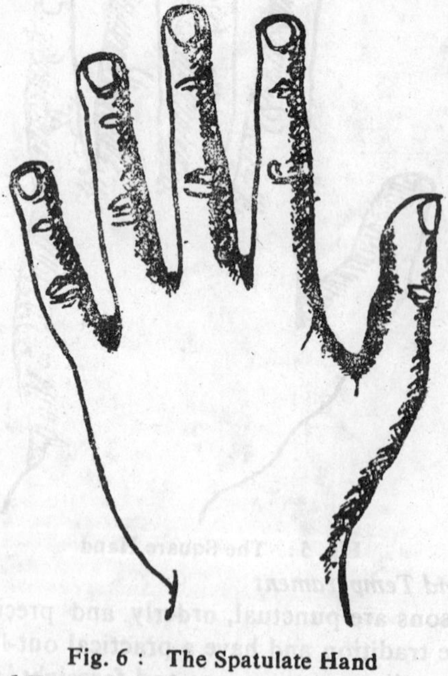

Fig. 6 : The Spatulate Hand

b) *Nature and Temperament*

1) Such persons are original and energetic.

2) They hate custom, tradition and regularity. They take any course they please and care little for what others say.
3) If the hand is hard and firm, it indicates a nature which is restless and excitable but full of energy and enthusiasm.
4) If the hand is soft and flabby, it shows a spirit which is restless but irritable.
5) Great navigators, explorers, discoverers, engineers and mechanics have spatulate hands.

*

iv) The Conic Hand (Fig. 7)

a) *Characteristics*

The conic hand is characterised by smooth fingers and conic tips. By smooth finger is meant the absence of knots between the joints of the fingers. The palm proper is broad at the base and the sides go on narrowing on both the sides making a narrow angle at the base of the fingers. The fingers also are broad at the base and pointed at the tip.

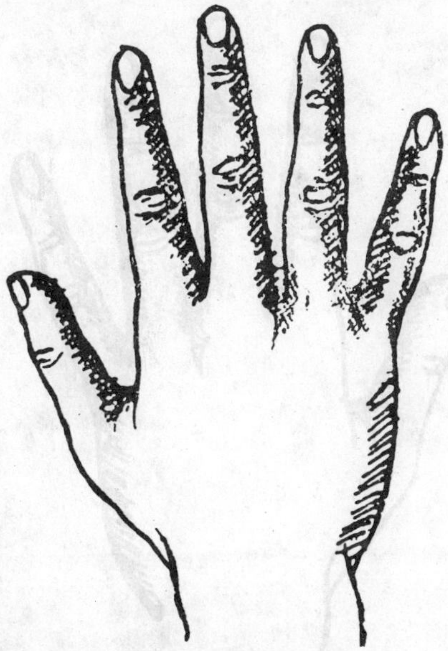

Fig. 7 : The Conic Hand

b) ***Nature and Temperament***

1) They are enthusiastic.

2) They appreciate beauty in nature and in life.
3) They are fond of leisure, novelty and liberty.

c) *Defects of the type*

1) The attraction for a thing is stronger than their sense of duty.
2) Such a person is incapable of obedience.
3) He does not understand the real value of a thing and seeks its superficial beauty.

*

v) The Psychic Hand (Fig. 8)

a) *Characteristics*

1) The Psychic hand is, of all hands, the most beautiful and consequently the most scarce, for rarity is one of the conditions of beauty.
2) It is small and fine in relation to the rest of the body.
3) A narrow palm, smooth fingers, the outer phalange long and drawn out to point, the thumb small and elegant.

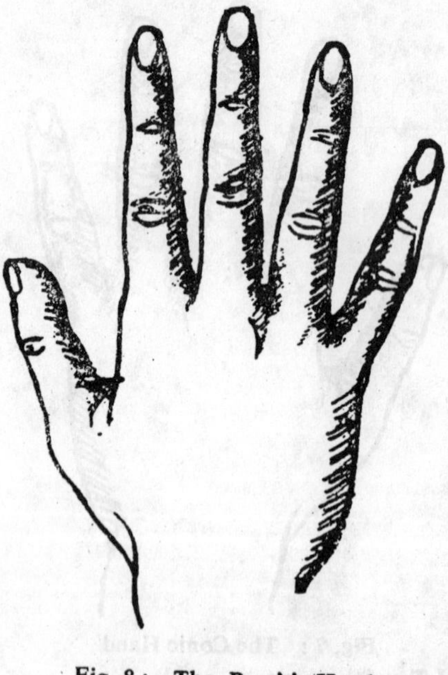

Fig. 8 : The Psychic Hand

b) *Nature and Temperament*

1) Such persons have imagination which is difficult for the other types to appreciate.
2) They live in a remote idealistic world. People with square or spatulate type, who go after precision or method, find it impossible to follow the ideas of the psychic type.
3) Square and spatulate types are carried away by war and its results; whereas the psychic type takes pleasure in the esoteric dreams of the soul and in contemplating intangible realities.

c) *Defects of the type*

1) Such a person has only a limited comprehension of the things of the outer world and of real life. He looks at them from too high a point to be able to see them clearly.
2) The talent for applied sciences is wanting in them.

Parents having such children do not know how to treat them. The strange thing is that they are often the offspring of matter-of-fact people.

*

vi) The Philosophic Hand (Fig. 9)

a) *Characteristics*

1) The Philosophic hand is the one where the fingers are long and the joints of the fingers well developed. These types of fingers are also called knotty fingers because the knots are developed. The word 'philosophic' is derived from the Greek 'philos'—love and 'sophia' wisdom.
2) The fingers are bony in appearance.
3) The palm proper is rather large and well-developed and the joints well marked in the fingers.
4) The top phalanges are half square and half conic, a combination producing on the upper joint a kind of egg-shaped spatula.
5) The thumb is large and indicates the presence of as much 'logic' as the 'will' since both the phalanges are of equal length.
6) The rest of the hand is either square, psychic or spatulate in appearance.

b) *Nature and Temperament*

1) Such persons have an analytical mind.

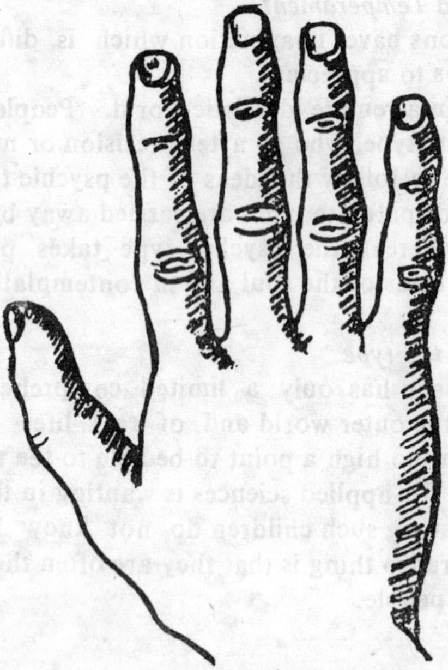

Fig. 9 : The Philosophic Hand

2) They are absorbed in thoughts about the creation, evolution, existence and destruction of themselves and of the the world at large.
3) Their ideas and beliefs are not borrowed from others but they are formed from their own experimental experience.
4) Their thoughts are occupied with details and with the mass, with the individual and with mankind, with the atom and with the universe.
5) They are students throughout their lives.
6) They are silent and secretive and very careful in using words.
7) They rarely forget an injury but wait patiently for an opportunity to take revenge.

c) *Defects of the type*

1) They are egotistic.
2) They are fanatical in religion or mysticism.

•

vii) The Mixed Shape of the Hand

a) *Characteristics*

The last of the seven types of the hand is the mixed type of the hand. This is so called because it does not have a particular type of shape but it is a mixture of two or more of the types described previously. This is a very difficult hand to read because it is often misleading. Sometimes, we think that it is a combination of square and conic, but in fact it may have a different formation.

In this type, the fingers may take a different shape from the shape of the palm proper, or the fingers may also differ from each other in their formation. The palm proper may be either square, spatulate, conic or psychic, or a combination of two or more of these types. The fingers also may belong to different types, often one pointed, one square, one spatulate etc.

b) *Nature and Temperament*

1) Such persons have ideas and versatility and are changeable.
2) They are adaptable and clever in the application of their talents.
3) They are brilliant in conversation and in any subject.
4) They are so versatile that they have no difficulty in getting on with persons of different dispositions.
5) Their most striking peculiarity is their adaptability to circumstances.
6) They never feel the ups and downs of fortune like other types.
7) They are generally inventive.
8) They are restless and do not remain long in any town or place.

*

The Indian System

In Indian Palmistry, there are ten signs which indicate good and praiseworthy hands. They are, 1) warm to touch, 2) coloured like the sky before dawn, 3) no light passes through the chinks if the fingers are brought close together, 4) bright hands as if they are oiled, 5) medium sized, 6) full and thick, 7) copper coloured nails, 8) long fingered, 9) wide and 10) no sweat, that is dry. A rich man has long fingers and good-looking palms.

If the hands of a woman appear as charming as a lotus, she is fortunate and will lead a happy life. Women with thin, skinny hands with protruding veins, with a network of lines and signs are not destined to be happy.

A heavily lined palm signifies misery and troubles in life, sometimes a short life. If there are very few lines, it is a sign of poverty. A clear yellow palm means the person will lose his patrimony. A palm with a distinct hollow is a sign of poverty.

CHAPTER 35

The Division of the Hand

In the previous chapter we studied the hand as a whole, that is, the hand from the wrist to the top of the fingers. Now we shall study the division of the hand in different sections. This division of the hand will assist a student to understand the psychology of the person whose hands are under examination.

The First System (Fig. 10)

The hand is divided into three worlds. The fingers constitute the first world, this is known as the mental world. The

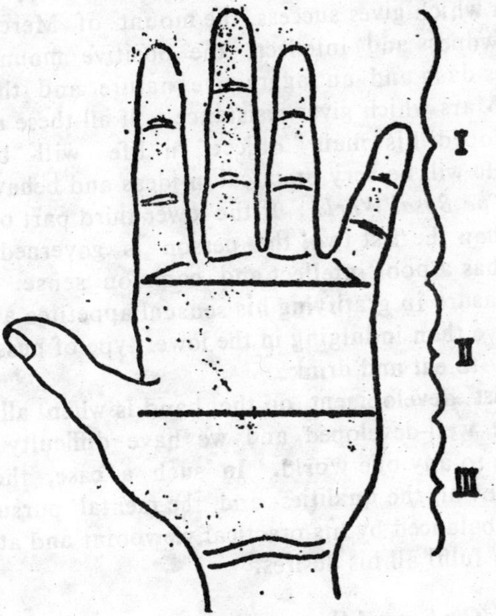

Fig. 10

second division is made from the base of the fingers to the imaginary horizontal line which runs from the top of the mount of Moon to the top of the mount of Venus. This is known as the material world. The third division constitues the part from the horizontal line to the wrist of the hand. This is known as the basal world.

i) *The Mental World*: When the hands are stretched and we find that the portion covered by the fingers is longer than either of the other two parts, the mental world is developed. This means that the person has good development of the brain and is fit for such intellectual pursuits as studies and research. However, if his mental activity is not backed by a good Line of Head or a square hand, he will simply be given to mental rambling without actually achieving anything. He lives in a realm of ideas without sufficient knowledge to follow his mental pursuits.

ii) *The Material World*: This division of the hand is composed of the mount of Jupiter which gives ambition, the mount of Saturn which gives wisdom and sobriety, the mount of the Sun which gives success, the mount of Mercury which gives shrewdness and intellect, the positive mount of Mars which gives dash and an aggressive nature and the negative mount of Mars which gives resistance. If all these mounts are well developed his main object in life will be to earn money. He will be very practical in ideas and behaviour.

iii) *The Basal World*: If the lower third part of the hand is longer than the first two, the person is governed by basal ideas and has a poor intellect and common sense. He takes intense pleasure in gratifying his sensual appetites and has no other motive than indulging in the lower type of passions. He knows only to eat and drink.

The best development on the hand is when all the three worlds are well-developed and we have difficulty in giving importance to any one world. In such a case, there is the balancing of all the qualities and the mental pursuits of the person are balanced by his practical viewpoint and at the same time he can fulfil all his desires.

The Second System of Division (Fig. 11)

The study of the hand, from the view point of this second

method, will give us further insight into the working of the mind of the person. According to this division, the hand is vertically divided into the Conscious Zone, the Sub-conscious Zone and the Social Zone.

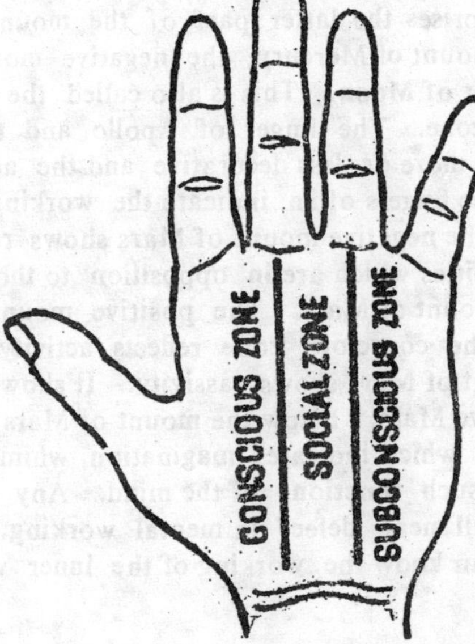

Fig. 11

The Conscious Zone

An imaginary line is drawn from the middle of the fingers of Jupiter and Saturn in a vertical manner which reaches straight to the bottom of the hand. This portion comprises the mount of Jupiter, the positive mount of Mars and the mount of Venus. This is called the Conscious Zone. The finger of Jupiter and the thumb which are characteristics of man only come under this zone. All our conscious actions such as picking up small things, writing etc are possible because of these two fingers. From the development of this zone we can easily see the ideas that rule the person and whether he is over-ambitious or lacks ambition and whether he has dash and aggression or he is mild, whether he is strong in passions and action or sober or imbecile. Similarly, his ego and his will, logic and reason, as shown by the thumb will indicate the function of his active mind.

The Sub-Conscious Zone

An imaginary line is drawn from the middle of the ring finger or the finger of Apollo to the bottom of the hand. This portion comprises the latter part of the mount of Sun or Apollo, the mount of Mercury, the negative mount of Mars and the mount of Moon. This is also called the passive zone or the ulner zone. The finger of Apollo and the finger of Mercury are more or less decorative and the act and talent shown by these fingers often indicate the working of the sub-conscious. The negative mount of Mars shows resistance and it has the qualities which are in opposition to those shown by the positive mount of Mars. The positive mount of Mars in the active or the conscious zone reflects activity whereas the negative mount of Mars shows passivity. It shows defence unlike the positive Mars. Below the mount of Mars is the mount of the Moon which indicates imagination, whimsey, ecstasy, fantasies and such functions of the mind. Any deformity of this mount will mean defect in mental working. Thus from this zone we can know the working of the inner world of the person.

The Social Zone

The portion that lies between the two zones described above is known as the middle zone or the zone of social conduct. In this zone come the mount of Saturn which shows sobriety, wisdom and materialism and the first half of the mount of Apollo which shows success in life. The line of Fate starts at the bottom of the hand in this zone and ends on the mount of Saturn. By the development or the course of this line, we can judge the social adaptability of the person. It has been observed that this line is the most unstable line on the hand because there are always changes in man's attitude and behaviour towards his social companions. As he gains more and more experience of the world, his ideas keep changing and thus it affects his behaviour. This line is present in most hands and its absence shows lack of sociability. Criminals and mental defectives who lack this super-ego and social adaptibility do not have the line of Fate. As this line is more concerned with social behaviour, it is usually more prominent on the hands of women than those of men because ladies are more social and adaptable than men.

Thus the division of the hand explains more of the individual and we can combine both the systems of division in order to arrive at a more detailed working of the mind of the individual.

CHAPTER 36

Skin, Colour, Consistency and Flexibility of Hands

Skin

The skin is either fine or coarse or elastic. This is known as the texture of the skin.

1) *Fine Texture* : It indicates a) a refined person in thought and deed. b) a person with pleasant actions, good manners and etiquette, c) a person who talks slowly, handles books very delicately and makes very little noise.

2) *Coarse Texture* : In this case the skin is rough, has big capillaries and the touch is unpleasant and coarse. It indicates a) dullness, b) lack of enthusiasm, c) impractical nature, d) cynicism and e) poor understanding.

3) *Elastic Texture* : This is a development which is neither very fine nor very coarse. The skin is elastic but not soft, it is firm but not hard. It indicates, a) a practical nature, b) common sense and good judgement. It is found on the hands of doctors, lawyers, businessmen and clergymen.

Colour

The colour of the hand gives an indication of the natural health and stamina of the person. However students should note that the colour changes according to the season of the year. In winter, a white pale colour of the hand is common while in summer dry hands with reddish dark colour are to be expected.

1) *Red Colour* : Red colour indicates strength, vigour and activity. The person who possesses it is intense in his desire and attempts purposefully to achieve his ends. Students should be able to combine the colour of the hand with its shape as well as with the most developed mount on the hand. Red

colour increases the coarse behaviour of the elementary hand and the activity of the spatulate hand ; it makes square hand more practical and enthusiastic ; it makes the philosophic hand develop a practical philosophy, a coniç hand more imaginative and a psychic hand more moody and so on.

2) *Yellow Colour* : This colour is peculiar to a Saturnian, though a Mercurian also shares it. The yellow colour shows melancholia and the person is shy. He is not joyous, bright and happy. This yellow colour will distort the qualities of the shape of the hand and also of the mounts on the hand.

3) *Blue or Purple Colour* : Blue or purple colour does not necessarily mean a poor quality. It shows a sluggish circulation. It means feebleness of the working of the heart and shows a dangerous stage. We should be careful to note the hand and the mount and to combine this colour with the type.

Thus we have studied how the colour of the hand helps us to find out the natural health of the person and its effect on his temperament.

Consistency of the hand

Consistency is of four kinds : a) flabby, b) soft, c) hard and d) elastic. We can study the consistency by shaking hands with the customer when we can press his hand with uniform pressure. It is through practice only that we can find whether the hand is flabby, soft or hard. It should be noted that hard developments on the mounts of the hand or at other places, due to games like cricket, hockey etc. or due to hazardous professions where certain portions of the hand become hard, should not be confused with hardness of the hand. Hardness or softness of the hand depends upon the resistence the hand gives us, under a particular pressure.

1) *Flabby Consistency* : We should hold the client's hand firmly in our two hands and then start exerting pressure on his hand. We shall know whether his hand is resisting our pressure. In this particular case, there will be no resistance and we get the feeling that the client does not have sufficient energy to resist our pressure. The muscles are very loose and we do not find the presence of bones in the hand. This is the flabby consistency which shows mental lethargy and laziness. He is merely

a dreamer and does not desire to bring into action his ambitions or ideas. He prefers an easy and comfortable life.

2) *Soft Consistency* : Next to flabby consistency is the soft consistency which looks like flabby consistency but which does not show as much laziness as flabby consistency. The difference between the flabby and the soft consistencies is that whereas we do not get the feeling of any bony structure in flabby consistency, we get that feeling in soft consistency. The intensity of laziness is therefore less in soft consistency and there is scope for the person with soft consistency to improve upon his inherent characteristics. Such persons have a delicate mind. Will-power is lacking. They cannot resist anything in life and suffer much if the odds are too many.

3) *Elastic Consistency* : This type of consistency shows energy, activity, vigour and enthusiasm. This is usually found in the hands of persons who are active in life. In this case there is a spring-like action as we press the hand and the mounts on the hand repel in a spring-like way. Elastic consistency shows an intelligent brain working behind the energy of the person.

4) *Hard Consistency* : Students may occasionally come across a hard consistency which is indicative of a brain which is not receptive and finds it difficult to absorb new ideas. When we press this hand, we find opposition to our pressure and feel the resistance. Hard consistency also shows an active brain not of the intelligent type but of one which would prefer manual labour to mental activity.

Flexibility of Hands

A hand is either stiff or flexible.

1) *Stiff Hand* : It shows 1) a stiff mind which is not prepared to modify its ideas, 2) an orthdox mind ; innovations are not acceptable to it, 3) a person who is narrow in ideas, selfish, stingy and unhelpful.

2) *Flexible Hand* : In this case, the fingers readily open and the hand becomes straight. It indicates 1) good understanding, 2) an active, intelligent and helpful nature.

In short, the skin colour, consistency and flexibility of the hand studied in this chapter throw more light on the character of a man and increase or decrease the qualities of the person as shown by the shape of his hand or the mounts on the hand.

CHAPTER 37

Fingers

Introduction

Fingers form a very important part of the palm. They are the instruments of the sense of touch and the means by which we obtain much of our information about the exterior world. In the evolution of man their place is striking as is shown by their length and by the development of complex and varied patterns of their papillary ridges. Besides their highly tactile sense, they possess a high degree of mobility of a kind, quite their own. The phalanges and length of the fingers enable them to perform a rich variety of movements. The most important function of the fingers is to receive the life's spark. The life current that runs through the human body is first received through the fingers.

Fingers are either smooth or knotty, long or short.

Smooth Fingers (Fig. 12)

a) *Characteristics* : When the joints or the knots of the fingers are not developed, they are known as smooth fingers. They are graceful to look at.

b) *Nature and Temperament* : 1) These persons take in ideas quickly and the waves of expression pass easily through these fingers into the brain. 2) They are endowed with the faculty of comprehension. 3) They proceed by inspiration rather than by reason, by synthesis rather than by analysis. 4) They have grace, spontaneity and insight. 5) They are very passionate and very hasty. 6) They are wrong in their intuitive deductions.

Knotty Fingers (Fig. 13)

a) *Characteristics* : When the joints or the knots of the fingers are developed, they are known as knotty fingers. In

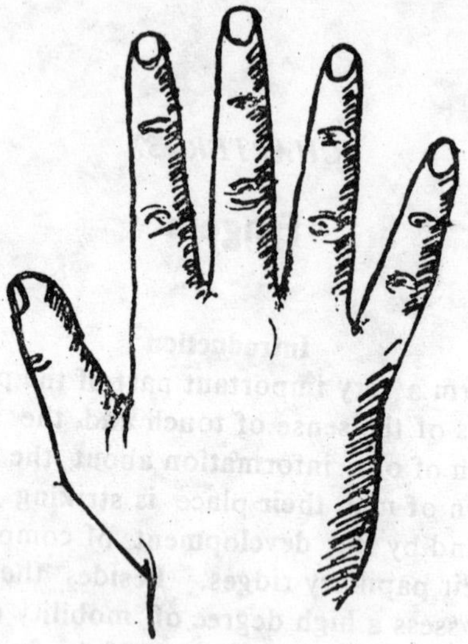

Fig. 12 : Smooth Fingers

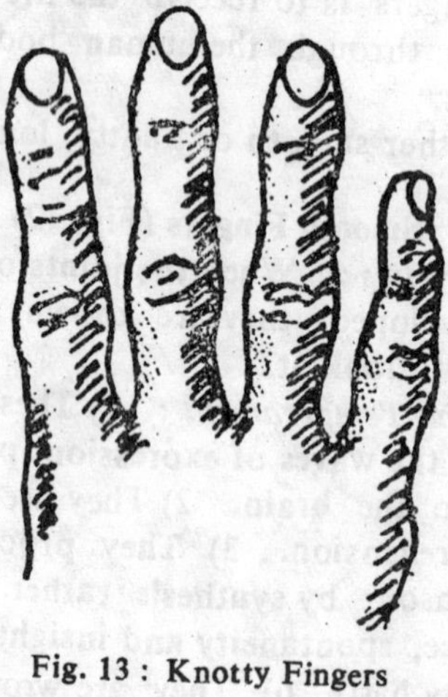

Fig. 13 : Knotty Fingers

this case, when all the fingers are touching each other, there is space between two fingers through which we can see the light. There are chinks between two fingers because the knots touch each other and the fingers cannot remain entirely closed.

b) *Nature and Temperament* : There are two knots to each finger. The nature of the person varies according to the first or the second knot developed. The first knot is between the top phalange and the middle phalange and the second knot is between the middle phalange and the basal phalange. Phalanges are counted from top to bottom. The topmost phalange is the first phalange, the middle phalange is the second phalange and the lowest one is the third phalange.

Knotty fingers display a nature which is contrary to the smooth fingers. Knotty fingers are generally the characteristic of those who are mature in thought. They indicate a) analysis, b) investigation, c) thoughtfulness and d) reasoning. These people love truth and are rightly called philosophers. They are not carried away by impulses and are seldom emotional. They act with their head and not with the heart. These fingers generally belong to scientists and historians who are studious and depend upon well-stored information, which they use when occasion demands.

a) *First Knot Developed*: It shows a) mental order, b) an intelligent person with systematic and careful thinking.

b) *Second Knot Developed* : It shows a) proper handling of things in material affairs, b) love of order at home, c) method in habits and in dressing.

Short and Long Fingers

a) *How to measure long or short Fingers ?* : If, when the fingers cover the palm, they reach the first bracelet on the wrist, the fingers are long (Fig. 14). If the fingers reach just upto the middle mount of Venus, they are of normal length. If, however, they do not reach the middle mount of Venus, they are short fingers.

b) *Short Fingers* : *Nature and Temperament* : a) A quick mind, b) Easy grasp of things, c) An active and alert mind, d) Ideas are brought into practice, e) Impetuous and hasty.

c) *Long Fingers* : *Nature and Temperament* : a) Slow going and slow talking, b) Love of details, c) A fault-finding and meddling disposition, d) If other signs on the hand are unfavourable, it is the poisoner's hand.

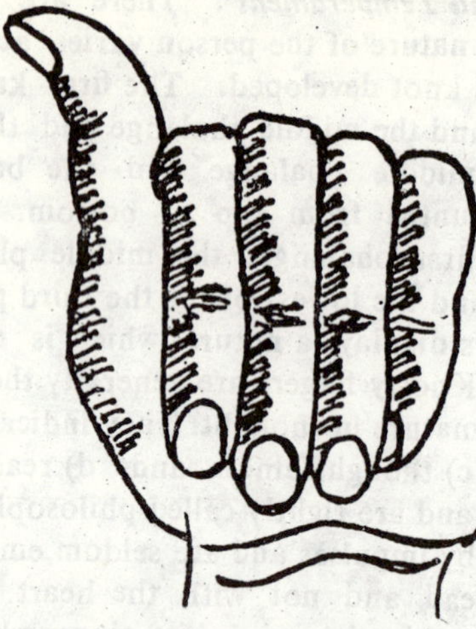

Fig. 14 : Long Fingers

Individual Fingers

a). *Length of the individual Fingers* (Fig. 15) : *Jupiter Finger* : To be normal in length, the Jupiter finger should reach the middle of the first phalange of the Saturn finger.

Saturn Finger : Normally, this is longer than the Jupiter and the Apollo (Sun) fingers.

Apollo Finger : Usually, this is equal in length to the Jupiter finger.

Mercury Finger : To be normal in length, this finger should reach the first knot of the Apollo finger.

We shall now study individual fingers in greater detail.

b) *The Finger of Jupiter* : The first finger is considered as the finger of Jupiter because it stands on the mount of Jupiter. It partakes all the qualities of Jupiter mount, and it is very important in judging the type of the subject. If the mount is slightly displaced, but the finger is strong and erect, the qualities of the mount which are lessened by its displacement may be enhanced by the firmness and the development of this finger. This finger shows a) pride, b) honour, c) religion, d) ambition, e) dignity, f) honesty, g) sacrifice, h) command, i) love of nature and such other qualities of Jupiter.

Long Finger of Jupiter : When this finger is very long, that is, as long as the Saturn finger, it shows an excess of the characteristics of a Jupiterian. The desire for power will be great.

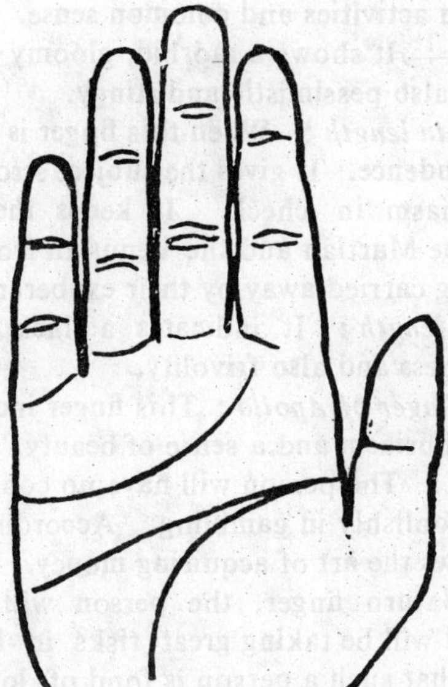

Fig. 15 : Normal Length of Fingers

If it is longer than the Saturn finger, it shows tyranny and a proud and dogmatic nature.

Moderate in length : When the finger reaches the middle of the first phalange of the Saturn finger, the Jupiterian desire for leadership will not be excessive and it shows moderate love of rule and an active disposition. The person is able and of good character. He is a leader and possesses a good and sweet tongue. He loves justice and prestige and craves for knowledge.

According to Indian Palmistry, he is happy in his relations with his brothers.

Too short a Finger of Jupiter: When this finger is short, the person is not a pure Jupiterian, even though he may have a strong mount of Jupiter. It shows a lack of the ability to lead, a dislike of responsibility and a lack of pride. The man will be unhappy in his relations with his brothers.

c) *The Finger of Saturn* : By virtue of its position on the hand, it is generally the longest of all the fingers. It is called the balance wheel because Saturn gives this finger, wisdom, sobriety and a balanced mind. It shows gloom, carefulness and a check in activities and common sense.

Very long : It shows a morbid, gloomy and melancholy person who is also pessimistic and stingy.

Moderate in length : When this finger is normal in length, it indicates prudence. It gives the subject strong power to hold undue enthusiasm in check. It keeps the Jupiterian, the Apollonian, the Martian and the Venusian from going too fast and from being carried away by their exuberant spirit.

Short in length : It indicates a lack of balance and untrustworthiness and also frivolity.

d) *The Finger of Apollo* : This finger indicates eloquence, brilliance, enthusiasm and a sense of beauty.

Very long : The person will have no control over himself and will lose foolishly in gambling. According to the Indian system, it shows the art of acquiring money. If the finger is as long as the Saturn finger, the person will have speculative tendencies and will be taking great risks in life. The Indian system states that such a person is fond of lottery and if the mount of Mercury is developed, he is a first class gambler and does not care for the future.

Moderate in length : According to the Indian system, the person has talent and loves to gain fame, honour and money through machinery. It shows brilliance and ambition.

Short in length : It shows a lack of a sense of beauty and artistic notions.

The Finger of Mercury : The best of talent in business and shrewdness in life is shown by this finger. Its development indicates either good or bad qualities of the mount underneath. A bad Mercury finger reveals a shrewd rogue or a clever criminal. This finger has a special reference to criminology.

Very long : It shows literary ability and fluency in speech and writing. It also shows crafty instincts. According to the Indian method, a very long finger indicates infidelity. The person enjoys all comforts in life and enjoys the love of his mother and of her relations. He is fond of sweet dishes and also adores women.

Moderate in length : It shows versatility and desire for general improvement. It also shows love of study and earning.

Short in length : It indicates lack of discretion and inability to judge matters. It also shows lack of tact as well as stupidity and a tendency to jump to conclusions.

General remarks : After discussing the length of the individual fingers, a general remark may be made that fingers which are evenly set on a line above the mounts indicate success. An absolutely even line is seldom seen. Any finger set below loses its power. When the Jupiter finger is low set, it gives social awkwardness. Saturn finger, when so found, loses the balance of the hand. Similarly, with the Apollo and the Mercury fingers, we find that they lose their power when placed at a lower level than normal.

Space between the Fingers

After stretching the hand and the fingers, if we find, a) a wide distance between the thumb and the Jupiter finger it indicates i) a nature full of noble human qualities ii) a mind which shows warmth, sympathy and generosity and iii) a love of independence, freedom and liberty.

b) a wide space between the Jupiter and Saturn fingers, it shows a man of thought. He forms his own opinion and is not held down by the views of others.

c) a wide space between the Saturn and Apollo fingers, it shows a person who is careless about the future.

d) a wide space between the Apollo and Mercury fingers, it shows a person who is shrewd and energetic and is a man of action.

Fingers closed together with no light passing through them : Sometimes we encounter a palm wherein the fingers are so close together that no light passes through them. Such a person is selfish and mean-minded. According to the Indian system, such a hand indicates wealth.

Fingers leaning towards each other

When the first finger leans towards the thumb, it leans a wide space between the first and the second fingers which means independence in thought. When this finger leans towards the second finger, it gets the morbid tendency of the second finger. This morbidity combined with the pride of Jupiter produces morbid pride. The ambition of the person will be more Saturnian and also hidden.

Second Finger : When the second finger leans towards the first, it indicates sadness because of superstition. The second finger exhibits its melancholy nature and in leaning towards Jupiter, it reduces the aspect of true religion which is inherent in Jupiter. So religion is misunderstood and the person becomes superstitious. Saturn makes him sad and depressed.

If the Saturn finger leans towards the Apollo finger, it loses some of its bad aspects and absorbs the characteristics of the Apollo finger. Thus, it indicates less morbidity. When both the fingers (the second and the third) lean towards each other, it shows a secretive disposition.

Third Finger : When the third finger bends towards the second, the vanity of the third finger gets the tinge of morbidity. The talent of the person shows crooked tendencies. When the third finger leans towards the fourth finger, it shows that the sense of beauty and the artistic talents in the man have a monetary object in view.

Fourth Finger : If the fourth finger bends towards the third finger, it means a marvellous combination of the two fingers. The business aptitude as shown by the fourth finger will have additional talent and the eloquence of the third finger.

Flexibility of Fingers

Three rules : a) A flexible object can adapt itself to a greater variety of conditions. b) A flexible object bends under pressure, a stiff object under the same amount of pressure breaks or remains immobile. c) As the fingers reflect the condition and quality of the mind, flexible fingers show a flexible mind and stiff fingers a stiff mind.

Stiff Fingers : When the fingers are stiff and cannot bend backwards, the person lacks flexibility or elasticity of mind and manner. He is narrow in his ideas and stingy in his ways but succeeds with his hard work.

Moderate flexibility : With this degree of flexibility, the person does not go to extremes. He is self-contained, listens readily and understands. He is neither held back by old fogism nor impelled to rashness or over-enthusiasm. He takes a bird's eye view of things and can appreciate the difficulties of others. He is thoughtful, broad-minded, earnest and sympathetic—yet all this within limits.

Extreme flexibiliiy (Fig. 16) : It shows a mind that is elastic and a brain that is susceptible to keen impressions. This person is adaptable and versatile.

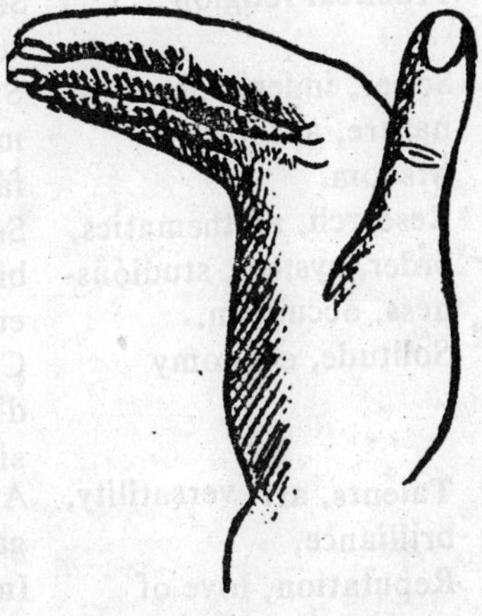

Fig. 16 : Flexible Finger

Phalanges of the Fingers

Order of Phalanges : The phalanges are counted from the tip of the finger towards the base, the upper phalange being the first, the middle the second and basal the third.

The First Phalange : If this phalange is more developed than the other two, it shows, a) mental development, b) idealistic views and c) marvellous schemes for life. We have to take into consideration the finger on which it is developed. On the finger of Jupiter, the man will have respect for religion and will think of achieving success in mysticism. On the finger of Saturn, the first phalange shows wisdom and a studious nature. On the finger of Apollo, it indicates high intellectual activity and ideal love. On the finger of Mercury it reveals interest in law and pursuit of scientific studies. Likewise, we have to combine the second and a third phalanges with the individual finger and arrive at a conclusion.

I give below a summary of the indications of the phalanges according to the finger on which they are developed.

Finger	*Phalange*	*Good qualities*	*Bad qualities*
Jupiter	I	Ambition, high moral sense, pride in religion, prestige, mysticism	Dictatorship, vanity, false pride.
	II	Dignity, courage, love of humanity	Tyranny, vulgarity, timidity.
	III	Practical religion	Sensuality, gluttony, dishonesty.
Saturn	I	Sober, independent nature, authority, wisdom.	Superstition, melancholia, fatalism.
	II	Research, mathematics, order, system, studiousness, occultism.	Secrecy, backbiting, treachery, envy.
	III	Solitude, economy	Cold nature, dislike for opposite sex, misery.
Apollo	I	Talents, art, versatility, brilliance,	Avarice, gambling.
	II	Reputation, love of wealth, integrity,	Infidelity, unsteady.
	III	Liberty, gaiety, freedom.	Audacity, stupidity.
Mercury	I	Intelligence, diplomacy, activity, law, scientific pursuits.	Crookedness, swindling.
	II	Business, law, invention.	Scandal, mockery,
	III	Shrewdness	Cheating, robbing.

Hair on the Fingers

a) *Black Hair* : It shows a) heat and warmth, b) vigour, c) restlessness, d) unsteadiness.

b) *Grey Hair* : It shows a moderate temperament, b) energy and vitality.

c) *White Hair* : It indicates a) a lack of iron pigments in the body, b) an easy going nature, c) less sensuality.

d) *Red Hair* : It shows, a) an excitable and quarrelsome nature, b) brutality, c) a revengeful attitude, d) a violent nature.

e) *Golden Hair* : It shows a combination of warmth and passion.

Whorls and Loops on Fingers

They have a medical significance as well as prophetic significance. We shall study only the prophetic significance. In Indian languages, whorls are known as Chakras and loops are known as Shankhas. There is one more pattern known as Shakti, the composite type.

Shankha

If the Shankha appears on—

one finger only, the person is happy,
two fingers, it is an unfavourable sign,
three fingers, also is a bad sign,
four fingers, it is not a good indication,
five fingers, it is not an auspicious sign,
six fingers, the person has prowess,
seven fingers, the person gets the comforts of a king,
eight fingers, the person is as good as a king,
nine fingers, the person lives like a king,
the Jupiter finger, the person is a spendthrift and is unsteady in life,
the Saturn finger, the person is wise, of a scientific outlook and of many accomplishments,
the Apollo finger, the person loses his wealth in business,
the Mercury finger, the person loses his money in manufacturing concerns.

Chakra

If the Chakra is found on

the thumb, and if the line of Life is long and good, the person inherits property,
two fingers, the person is honoured in courts of kings,
three fingers, the person becomes wealthy,
four fingers, the person becomes a pauper,
five fingers, the person enjoys pleasures,
six fingers, the person satisfies his passions,
seven fingers, the person is virtuous,

eight fingers, the person suffers from diseases,
nine fingers, the person becomes a king,
ten fingers, the person is very happy and he realises the 'self',
the Jupiter finger, the person benefits through friends,
the Saturn finger, the person benefits through religion or the church and is an authority on religion,
the Apollo finger, the person benefits through trade and enjoys a good reputation and happiness,
the Mercury finger, the person benefits through manufacturing concerns and is a scientist and an author.

Shakti (Composite)

If it is seen on
one finger, the person is very happy,
two fingers, the person is an orator,
three fingers, the person is very rich,
four fingers, the person is virtuous,
five fingers, the person is a vedantin (philosopher),
six fingers, the person has a high level of thinking,
seven or more fingers, the person is successful in life.

Signs on the Fingers

The Jupiter finger

a) A line encircling the first joint shows a scar on the skull.

b) A cross line on the second joint shows a harmful and dishonest person.

c) A cross line on the third joint shows acquisition of other people's money.

A Star on the finger of Jupiter

a) A star on the first phalange shows honour and fame.

b) A star on the second phalange shows an obstinate and rigid person. The person is very courageous.

Lines on the Jupiter finger

a) Four vertical lines each on the second and third phalanges show a virtuous and happy person.

b) Three vertical lines on the third phalange plus a star on the bracelet show acquisition of other people's money.

c) A line starting on the Jupiter finger and ending on the first joint of the thumb indicates crime and a death sentence.

d) A broken line at the root of the finger shows robbery by a person appointed for performing religious duties.

The Saturn finger : Lines on the Saturn finger

a) A line starting from the root of the Saturn finger and going straight upto the first phalange of the finger shows a learned and wealthy person. If however, the above line is not straight, the person dies in war.

b) Vertical lines on the middle phalange show riches and interest in occultism.

c) A few lines from the root to the top of the finger show success in business connected with minerals.

d) Vertical lines on the first phalange indicate a jealous person.

e) Vertical lines on the third phalange and very near the root of the finger indicate ill-luck.

Stars on the Saturn finger

a) Two stars on the third phalange with a break in the Head line under the mount of Saturn show death. If found on a woman's hand, it means suicide in water.

b) A star on the first phalange denotes unhappiness.

c) A star on the third phalange shows death through weapon or poison.

d) A star at the root of the finger denotes the sterility of the wife.

Triangle on the Saturn finger

a) A triangle on the first phalange denotes a person who will go to any extent to accomplish his selfish motive.

b) A triangle on the third phalange denotes immoral character.

Spot on the Saturn finger

a) It denotes theft by one in his own family.

b) A spot on the third phalange indicates loss of money through women.

Island or Yava on the Saturn finger

An island on the second joint of the finger brings wealth, either through adoption, lottery or inheritance.

Sign of an Angle

On the second phalange, it indicates a gambler. He may also be a good conversationalist.

Sign of a Trident

On the third phalange, it means a person who is surrounded by difficulties. He is tempted to commit theft and suffers from difficulty in breathing.

The Finger of Apollo

Lines : Lines starting at the root of the finger and going upto the first phalange indicate a person who is very lucky, wealthy and even an owner of mills. If there are many such lines, the person spends lavishly for his fiancee.

Vertical lines on the first phalange indicate a learned and wise person. If any one of these lines bends towards the sides of the finger near the knot, he acquires fame and reputation.

A line crossing the third phalange, the person will come out successfully through all difficulties and impediments.

A star on the Apollo finger

It shows a spendthrift person.

Cross on the Apollo finger : On the first phalange of a woman's hand, it indicates chastity.

The Finger of Mercury

Lines : a) A line starting from the bottom of the finger and going upto the first phalange shows a scientist and a noble heart.

b) Three lines show a dreamer.

c) Strong vertical lines on the first phalange show ill-health.

d) Two or three lines on the second phalange show interest in occult subjects. However, if these lines are broad and wavy, the person loses all bonds of morality.

e) A line from the bottom of the finger to the second phalange signifies an orator. If this line is not straight, the person is obstinate and sticks to his opinions rigidly.

Cross on the Mercury finger (on the first phalange)

It shows that the person may not marry.

Zodiacal Signs on fingers (Fig. 17)

Students will be astonished to know that according to Indian Shastra (science), there are definite methods of calculating the exact day, the month and the year of birth from an examination of the hand. By the study of these methods, we can chalk out an exact horoscope of the person. But since the preparation of the natal-chart from the hand is an independent subject by itself, it will be out of place to deal with it in these pages. However, for the interest of the readers I produce herewith a figure which shows the Zodiacal signs and the months on the phalanges of the fingers (Fig. 17).

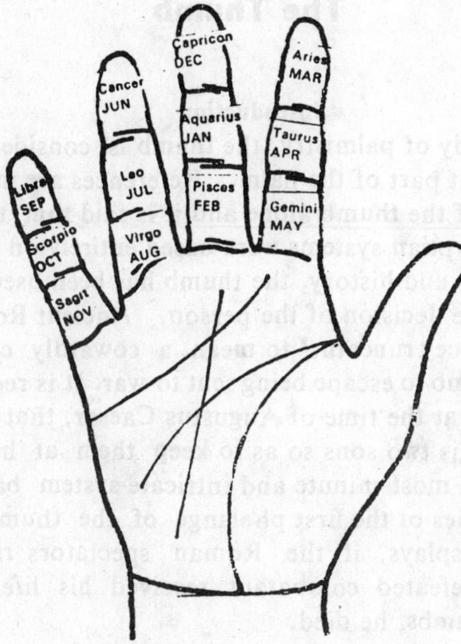

Fig. 17 : Fingers and Months, Fingers and Zodiacal Signs

CHAPTER 38

The Thumb

Introduction

In the study of palmistry, the thumb is considered as the most important part of the palm. References are made to the examination of the thumb alone and it is said that the ancient Hindu and Egyptian systems were based entirely on the thumb.

In religion and history, the thumb has been used to signify the will and the decision of the person. Ancient Romans used the word 'pollice truncatus' to mean a cowardly citizen who cut off his thumb to escape being sent to war. It is recorded of a Roman citizen at the time of Augustus Caesar, that he cut off the thumb of his two sons so as to keep them at home. The Chinese have a most minute and intricate system based solely on the capillaries of the first phalange of the thumb. In the gladiatorial displays, if the Roman spectators raised their thumbs the defeated combatant received his life. If they lowered the thumbs, he died.

Evolution

In the evolution of living beings we find the existence of the thumb in the monkey. But its thumb is not fully developed. Sir Charles Bell has called attention to the fact, that in the paw or the hand of the chimpanzee, which is the nearest approach to a human being, the thumb, although well formed in every way, does not reach the base of the first finger. The deduction therefore is that the longer and better formed the thumb, the higher the man has developed beyond brute creation. In the case of the monkey's thumb, we find that it is very weak and high set. It also lacks the ability to oppose the fingers. The more intelligent the monkey, the more developed the thumb. In man only we find the thumb most developed showing the development of the will-power and the equipment of the brain for higher thinking.

Large and Small Thumbs

A large thumb indicates a) trustworthiness, b) intellectual ability, c) a strong will-power, d) determination, e) reason f) a love of history and g) force of character.

A small thumb indicates a) sentiments and emotions, b) an irresolute mind and a wavering disposition, c) tolerance, d) impartiality.

The Position of the Thumb

There are three positions of the thumb on the hand, a) high set, b) low set and c) medium set.

High set thumb

The carriage of the thumb is close to the hand and its position on the hand is at a high level. This thumb indicates a) poor human understanding, b) lack of moral force, c) lack of independent thinking, d) lack of social adaptability, e) mean-mindedness, f) selfishness and g) crookedness.

Low set thumb

When the hand is stretched before us we can at once recognise the low set thumb by its low position on the mount of Venus and quite away from the finger of Jupiter. It indicates a) loftiness of mind, b) sympathy, c) generosity, d) a good understanding, e) sincerity and f) common sense.

Medium set thumb

This is the thumb which is neither too high nor too low on the hand which by its medium position gives a good shape to the hand. It indicates a) common sense, b) materialism, c) a practical outlook, d) enthusiasm and e) reason and sentiments appropriate to an occasion.

The Shape of the Thumb

i) *An Elementary Thumb*

This thumb does not create a good impression upon our mind. It looks dull and dead. It looks like a red potato. It indicates a) sluggishness, b) absence of enthusiasm, c) a vacant mind and d) lack of grace, tact or elegant manners.

ii) *A Strongly Developed Thumb*

This thumb is attractive and has grace by its position on the hand. When observed from the nail side it has a strong appearance and we can see it can go far against the fingers. The phalanges are strong and well developed which show strong determination and a good practical outlook.

iii) *The Nervous Thumb* (Fig. 18)

The nervous thumb can be recognised by its weak position and carriage on the hand. This is a flat thumb and it looks as if all its energy has been taken away. It hangs loose by the side of the hand. It indicates a) a lack of nervous energy, b) lack of force, c) absence of mental strength, d) lack of self-confidence and e) fear of public rumours and scandals.

iv) *The Diplomatic Thumb* (Fig. 19)

This thumb is uniform throughout and the phalanges are well developed. The tip of the thumb is usually strong and the whole thumb looks attractive.

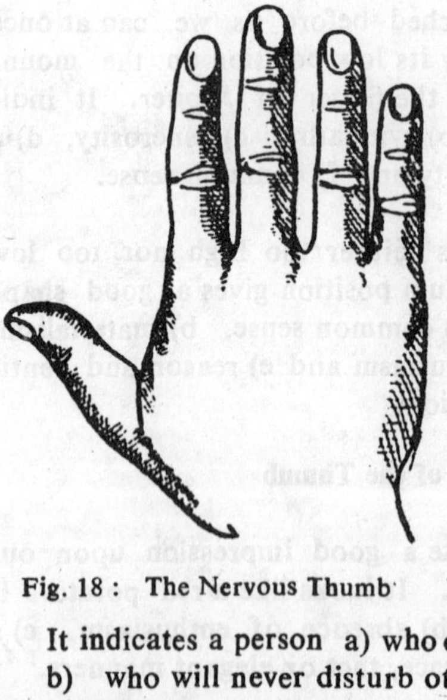

Fig. 18 : The Nervous Thumb

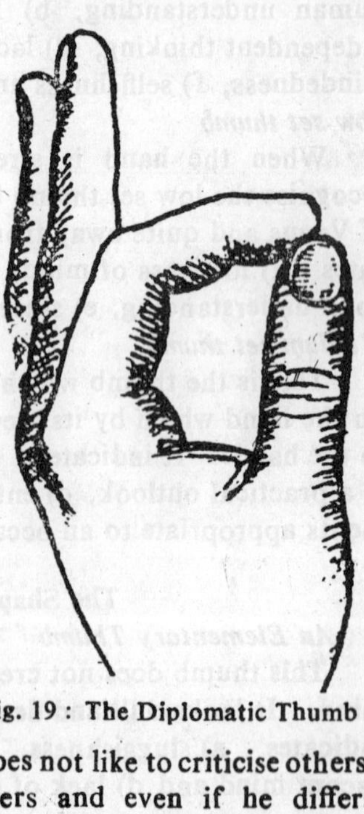

Fig. 19 : The Diplomatic Thumb

It indicates a person a) who does not like to criticise others, b) who will never disturb others and even if he differs from them will never attack them,

c) who gets all he wants but at the same time will never burden others,

d) who is very social but original in his opinions and ideas, and

e) who has tact, refinement and elegant manners.

This is a beautiful thumb, that of a man who attracts others and fills their lives with beauty.

v) *The Clubbed Thumb* (Fig. 20)

Every student of Chirosophy has heard about the clubbed thumb but I think very few of them would have seen one. The clubbed thumb has been marked as the murderer's thumb because it has been observed on the hands of many murderers. But that does not mean that all those who possess it will commit a murder. Since the hand has a psychological significance, it can truthfully be said of such a thumb that the person has cruel and murderous instincts which may be dormant in him. These instincts may not show themselves during the man's entire life because of lack of opportunity.

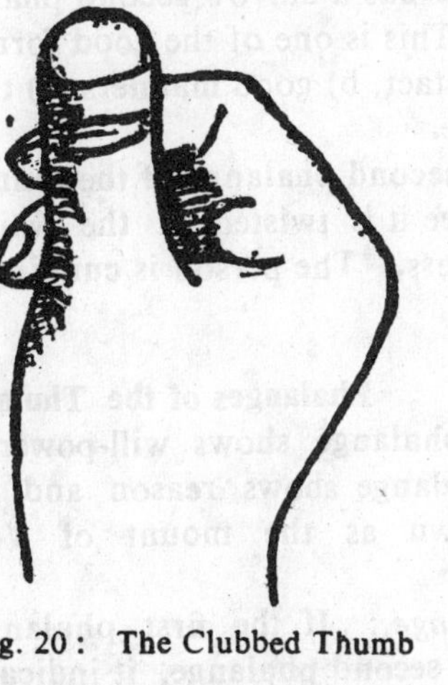

Fig. 20 : The Clubbed Thumb

The peculiarities of this thumb are a) it is very thick and broad in the first phalange, b) the nail is short and coarse.

The thickness of the first phalange shows obstinacy and shortness shows violent temper.

vi) *Paddle-shaped Thumb*

This thumb at first sight resembles the clubbed thumb. The similarities are

a) both the thumbs are broad in shape

b) in both the first or the top phalange is broad.

The differences are

a) the first phalange of the clubbed thumb is short and thick in addition to being broad,

b) the paddle-shaped thumb is only broad and not very thick, and

c) the clubbed thumb is usually found on the hand of a person who is robust, whereas the paddle-shaped thumb is found on the hands of men who generally are weak in constitution.

The paddle-shaped thumb shows strong determination and tenacity of purpose. Also, though the health of the person is not very strong, the development of the first phalange shows that the person is backed by strong nervous force.

vii) *The Waist-Like Thumb*

This thumb has a narrow second phalange and looks as if it is twisted. This is one of the good formations of the thumb. It indicates, a) tact, b) good manners, c) talents, d) intelligence and e) elegance.

Since the second phalange of the thumb shows logic and reason and since it is twisted in the waist-like formation, it shows shrewdness. The person is cunning and his reasoning is very shrewd.

Phalanges of the Thumb

The first phalange shows will-power and determination, the second phalange shows reason and logic and the third which is known as the mount of Venus shows love and sympathy.

First Phalange : If the first phalange of the thumb is longer than the second phalange, it indicates a) strong determination and strong will-power, b) hasty steps, c) tyranny and foolish obstinacy, d) stubbornness and fighting to the last, e) a person who acts first and think later. He is impetuous and hard to convince.

This is the type which shows how the good qualities in a man, if in excess, make him unsuccessful in life.

Second Phalange : If the second phalange of the thumb is longer than the first one, it shows a person whose logic and reason are more developed than determination. It means a) an intelligent person who grasps things very quickly, b) a person of sound judgement, c) a person who only reasons out things and is a sophist, d) a person who is only a talker without action.

Third Phalange : The third phalange of the thumb is the mount of Venus and since this phalange is usually the most developed one, the person acquires the qualities of that mount which are sympathy, love, co-operation, generosity etc. We shall study these in greater detail while studying the mount of Venus.

Knots and Flexibility of the Thumb

We have studied the characteristics shown by the knots of the fingers and also the flexibility of the fingers. The same principles apply to the thumb and we have to study whether the first or the second knot is developed and how flexible the thumb is.

Signs on the Thumb

Signs on the first phalange of the thumb

Vertical lines : a) Vertical lines on the first phalange of the thumb indicate will-power. But the number of such lines should not exceed three. More than three lines mean obstacles in the way of success.

b) Small vertical lines near the nail show legacies.

c) A line from the first phalange to the line of Life shows death from a metalic weapon like a sword or a dagger.

d) Two lines running from the first phalange to the line of Life indicate riches and wealth. If these two lines run very near to each other, almost touching each other, the person loses all his estate in lottery and speculation.

Cross : a) A cross on the upper side of the first phalange indicates lack of chastity. This is particularly so if the mount of Venus is prominent.

b) Two crosses show that the person is fond of luxury.

Star : a) A star on the first phalange of the thumb indicates immorality.

b) Two stars indicate a captious and fault-finding person.

Triangle : It shows great concentration in the scientific field.

Circle : It is a good sign on the first phalange and indicates success in the end.

Square : a) It means concentration in one direction.

b) Sometimes it means a tyrannical disposition.

Grill : It is a very dangerous sign especially when it is near the nail. It shows danger to the spouse of the person.

Chakra (Whorl) : a) If this sign has a southward direction, it is a lucky mark.

b) On the hand of a woman with the middle portion of the thumb being big and round, it shows infidelity and immorality.

Island or Lotus : It is a sign of a legacy.

Rainbow : It shows wealth, comforts and luxury in life.

Signs on the first joint of the thumb

a) A slanting line on the first joint shows wealth.

b) Two or three lines running down from the joint show a person good at heart and of a loveable disposition.

c) A line encircling the thumb on the first joint shows end of life on the scaffold.

Signs on the second phalange of the thumb

Vertical lines : Two or three lines on the second phalange show sound reasoning power.

Cross lines : They show lack of reasoning and common sense.

Cross : It shows the influence of others' views and opinions.

Stars : One or two stars show vulgar passions.

Triangle : It means scientific and philosophical talents.

Squares : It means blind stubbornness.

Circle : It shows success in argument.

Grill : It means lack of moral sense.

Line : A line from the second phalange to the line of Life shows troubles in married life.

Signs on the second joint of the thumb

Lines : a) A single line from the second joint of the thumb to the Life line shows wealth.

b) A thin and single line from the second joint of the thumb to the Life line shows inheritance.

c) Two or more lines show riches.

d) Vertical lines on the joint show brothers and sisters.

Yavas or Islands : They show the number of children.

CHAPTER 39

The Nails

Most students of Palmistry ignore nails in their study of the hand. As a matter of fact, nails are also very important in revealing the temperament of the person in general and his state of health in particular. Here is some information regarding nails and their significance.

Evolution

The evolution of nails depends upon their functional role. In animals, they serve as organs of attack and of apprehension. In man, these functions have become atrophied. It is true our nails are still to a small extent organs of apprehension, as for example, when we use them for picking up pins or other minute objects, but in general they are little more than a shield to protect the finger tips. The nails are the first tissues of the body to appear as early as the ninth week of prenatal life. The embryonic nail, which is delicate and transparent and without moons differs from the adult nail in texture.

Normal Development

The normal development of the nail is even and smooth in surface and it is not composed of ridges or flutings. It must also look alive and elastic. It should be pliable and not brittle. Once we know the normal nail, we can distinguish other nails from the normal one.

Fluted Nail (Fig. 21–a)

In this case, the nail, instead of growing over the end of the finger in a protecting way, goes away from the flesh. It shows a serious condition in a person. The white spots on the nails indicate a beginning of the loss of vitality and are nature's first warning of trouble ahead.

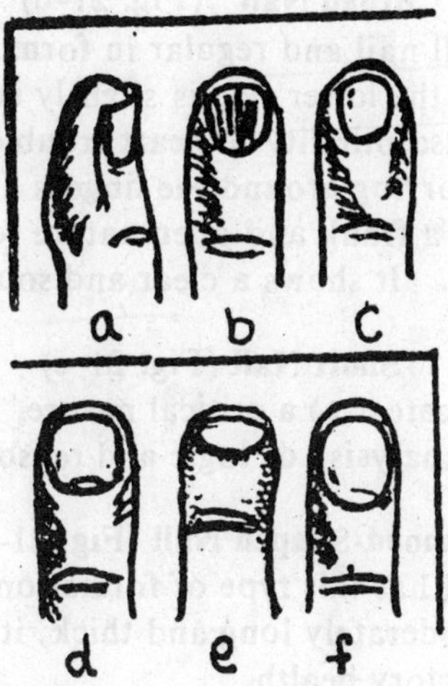

Fig. 21

a) If the spots go on increasing, the nail loses its graceful shape and turns high on one side and low on the other. This shows a grave danger of paralysis.

b) If the nail is long, thin and curved with ridges, it is a sign of consumption (Fig. 21–b).

c) The ridges on the nail are a product of chronic infection and remain as long as the illness.

d) These ridges indicate colitis and rheumatism with a focus of infection either in the roots of the teeth or the bowels. These ridges can be heriditary, indicating a rheumatic tendency in the family.

e) Ridges on a particular finger only indicate devotion and aptitude to the particular art or profession indicated by that finger.

Narrow Nail (Fig. 21–c)

It indicates nervous energy. Blue colour at the bottom of the nail shows poor blood circulation.

a) A narrow nail, which is also short and curved, shows spinal cord weakness.

b) A narrow as well as long and thin nail shows timidity and cowardice.

c) A long, narrow and shiny nail with a large opaque moon indicates hyperthyroidism.

Broad Nail (Fig. 21–d)

This is a small nail and regular in form. The end of this nail is square and the lower side is slightly small in breadth.

It indicates susceptibility to heart trouble. If the nail is broad at the tip curving around the fingers and broadening at the base, it shows a frank and open nature to which honesty of thought is natural. It shows a clear and sound judgment.

Short Nail (Fig. 21–e)

This nail indicates a) a critical nature, b) inquisitiveness and intuition, c) analysis, d) logic and reason.

Almond-Shaped Nail (Fig. 21–f)

When the nail has this type of formation and is naturally polished and is moderately long and thick, it denotes a happy nature and satisfactory health.

Indian system on spots on Nails

Spots on the nail of the thumb

Black spots on the nail indicate grief and sorrow. White marks on the nail indicate a reciprocated attachment. A star-shaped white mark indicates an illusion in life, unrequited love, self-deception and a vain worship of things and persons one cares for.

Black spots on the nail of the thumb indicate crimes caused by passion.

Spots on the nail of the first finger

A white mark on the nail of the Jupiter finger shows gain, a black mark shows loss.

Spots on the nail of the Saturn finger

A white mark on the nail indicates foreign travels. Yellow spots indicate worry and loss of brothers or wife. Black spots denote incoming danger.

Spots on the nail of the Apollo finger

A white spot on the nail denotes honour and wealth.

A black spot indicates loss of reputation.

Spots on the nail of the Mercury finger

A white spot on the nail denotes success in business.

A black spot signifies business failure.

CHAPTER 40

The Mounts on the Hand

Introduction

The study of mounts on the hand is very important to a student of palmistry. At the same time it is very difficult to find out the most prominent mount and the subsidiary mount or in other words, the principal mount and the secondary mount. However, I shall explain each mount in a simple way.

Uptil now only seven mounts on the hand have been recognised by all the authors on this subject. Mars is split up into two and so the number becomes eight. But in this course I have allotted space to the planets Uranus and Neptune also and the interpretations of these given later on will justify my method.

The Psychological Aspect of the Mounts

Mounts are the flabby pads which rise high on the hand. They are sensitive pads which consist of a network of nerves. The centre of these nerves is called the apex of the mount. This apex is of great importance in locating the correct position of the mount. The hand-print will give us a clear idea of the real development of the mount. The tissues that are just below these pads have various degrees of elasticity and the mounts become more or less sensitive depending upon the tissues underneath.

The Psychological Aspects of the Mounts

Why the particular mounts on the hand were allotted particular places only is a matter for consideration. It seems that the ancient scholars of the subject, who were also the masters of astrology, found that the persons who have Jupiter powerful in their horoscope have a powerful mount developed under the first finger which they called the mount of

Jupiter and the finger of Jupiter respectively. In this way, persons having powerful planets were seen to have certain places more developed on the hand, and these were named after those planets.

The mental behaviour of the person, his characteristics, his ideas, his ambition, his sub-conscious mind and such other aspects are determined by the particular type of mount to which he belongs. There is not the least doubt that the planets exert their influence on human life. This has been proved by the science of casting a horoscope from the hand. In palmistry these planets are seen in the form of mounts on the hand. The nine mounts whose influences are seen on mankind are as follows.

1	Mount of Jupiter	Pitru Sthana	Father
2	Mount of Saturn	Matru Sthana	Mother
3	Mount of Apollo	Vidya Sthana	Education
4	Mount of Mercury	Jaya Sthana	Wife
5	Mount of Mars :		
	Negative	Dharma Sthana	Religion
	Positive	Shatru Sthana	Enemies
6	Mount of the Moon	Kalpana Sthana	Imagination
7	Mount of Venus :		
	Upper	Bhratru Sthana	Brothers
	Lower	Bandhu Sthana	Relatives
8	Mount of Uranus	—	—
9	Mount of Neptune	—	—

The chart (Fig. 1) shows their positions as well as their symbols.

It is very difficult to determine the mount type of the individual because a pure specimen of the type is rarely seen. In olden days it was possible to determine this because the Roman race and the Aryan race were available and these were governed by particular mounts. However as races got mixed up, pure specimens became rare.

Once we find out the principal mount and the secondary mount, we can know the i) nature, ii) health, iii) financial position, iv) marriage, v) vocation etc of the individual.

Valuable tips for locating the prominent mount

Mounts on the hand may be either a) developed or b) flat

or c) under-developed. In order to accurately judge the development of the mount, we shall have to apply the following tests.

i) Finger, phalanges and tips of the finger.
ii) Apex of the mount.
iii) Signs on the mount.
iv) Elasticity of the mount.
v) Hardness or flabbiness of the mount.

Finger, Phalanges and Tips of the Finger

A finger, normal or greater in length, adds to the strength of the mount. Even if a mount is developed but the finger on that mount is underdeveloped, the qualities of the developed mount are lessened and diminished. Similarly, long fingers, short fingers, smooth fingers or knotty fingers add their qualities to that mount. From the development of the phalanges, we shall know which world governs the mount. The tips also indicate the bias of the qualities shown by the mount, whether the qualities are original, practical, or emotional.

Apex of the mount (Fig. 22)

Fig. 22 : Apex

The mount is in its normal position if the apex is in the centre of the mount and also exactly below the finger to which it belongs. If the apex is shifted to any other side, it means that the mount is displaced.

a) If the apex is towards the finger, it elevates the qualities of the mount.

b) If the apex is nearer the base of the mount, it lessens the qualities of the mount.

c) If the apex leans towards another mount, it gives away its qualities and takes the qualities of the mount towards which the apex leans.

Thus, the position of the apex adds to or diminishes the qualities of the mount.

Signs on the mount

There are good or bad signs which can be seen on the mount.

A) *Good Signs*

i) A single vertical line is a good sign and adds to the qualities of the mount. Even on a flat mount, this vertical line increases the prominence of the mount.

ii) Star, triangle, square and circle are considered to be auspicious signs and they add to the qualities of the mount.

B) *Bad Signs*

i) Cross lines, grills and two or more vertical lines diminish the qualities of the mount and they show hindrances in acquiring the qualities of the mount.

ii) Island, dots and spots are considered as inauspicious signs on the mounts and they exhibit dangers, accidents, losses and troubles.

Elasticity of the mount

In order to find out the elasticity of the mount, it is better to take a brand new pencil which is not sharpened and press it on the mount with even pressure. We notice that the mount when pressed comes to its original bulging in a rebounding way. It has a springlike action. We have to study this springlike action of each mount. A mount which rebounds in a quick and consistent manner is said to have good elasticity. An elastic mount adds to the qualities of the mount.

Hardness or flabbiness of the mount

Hardness adds to the strength of the mount. A hard mount, even though it is less developed, adds strength to that mount. A flabby mount lessens the qualities of the mount.

From the above study, we are in a position to find out the prominent or the principal mount and the secondary mount. We shall now proceed further with the study of individual mounts.

The Mount of Jupiter (Pitru Sthana—Father)

A Jupiterian is a good type. He is confident. He is self-reliant and takes his own decisions. He has the habit of talking loudly. He is fond of show and likes to observe form, order and law. He is jovial in spirit and cordial in manner. His passions are healthy, spontaneous and without inhibitions. He is free in his expression.

Jupiter stands for a) morality, b) pure love, c) justice, d) sympathy, e) ambition, f) leadership, g) religion, h) pride,

i) honour, j) enthusiasm, k) generosity, l) respect and m) reverence.

A) *Development of the mount of Jupiter*

i) If the mount is developed in a normal way, it shows a) high religious ideas, b) lofty pride, c) pride in everyday life, d) pride in great enterprises. The person has an attractive personality and powerful looks. He enjoys a luxurious and happy life. He is very popular and attains distinction with kings and princes. He is generous, lucky, courageous, straightforward, noble, calm and strong. He gains victory over his rivals. He is religious and remains busy in his own activities.

ii) If the mount is overdeveloped, the person has a) arrogance, b) boastfulness, c) vindictiveness, d) criminal jealousy, e) tyranny, f) superstition. He is also egoistic, selfish and shrewd.

iii) If the mount is underdeveloped, it means a) absence of veneration, b) vulgarity, c) lack of self-respect. He lacks ambition and does not take steps to improve his lot in life. He feels nervous, shy and awkward in the presence of strangers.

B) *Placement of the mount of Jupiter*

The mount of Jupiter has five positions of placement. They are judged by the position of the apex.

i) When the apex of the mount leans towards the first finger, it shows egotism and vanity.

ii) If the apex leans towards the mount of Saturn, it means that Saturn will influence the Jupiterian ideas, and sobriety and sadness will hold down the Jupiterian ambition.

iii) If the apex leans towards the outer edge of the hand, it means a selfish motive and pride in one's family.

iv) If the apex leans towards the line of Heart, it shows pride in affection and ambition for the loved ones. Such a person is lucky, benevolent, rich and religious.

v) If the apex leans towards the line of Head, the Jupiterian ambition will be directed to intellectual pursuits. It shows pride in the intellect.

C) *Combination of the mount with different aspects on the hand*

After studying the basic characteristics of a Jupiterian, we should be able to combine these qualities with texture, flexibility, length of the finger of Jupiter and other factors like smooth fingers, knotty fingers, phalanges of the Jupiter finger, tips of the finger etc., etc. For instance,

a) The texture of the hand will indicate whether the Jupiterian qualities are fine or coarse.

b) Flexibility will show whether adaptability will bring the Jupiterian success or whether his stiff demeanour will obstruct his ambition.

c) Consistency will help us to know the energy behind his ambition.

d) If the Jupiter finger is as long as the Saturn finger, the desire for power will be great. If it is longer than the Saturn finger, the person will be a tyrant.

e) Smooth fingers will add to his intuition, impulse and inspiration. They mean brilliant thinking.

f) Knotty fingers develop organising capacity, orderliness and discipline.

g) Long fingers will make a Jupiterian slow in thinking. However these fingers will assist him to go into details and will make him studious.

h) Short fingers will increase his brilliance and will make him go for big projects.

i) If the first phalange of the Jupiter finger is developed, it gives him intuition. If the second phalange is developed, it makes him more practical in life regarding his religious thinking. If the third phalange is developed, it gives him good taste and also makes him a glutton.

j) Square tips will mean high religious ideals if the mount is normal in development. In an excessively developed mount they means superstition, whereas when the mount is flat or underdeveloped they shows absence of veneration.

k) Spatulate tips to the normal mount of Jupiter show pride in great enterprise. They mean boasting and arrogance when the mount is excessively developed and they indicate vulgarity if the mount is underdeveloped.

l) Conic and pointed tips to the normal mount mean lofty pride and religious ideals ; to the excessive mount, they mean artistic concept and superstition, to the underdeveloped mount, they mean lack of respect for others.

D) *Signs on the mount of Jupiter*

Good signs on the mount of Jupiter are a star, a cross, a

circle, one vertical line, a triangle, a square and the ring of Solomon.

Bad signs on this mount are a spot, a bar, a grill, a ladder-like formation, an island, capillary cross lines and a spring.

1) *Star* : A star on the mount of Jupiter is an excellent sign. It indicates a) realisation of ambition, b) fame, c) sudden rise in life.

The period of rise in life can be calculated by studying the position of the star. If it is at the bottom of the mount it means rise in early life. If it is in the middle of the mount, it shows success in the middle of life, *i.e.*, between 30 and 45 years, and if the star is found on the upper side of the mount, it indicates success in old age.

ii) A star on the outer edge of the mount of Jupiter shows accident through fire. If there is a square around this star, it gives protection from danger.

iii) A star at the edge of the mount and touching the line of Life at its beginning shows loss of mother after the birth of the person.

iv) If the above star does not touch the line of Life, it shows an illegitimate birth.

v) When a branch of the star on the mount of Jupiter is continued by a line which cuts the line of Apollo on the mount of Apollo, it shows that a revengeful enemy has interfered with the ambition of the person.

2) *Cross* : A cross on the mount of Jupiter shows a) happy married life, b) popularity among ladies.

3) *Circle* : A circle shows a) success, b) remembrance of previous birth.

4) *Vertical line* : A single vertical line when bright and uncrossed by other lines shows success.

If there are five vertical lines between the mounts of Jupiter and Saturn, they mean that the person has many friends as well as enemies.

5) *Triangle* : It shows a) diplomatic cleverness, b) that the person will be a politician.

6) *Square* : It means a) protection from scandal, b) protection from social failure, c) a good sober sense which guides ambition.

7) *Ring of Solomon* : A line placed at the root of the finger of Jupiter and in a semicircular shape, which encloses a portion of the mount, is known as the Ring of Solomon. As the name signifies, it shows knowledge and wisdom. It is a symbol of occultism. It gives one prophetic vision.

8) *Spot* : A black or red spot on the mount shows misfortune and loss of reputation.

9) *Bar* : A cross bar denotes failure and difficulties. The difficulties may be due to ill-health. A bar crossing a branch of the line of Heart indicates misfortune through love.

10) *Grill* : A grill pulls down the virtues of the mount. It destroys the efficiency of the mount. It also turns good qualities into defects and vices. It means loose morals and superstition.

11) *Ladder* : A ladder-like formation shows a poor life, suffering losses.

12) *Island* : It indicates the ruin of an ambitious career by the conduct of a close relative or a friend.

13) *Capillary cross lines* : They show a wound to the head.

14) *Spring* : A sign like a spring shows apoplexy.

CHAPTER 41

The Mount of Saturn (Matru Sthana-Mother)

A good mount of Saturn shows extreme sense of discipline and it represents steadfastness, constancy and dutifulness. This man has a sober and solitary personality. He is very conservative and does not do anything hastily. He is a lover of classical music but mostly of the melancholy type. He is also a lover of art but he loves landscapes, natural scenery and flowers. His melancholic nature has a depressing effect upon others also. He lacks imagination and is sceptical. Even though he is passionate, he has no capacity to appreciate the good qualities of his wife and thus he is unsuccessful in his married life.

Saturn stands for a) endurance, b) politeness, c) system, d) method, e) wisdom, f) sobriety, g) purity, h) justice, i) chastity, j) economy, k) thrift, l) industry, m) perseverance and n) veneration and love of truth.

Development of the mount of Saturn

1) If the mount of Saturn is developed in a normal way, it shows a) suspicion, b) conservatism, c) prudence and d) caution. It shows a studious person, especially in abstruse subjects such as science, astrology, palmistry and mysticism.

2) If the mount is over-developed, it indicates a) morbidity, b) melancholia, c) pessimism and d) a stingy nature. The exaggerated prominence of this mount shows the negative side of the good qualities of the mount. Love of solitude and seclusion is converted to intense dislike of society, even to the extent of hatred of mankind. There will be extreme selfishness and avarice. Excessive development of this mount shows a tendency to commit suicide and a secretive temperament which will not disclose the method employed in doing this.

3) Underdeveloped mount of Saturn : Saturn is considered as a balance wheel and when its mount is absent on the hand, it means want of harmony in the balance of the personality. Such a person will be callous and he has to work very hard with a suppressed sense of misfortune. He has to face public mistrust and undergo corporal punishment. He is vicious and unreliable.

Placement of the Mount

The mount of Saturn has five positions. They are judged by the position of the apex.

i) When the apex of the mount leans towards the Saturn finger, it intensifies the qualities of the mount and shows a) intense love of solitude and conservatism, b) shyness and c) repulsion for the opposite sex. Such a person lacks grace. He is awkward in his manners and tactless.

ii) If the apex leans towards the mount of Jupiter, it partakes the qualities of Jupiter and makes the person morbid in pride. He suffers because of brothers and relatives. He has danger from the head of the country. He is always worried and sad. However, after his middle life, he enjoys the company of his children and spends his life in good company.

iii) If the apex leans towards the mount of Apollo, it partakes the joyfulness of the mount of Apollo and makes him less melancholy and less gloomy.

iv) If the apex moves towards the line of Heart, it shows anxiety for the loved ones and sincerity in love.

v) When the apex is centrally located, it means that the person is a Saturnian in its real sense and the mount is the balance wheel as described earlier.

Combination of the mount with different aspects on the hand

After studying the basic qualities and characteristics of a Saturnian, we should be able to combine these qualities with texture, flexibility, length of the finger of Saturn, smooth fingers, knotty fingers, phalanges of the Saturn finger, tips of the finger etc., etc. For instance.

a) Fine or medium texture is the best for the Saturnian since it would make him sensible in his thinking and he can be more refined in his behaviour in society. The fine texture will lessen his shyness and he will be able to mix in society.

Coarse texture makes a man rough, arrogant and curt. It increases his hatred for mankind.

b) A flexible hand makes the man enjoy the society of his fellowmen and heightens the good qualities of the Saturnian. A stiff hand makes him hate mankind and makes him more selfish.

c) Flabby consistency makes him lazy. Elastic consistency reduces his gloomy and morbid tendencies.

d) Knotty fingers make him systematic and methodical in his work and he succeeds in scientific pursuits. He can be a writer on scientific subjects as well as on philosophy.

e) Smooth fingers increase his intuition and reduce his shyness and retiring disposition.

f) Long fingers make a Saturnian successful in studies where research is needed for a long time. He will be free from excitement and confusion.

g) Short finngers make him more critical and sceptical and less analytical. This adds to his loneliness and his nature, by virtue of short fingers, to jump to conclusions deceives him in life.

h) *Phalanges* : If the first phalange of the Saturn finger is developed, he will be a thinker and inclined to occult subjects and superstitions. If the second phalange is developed, that would create interest in critical and scientific investigations such as those in physics, chemistry, mathematics etc. If the third phalange is the longest, he will be a money worshipper and will evaluate everything in terms of money ; he will be a miser.

i) *Tips* : A conic tip to a Saturnian and to the Saturn finger is not a happy sign as it disturbs the characteristics of the balance wheel.

j) A square tip adds to the man's love of mathematics and solitude.

k) A spatulate tip adds to his love of agriculture.

Signs on the mount of Saturn

As single signs or in combination, a triangle, a square, a single vertical line, a circle etc. strengthen the mount of Saturn. On the other hand, a cross bar, grill, island and cross weaken the characteristics of the mount.

1) *Star* : A star on the mount of Saturn is not a good sign and it indicates a) a mysterious force working to raise the Saturnian to greater heights but only to pull him down to suffer the worst fatality, b) paralysis and an incurable disease, c) death on the scaffold, d) danger of assassination if it is at the end of a deep line of Fate.

2) *Cross* : A cross means a) misuse of occult powers, b) childlessness, c) death on the scaffold.

According to Hindu Palmistry, it means riches.

3) *Circle* : It means spiritual attainments.

4) *Whorl or loop (Chakra or Shankh)* : According to Hindu Palmistry, this sign means a person who is learned, religious, popular, benevolent, courageous, outspoken and virtuous.

5) *Vertical line* : A single vertical line on the mount gives prominence to qualities of the Saturnian. It means a) satisfaction in life, b) a successful and happy old age, c) good luck.

6) *Triangle* : It indicates a) success in scientific pursuits, b) a deep insight into occult and mystic subjects.

7) *Square* : This sign will reduce the intensified qualities of a bad Saturnian and will save him from fatality.

8) *Ring of Saturn* : It means delays and difficulties in the career of the person.

9) *Spot* : It shows an evil influence.

10) *Bar* : It indicates an unavoidable misfortune.

11) *Grill* : It shows a) ill-luck, b) an unscrupulous and untrustworthy person, c) a culprit and d) imprisonment.

12) *Island* : It shows a) trouble, b) loss of memory, c) deafness.

13) *Capillary cross lines* : They indicate a wound in the chest.

CHAPTER 42

The Mount of Apollo (Vidya Sthana-Education)

The third mount on the hand for our study is the mount of Apollo. This is also called the mount of the Sun. When the mount is found well-developed with the apex centrally located, the finger of Apollo long and strong, it shows that the person is an Apollonian. This mount, however, does not have a bulge like Jupiter or Mercury mounts and the bulge may be on the side, more probably on the Mercurian side. The development of the mount of Apollo also shows the prominence of the Sun in the horoscope and the astrological attributes of the Sun are applicable to the Apollonion.

Apollo stands for a) originality, b) art, c) brilliance, d) spontaneity, e) adaptability, f) energy, g) enthusiasm.

Development of the mount of Apollo

1) If the mount is developed in a normal way, it shows enthusiasm, eloquence, oratory and a life full of energy. Such persons are also dreamers and idealistic artists.

2) If the mount is overdeveloped, it shows the wrong side of the Apollonian attributes and indicates vanity, ostentation and a passion for wealth and luxury. The man's talents and brilliance may result in insanity. He is overtalkative and has a craze for showing off his talents to others. But his superficial knowledge of any subject exposes him soon and he often becomes the subject of abuse.

3) If the mount is underdeveloped, the usual enthusiasm and energy are lacking and art has no place even in his dreams.

Placement of the mount of Apollo

There are four positions for this mount.

i) When the mount of Apollo is leaning towards the finger of Apollo, it shows love for public life.

ii) If the apex is leaning towards the mount of Mercury, it means that the shrewdness and the business qualities of the Mercurian are absorbed by the Apollonian and he can make money out of his talents. It also shows love of children and animals, especially domestic pets.

iii) If this mount is leaning towards the mount of Saturn, it denotes an Apollonian with a selfish attitude and sometimes diffident about his abilities.

iv) We may also find this mount leaning towards the line of Heart in which case the man is sentimental and emotional and his talents and talk have a personal and emotional touch.

Combination of the mount with different aspects on the hand

We shall now combine the different aspects on the hand with the developed mount of Apllo.

a) Normally, smooth texture is expected in an Apollonian's hand, as it shows refinement of character. Rough texture therefore reduces to a great extent his enthusiasm, ability, instinctiveness and intuition.

b) An Apollonian is expected to have more flexible hands. This is because he is more social and has an aptitude to mix in society. Stiff hands will have a check on his natural aptitude and talents.

c) Flabby consistency shows a man of talk and not of deeds.

d) *Knotty fingers* : A developed first knot indicates an artist who is endowed with high ideals. A developed second knot develops his talent in instrumental music, dancing and such other arts which involve physical activity. An Apollonian with either of his knots developed will be studious and thoughtful.

e) *Smooth fingers* : He will have an easy grasp of any subject but he will try to make a show of the little knowledge he acquires.

f) Long fingers will make him slow in his talents.

g) Small fingers will make him cautious in expression.

h) If the first phalange of the Apollo finger is developed, he will be given to mental roaming and will only dream of high ideals.

If the second or the middle phalange is developed, he will have a better understanding of human life.

If the third phalange is found more developed, he will have friends for the sake of company only and he will enjoy life for the sake of enjoyment,

i) A conic tip will add to the artistic nature of the person.

j) A square tip will make him more practical.

k) A spatulate tip will make him influence others with his originality, but at the same time he will not like much to mix with ordinary people who are not as intelligent as he.

l) If the Apollo finger is longer than the Jupiter finger, he will be overenthusiastic. If it is longer than the Saturn finger, he will lose foolishly in gambling. If this finger is crooked, it shows a tricky gambler.

Signs on the mount of Apollo

1) *Star* : It shows a) distinction, b) accession of wealth, c) reward, d) reputation and e) social standing.

2) *Cross* : It means a) success in life, b) learning.

If the line of Apollo is absent on the hand, a cross shows c) disappointment in the desired pursuits, d) difficulties. On the hand of a woman it means an avarice and unscrupulousness.

3) *Circle* : If the line of Apollo is poorly developed, and the circle is towards the line of Heart, it shows heart trouble as well as eye trouble.

4) *Vertical line* : A deep and straight vertical line indicates a) domestic happiness, b) wealth and c) fame.

5) *Triangle* : It shows reputation in pursuits.

6) *Square* : It means protection from jumping to unwarranted activities and from bad results of over enthusiasm. According to the Hindu system, it means success in business.

7) *Spot* : It indicates evil influence.

8) *Bar* : It means difficulties in enterprise.

9) *Grill* : It shows vanity and little possibility of development of talents and of success.

10) *Island* : It shows danger to health.

11) *Many hair-like lines* : The person is uneasy, changing, unlucky and dull.

CHAPTER 43

The Mount of Mercury (Jaya Sthana-Wife)

This is the fourth mount for our study. It has peculiar characteristics and we have to be very careful in making our judgement about the good or the bad development of the mount. We can use the same knobs in determining the development of this mount. The apex should be in the centre of the mount and the Mercury finger straight and well-developed. On its good side, it is one of the best and most successful of all the types, but at the same time, the greatest swindlers, cheats or liars can be found in this type only.

The main characteristics of the Mercurian are a) shrewdness, b) quickness, c) scientific pursuits, d) business ability, e) industry, f) intuition, g) diplomacy.

Development of the mount of Mercury

1) If the mount is developed in a normal way it shows intelligence, an aptitude for the occult, diplomatic shrewdness, legal profession, oratory, talents, dexterity, love of travel and experiments, eloquence and intuition.

2) If the mount is overdeveloped, it shows deceit, hypocrisy and dishonesty. The man is likely to be callous and criminal.

3) If the mount is underdeveloped it means failure in personal, social and domestic life.

Placement of the mount of Mercury

There are six positions for this mount.

i) If the apex of the mount is in the centre, the person has balanced qualities. He will be reasonable in all his dealings and will have normal emotions, feelings and discretion.

ii) If it is leaning towards the finger of Mercury, it shows eloquence and humour.

iii) If it leans towards the mount of Apollo, it indicates enthusiasm in the field of business and a life more dominated by energy but less by Mercurian shrewdness. According to the Hindu system it means on the hand of a woman, a vicious husband and widowhood.

iv) If it leans towards the percussion, it shows success in business through perseverance and industry.

v) If it is towards the negative mount of Mars, it means self-confidence and hypnotic power. This person will never shed tears nor will he care for others' miseries.

vi) If it leans towards the mount of Uranus (which lies between the lines of Heart and Head), the Mercurian will have an aggressive spirit.

Combination of the mount with different aspects on the hand

a) *Flexibility* : Flexible hands make a Mercurian brilliant and shrewd in his profession.

Stiff hands make him follow old fashions, traditions and notions.

b) *Texture* : A fine texture means good judgement and common sense. It will give intuition to a doctor, sound arguments to a lawyer and refined manners to a businessman.

Coarse texture to a bad Mercurian shows criminal acts.

c) *Consistency* : Elastic consistency means sharpness in thinking, arguments and advocacy.

Flabby consistency weakens the qualities of the Mercurian.

Hard consistency is expected on a bad mount and with coarse texture, it means a scoundrel who will not stop at anything in order to achieve his aim.

Soft hands make a Mercurian less intuitive.

d) *Knotty fingers* : If the first knot is developed, the person is an inventor and likes to work in scientific pursuits.

If the second knot is developed, his thinking, writing and scientific pursuits are towards materialistic things.

e) *Smooth fingers* : A smooth finger adds to the intuitive ability of the Mercurian and he will have an easy and quick understanding of his fellow beings.

f) *Long fingers* : A person with a long finger of Mercury enjoys comforts in life and also maternal love.

g) *Short fingers* : A short finger indicates lack of discretion and inability to judge matters.

h) *Phalanges* : If the first phalange of the Mercury finger is developed, it shows law-mindedness, cleverness in speech and eloquence.

If the second phalange is developed, the man is fit for commercial positions. Excessive development of this phalange shows a criminal aptitude.

If the third phalange is developed, the person will spend his money in buying comforts and pleasures for himself. On the hand of a bad Mercurian the developed third phalange shows a disposition to crime.

i) *Tip of the finger* : i) A pointed tip gives psychic powers and intuition.

ii) A conic tip indicates an artist who will make plenty of money.

iii) A square tip shows a methodical and practical businessman.

iv) A spatulate tip gives good success.

Signs on the mount of Mercury

1) *Star* : It shows a) sense in business, b) unexpected luck.

2) *Cross* : It adds to the talent and diplomacy exhibited by the Mercurian. On an overdeveloped mount, it means a gambler.

3) *Circle* : It shows danger from water and poinsoning.

4) *Vertical line* : It means unexpected accession of wealth. Many vertical lines on the mount of Mercury are called medical stigma and they show an inclination to medical studies.

5) *Triangle* : It adds to the diplomacy and cleverness of the person,

6) *Square* : It saves a Mercurian from financial losses.

7) *Spot* : It indicates accidents or illness. If it is connected with the line of Marriage, it shows trouble in married life.

8) *Bar* : It shows troubles and obstacles in business.

9) *Grill* : It indicates temptation to commit suicide after a crime is committed by the person.

10) *Island* : It means betrayal of trust by the person.

11) *Many hair-like lines* : On a woman's hand, they show a chattering nature.

CHAPTER 44

The Mount of Mars

i) Negative Mars – Dharma Sthana—Religion
ii) Positive Mars—Shatru Sthana—Enemies

There are two positions for the mount of Mars on the hand (Fig. 1). One of them is located below the mount of Mercury and above the mount of the Moon on the side of percussion. This mount is called the upper mount of Mars or the negative Mars. The other position is situated inside the line of Life above the mount of Venus. This is called the positive Mars or the lower Mars. These positions of Mars were located on the hand at a very late stage in the study of palmistry.

The main characteristics of a positive Martian are a) aggression, b) fighting to death, c) intolerance of injustice, d) dash, e) courage, f) activity.

The negative Martian has all the above qualities but in a subdued form. His characteristics are a) resistance, b) defence, c) tolerance, d) carefulness.

Development of the Upper Mount of Mars

a) Normal development of this mount shows the courage of a soldier, a martyr or a patriot.

b) Excess development shows a violent temper.

c) An underdeveloped mount means a coward. It shows absence of resistance and surrender to fate. It also shows a suicidal tendency.

Development of the Lower Mount of Mars

a) If this mount is developed in a normal way, it shows a resigned person who is careless about dangers.

b) If the development is in excess, it means a hard-hearted person.

Placement of the mount of Mars

Placement of the negative (Upper) mount of Mars

i) If this mount is leaning towards the mount of Mercury, it will make the Martian a businessman who has the power of resistance and who will not be discouraged in emergencies.

ii) If it inclines towards the middle portion of the line of Heart, it shows patience in love affairs.

iii) If it is inclined towards the mount of Uranus (middle portion of the hand), it indicates intelligence and energy.

iv) If this mount is leaning towards the mount of Moon, it means a) protection from laziness and dreaming, b) power of hypnotism.

v) If it is bulging towards the purcussion, it means the Martian qualities are intensified.

Placement of the positive (Lower) mount of Mars

This mount does not have an apex but we can find out the development from the bulging it has.

i) If it leans towards the mount of Venus, it shows a) power of endurance through affection and attachment, b) the vigour of Mars gets an outlet in the company of members of the opposite sex and leads to polygamy.

ii) If it is deflected towards the thumb, it means determination.

iii) If it is inclined towards the interior of the palm, it shows unexpected changes in life and upheavals due to the aggressive nature of the Martian.

iv) If the mount is inclined towards the line of Head, it means a combination of intellectual strength and discrimination.

Combination of the mount with different aspects on the Hand

The combination is applicable to both the mounts, the positive mount as well as the negative mount of Mars.

a) *Flexibility* : A very flexible hand shows versatility. A stiff hand will make the Martian more obstinate, quarrelsome and a person with fixed ideas.

b) *Consistency* : Elastic consistency will help a Martian to push his strong qualities within reasonable limits.

Flabby consistency is not fortunate for a Martian as it would reduce the qualities of a fighter.

Hard consistency shows less adaptability and it is a bad combination on the hand of a Martian with the lower mount developed.

c) *Texture* : A fine texture will lessen the brutality of a Martian.

Medium texture will be found on the hand of a Martian who moves in good society. If the upper mount of Mars is developed, a medium texture means refined resistance under disappointment.

Coarse texture will make a Martian a disagreeable fellow.

d) *Knotty fingers* : If the first knot is developed, it shows intelligence and order in plans.

If the second knot is developed, the person will be neat and tidy in clothes and at work.

e) *Smooth fingers* : They indicate a quick grasp of the situation ; such a Martian overcomes his opponents by taking quick decisions.

f) *Long fingers* : A Martian with such fingers will not be impulsive ; he will take decisions cautiously and slowly.

g) *Short fingers* : The impetuous nature of the short fingers will make a Martian commit blunders.

h) *Phalanges* ; If the first phalange of the fingers is developed, it means a Martian who is fearless and sometimes fanatical in his aggressive moves.

If the second phalange of the fingers is developed, it shows enthusiasm and courage in public life.

If the third phalange is developed, it means a vulgar Martian who is a sensualist, a heavy eater and one who hates intellectual pursuits.

i) *Tip of the fingers* : i) Pointed tips : If the mount is normally developed these tips show courage. If it is developed in excess, the tips mean violence. If the mount is lacking, the man is a coward.

ii) Conic tips : With normal development of the mount, these tips indicate a patriot. On an excessively developed mount they show vanity.

iii) Square tips : If the development is normal, these tips show courage. If it is in excess, the tips indicate the violence of a disappointed schemer. If the mount is lacking, they indicate a coward in everyday life.

iv) Spatulate tips : On a normally developed mount, they mean an explorer. On an excessively developed mount, they mean a rough Martian. If the mount is absent, they mean a coward on the battlefield.

Signs on the Mount of Mars (either positive or negative)

1) *Star* : It shows courage and military honour.

2) *Cross* : It shows danger through a quarrelsome and stubborn nature.

3) *Circle* : It means a wound in the eye.

4) *Horizontal line* : A single horizontal line, rising from the line of Life and going into the positive or negative Mars, shows severe illness, sorrow or death.

5) *Triangle* : It shows a) military skill, b) aptitude for and gain from mining and geology.

6) *Square* : It shows control over a violent temper and protection from harm.

7) *Bar* : It shows enemies who stand in the way of success.

8) *Spot* : It means a wound in a fight.

9) *Grill* : It indicates a) violent death, b) murderous instincts.

10) *Island* : It means obstacles in life.

11) *Many hair-like lines* : They mean obstacles, violence of temper and brutality in love.

CHAPTER 45

The Mount of Moon (Luna)

(Kalpana Sthana)

This mount is located under the upper mount of Mars and is the biggest mount on the hand. This mount is divided into three sections: a) upper mount, b) middle mount and c) lower mount. This division is useful in order to study the health defects of the Lunarian (another name for Moon). This mount shows high imagination, idealism and dreamy nature. It is necessary for every individual to have this mount developed to a certatin extent. Imagination is the natural faculty of a human being and, if it is withdrawn, our life will have no charm. A person who lacks the mount is a very dull person spending his life in a routine way, without a lively spirit or enthusiasm or idealism. A Lunarian has fantasies and he lacks a practical approach to life. He lives in his own dreams and therefore shuns society.

The main characteristics are a) imagination, b) love of travel, c) an unsteady mind, d) moodiness, e) a love of mystic subjects and f) coldness.

Development of the Mount of Moon

1) If the mount is developed in a normal way but on the lower side towards the wrist, it indicates power of foretelling events.

2) If the mount is developed in excess, it is a danger and it means extreme sensuality. It develops hysteria, insanity and nervousness. Sometimes the overdeveloped mount may be in the form of a narrow strip along the percussion. It shows a strong power of meditation and concentration but more seclusion and a lack of mental force.

3) An underdeveloped mount of Moon shows a cynical person who lacks imagination.

Placement of the Mount of Moon

There are five positions of placement for this mount.

i) When the mount leans towards the rascette, it adds to the power of meditation.

ii) If the mount leans towards the mount of Venus, the person will imagine things very beautiful and idealistic. This will, however, make the Lunarian more effeminate.

iii) If the mount is deflected towards the Plain of Mars or the mount of Uranus, it will produce drastic results and the person will have to suffer from the greatest blows in life.

iv) If it leans towards the upper mount of Mars, the person will have an automatic check on his foolish ambitions.

v) If the mount inclines towards the percussion, it enhances the creative power of the Lunarian.

Combination of the Mount with different aspects on the hand

a) *Texture* : Medium texture is best for the highly imaginative nature of the Lunarian. This will give him practical idealism.

Fine texture will lead him to fantasies and lunacy.

Coarse texture will make him sluggish.

b) *Flexibility* : Flexible hands will create a person with extreme views and moods which change from time to time. Stiff hands will make him obstinate in his beliefs.

c) *Consistency* : Flabby consistency depicts idealism, fancy, dreaminess and laziness.

Elastic consistency will make him intelligent and reduce his lethargy.

Hard consistency shows distorted views on religion, restlessness and attraction for travels.

d) *Knotty fingers* : These fingers will be an advantage to a Lunarian as he will get the power of reasoning and analysis.

e) *Smooth fingers* : They will make him more intuitive and revel in fancies.

f) *Long fingers* : Such fingers will make him dull and indolent.

g) *Short fingers* : A Lunarian with short fingers will jump to conclusions and misunderstand others.

h) *Phalanges*: The first phalange, more developed, shows fantasies and hallucinations.

The middle phalange, more developed, will make him a creative thinker.

If the lower phalange is more developed, he will indulge in his lower passions.

i) *Tips of the fingers*: i) Conic tips will make it difficult for the Lunarian to control his sensual nature.

ii) Square tips indicate a good poet or a writer and healthy idealism.

iii) Spatulate tips create many conflicts and contradictions in the mind of a Lunarian.

iv) Pointed tips show feeble-mindedness and madness.

Signs on the Mount of Moon

1) *Star*: A star, when small and well formed, is a good sign. With the presence of line of Apollo and Saturn, it shows success through the imagination.

A star on the lower Luna and connected to a line of a Voyage from the line of Life shows great adventures and mysterious experiences.

A star connected with an influence line from the mount of Venus shows an erotic nature.

A star on the voyage line from percussion shows danger from voyage and ship-wreck.

2) *Cross*: It shows a superstitious and dreamy nature. A large cross shows an unreliable and deceiving nature.

3) *Circle*: It means danger from drowning.

4) *Vertical line*: It shows a tendency to rheumatism.

5) *Horizontal line*: It shows a chronic disease of the partner and allergy to allopathic drugs and injections.

6) *Triangle*: It indicates a highly imaginative faculty used with understanding and good sense.

7) *Square*: It means protection from danger arising from bad signs or the overdevelopment of the mount.

8) *Spot*: It means danger from drowning.

9) *Bar*: It indicates a weak, inconstant and unreliable nature.

10) *Grill*: It shows a worrying and discontented nature.

11) *Island*: It means worries, obstacles and danger from voyage,

CHAPTER 46

The Mount of Venus

Upper—Bhratru Sthana—Brothers
Lower—Bandhu Sthana—Relatives

The seventh mount for our study is the mount of Venus. This is also a large mount. A Venusian is a most beautiful and attractive person. He is always governed by love, sympathy and adoration. His talk is interesting and lively.

The main characteristics of a Venusian are a) beauty, b) vitality, c) warmth, d) sympathy e) love, f) music, g) art.

Development of the Mount of Venus

1) If the mount is developed in a normal way, it means on the hand of a woman, a) sincere love, b) an aptitude for artistic and beautiful things, c) a fancy for beautiful clothes, d) a desire for wealth, luxury, jewellery and perfumes. On the hand of a man it means a) love of music, b) grace, c) passion, d) generosity, e) love of social life.

2) Excess development of the mount shows a) sensuality and inconstancy, b) vicious thinking, c) selfishness, d) immorality and profligacy,

3) An underdeveloped mount of Venus indicates a cold nature and indifference to sex and the charms of the other sex.

Placement of the Mount of Venus

There are four positions for this mount.

i) If it leans towards the positive Mars, it means an aggressive approach to love and a purely sensual nature.

ii) If it leans towards the thumb, the person is more realistic in his artistic pursuits and gets reputation and money by his art.

iii) If the mount leans towards the rascettes, it means, in the case of a woman, difficulties in child-bearing.

iv) If the mount is deflected towards the mount of Moon, the person is more sensual and foolishly involved in love affairs.

Combination of the mount with different aspects on the hand

a) *Texture* : A fine texture shows natural understanding and appreciation of the feelings of colleagues and friends, and an aptitude for creative arts such as music, painting and sculpture.

A coarse texture indicates indulgence in vices and selfish and vulgar passions.

b) *Flexibility* : A Venusian usually has flexible hands which show a knack for developing his ideas.

Stiff hands indicate an artist with rigid and fixed ideas.

c) *Consistency* : A flabby consistency shows a Venusian who is a lazy artist who does not achieve anything in life.

A Venusian with soft consistency is attracted to the fair sex. He will be practical in his idealism.

An elastic consistency adds moral responsibility to the flirting nature of the Venusian.

A hard consistency diminishes the love and the sympathy which are the main characteristics of a Venusian. He will be cold in his passions and will be rough and arrogant in his approach to the opposite sex.

d) *Smooth fingers* : They give insight and quick grasp. Such a man is impetuous in his passions and approach to the opposite sex.

e) *Knotty fingers* : These fingers give a Venusian an analytical mind, and system and method in his profession.

f) *Short fingers* : Short fingers indicate a nature which is hasty and impetuous and a tendency to jump to conclusions. A Venusian with such fingers will be changing and fickle-minded and will hardly be successful in his love and profession.

g) *Long fingers* : A Venusian with long fingers will show interest in details and, if he is an artist, will show the details of the leaves of a tree, will portray the small shades on a face and will paint landscapes with the utmost care.

h) *Phalanges* : If the first phalanges of the fingers are

developed, he will have an ideal love. He will master a creative art, may be music or painting.

If the second phalanges are developed, he will be an artist with a practical outlook and will earn by his art.

If the third phalanges are developed, the Venusian will be selfish and desire gratification of his lower passions.

i) *Tips of the fingers* : i) Pointed tips give ideal love and a vicious imagination.

ii) Conic tips mean a poet or an artist wedded to his art.

iii) Square tips show a successful artist.

iv) Spatulate tips indicate a good husband or a wife if the mount of Venus is developed in a normal way, but if it is developed in excess, spatulate tips show a flirting and debaucherous nature.

Signs on the Mount of Venus

1) *Star* : The significance of this sign on the mount of Venus varies according to its position on the mount.

i) A star on the centre of the mount shows success in love.

ii) On the side of the mount and nearer to the thumb, it shows love for a person of distinction.

iii) Between the second phalange of the thumb and the mount of Venus, it means unhappiness caused by the opposite sex.

iv) At the outer side and at the base, but far removed from the rascette, the star produces the same result as described in (iii) above.

v) At the base of the mount and near to the rascette, it shows successful, unopposed and distinguished love.

2) *Cross* : It shows patience in one's affection. If it touches the line of Life, it means trouble with relatives.

3) *Circle* : It means ill-health.

4) *Vertical line* : A single vertical line going up to the mount of positive Mars shows a love-affair. Two vertical lines show inconstancy in love.

5) *Horizontal line* : A single horizontal line from the second phalange of the thumb to the line of Life shows troubled married life.

6) *Triangle* : It shows prudence and a calculating attitude in love.

7) *Square* : It means protection from the trouble brought about by passion. Two squares close to each other and on the upper mount of Venus show litigation.

8) *Spot* : It shows frustration in love and trouble from relatives.

9) *Bar* : It indicates obstructions in getting hereditary property.

10) *Grill* : It shows lasciviousness and morbidity.

11) *Island* : It means susceptibility to love affairs.

CHAPTER 47

The Mounts of Uranus and Neptune

Until recently the above mounts were not alloted any space on the hand ; their influence on the hand was also not observed. However, after the discovery of these planets and their influence on human life, it was necessary to study whether these planets also showed their importance in the hand. It was, therefore, observed that what is called the Quadrangle (space between the lines of Head and Heart) or more specifically, the space between the positive mount of Mars and the negative mount of Mars (also known as the plain of Mars), represented the mount of Uranus and the portion near the wrist, between the mounts of Venus and Moon, represented the mount of Neptune.

Even though these planets influence human life, they do not indicate any distinctive personalities as other mounts do. We, therefore, do not have a Uranian or a Neptunian.

Though they do not indicate any individuality or a distinctive personality, their development on the hand elevates the importance of other mounts such as those of Jupiter, Saturn etc. The mounts of Uranus and Neptune have a subtle and magical influence on the activities of other mounts. These mounts show progress, elevated ideas and interest in spiritual life.

The Mount of Uranus

The portion covered by this mount is the plain of Mars and we can study the development of this mount by the bulging of this portion or by the sign of Uranus in this area.

The mount of Uranus shows revolution and unexpected happenings in life. Usually, the changes that take place are for the better and the mount represents the higher faculties of the mind. The mount shows activity and intelligence engaged for the betterment of human life. The peculiar characteristic of this mount is that it constantly aims at changes in life and society and at the liberation of the mind from the bondage of environment and society.

Development of the Mount of Uranus

If the mount is normal in its development, it shows clear understanding and a steady mind.

A better developed mount shows love of money and a tendency to amass wealth.

An underdeveloped mount shows a stingy nature.

Signs on the Mount of Uranus

1) *Cross* : A distinct and independent cross on the mount of Uranus is known as St. Andrew's Cross or the Mystic Cross. It indicates an aptitude for abstruse subjects and a love for occultism.

A cross under the mount of Saturn and in the plain of Mars touching the Fate line shows a fortunate and lucky life. It also shows a religious aptitude and this is found on the hands of religious preachers.

2) *Star* : It is a good sign and shows success in life.

3) *Square* : It shows a kind and sympathetic heart.

4) *Triangle* : It indicates love of deep studies.

5) *Circle* : One circle shows eye trouble. Three circles one touching other mean epilepsy.

6) *Grill* : It indicates madness.

7) *Lines* : Many small lines on the mount of Uranus show a weak and nervous mind and restlessness.

8) *Dots* : A red dot indicates murder or a serious wound. A white dot means a general weakening of the system.

The Mount of Neptune

This mount lies between the mounts of Moon and Venus and at the centre and at the base of the palm, just above the rascettes. This mount has control over the mind. A person with this mount prominent on the hand has to undergo a number of experiences in life and often he is a rolling stone which gathers no mass.

This is a spiritual mount and Supreme Consciousness is developed in this individual. He is like a free bird and likes to break the traditional bonds and restrictions. It is possible that the greatest of the prophets and spiritualists have this mount well developed on their hand.

Neptune shows love of travel, and change in life. The person is restless, uneasy and whimsical. He is often absent-minded and his behaviour is a mystery to others.

The other aspects such as placement, development of the mount and signs on the mount do not exist in the case of this mount.

The study of palmistry explained so far is known as Chirognomy. The success of hand-reading depends upon the combinations of various aspects on the hand and in order to study the hand in a scientific way, I am giving a model chart, which when completed will give a complete picture of the client.

The Model Chart

1) *The shape of the hand* :
2) *Skin* : a) fine, b) medium, c) coarse.
3) *Colour* : a) red, b) pink, c) blue, d) yellow, e) white.
4) *Consistency* : a) flabby, b) soft, c) elastic, d) hard.
5) *Flexibility* : a) stiff, b) normal, c) excessive.
6) *Finger* : a) smooth, b) knotty, c) short, d) long.
7) *Finger tips* : a) square, b) spatulate, c) conic, d) pointed.
8) *Tips of individual fingers* : a) Jupiter, b) Saturn
   c) Apollo, d) Mercury
9) *Length of fingers*: a) Normal, b) in relation to each other.
10) *Space between the fingers* :
11) *Leaning of fingers* :
12) *Phalanges* : Jupiter finger : 1st or 2nd or 3rd ?
    Saturn finger : —do—
    Apollo finger : —do—
    Mercury finger : —do—
13) *Signs on fingers* :
14) *Thumb* : a) large, b) small, c) position : i) high set
    ii) low set
    iii) medium set
    d) length of the thumb :

e) shape of the thumb : i) elementary
ii) nervous
iii) strongly developed
iv) diplomatic
v) clubbed
vi) paddle shaped
vii) waist like

f) phalanges :

g) tips of the thumb : i) pointed
ii) conic
iii) square
iv) spatulate

h) knots : 1st knot or 2nd knot

i) flexibility :

j) signs on the thumb :

15) *Nails* : a) fluted, b) narrow, c) broad, d) short, e) almond-shaped.

16) *Mounts* : a) Which is the principal mount ?
b) development of the mount
c) placement of the mount
d) signs on the mount

CHAPTER 48

The Lines on the Hand

Introdaction

After discussing Chirognomy, which forms the first part of our study, I shall proceed further to explain the other part which is known as Chiromancy. This is also called palmistry or Chirology. It deals with the lines on the hand and has a prophetic aspect. Scientists believe that every detail in the human body has a purpose and nothing has been created without a purpose. We have therefore to believe that the lines have some function to perform and, as experience shows, the lines have close relation to the mind and have a psychological, biological and prophetic significance.

The Study of Lines

A hand may have a few lines or many lines. Few lines do not mean that there are no important events in the life of the person and that there is nothing special which we can tell the person. Similarly a number of lines or a complicated pattern of lines do not mean that the life is full of events. The opposite may be the truth. However, if we find that the entire hand is covered with irregular lines running in several directions, the lines exhibit a worrying nature and a nervous temperament.

Different hands show different markings and formation of lines. If the same pattern of lines is found on two different hands, it does not mean that the interpretation is the same. This is because we have to interpret the lines in relation to the other factors of the hand. Similarly, there is a difference in the pattern of lines on the left hand and the right hand. In case there is no difference, we can conclude that the person is lethargic and that he is happy with what he has and that he has no dynamism. Such a person is averse to progress.

As regards the formation of lines and defects in them, it is always better to study both the hands before pronouncing judgement. We may find a break in the line on the left hand but it may be bridged over on the right hand. This means that the danger shown on the left hand has not been shown on the right hand and the person may not suffer the calamity. However, if the danger is shown on both hands, we may be sure that the event will take place.

Basic facts about the Lines

Before studying the lines, we have to study the basic facts of the lines and observe certain rules.

1) We have to observe whether the lines are in proportion to the hand. On a large hand we expect deep and large lines whereas on a small hand we expect delicate lines. If this proportion is not maintained, we may expect the lines to have bad effects.

2) We should study each line in detail, its starting position, its course and the ending position. Similarly, we should study the defects on the line and consider how much importance we should give them.

3) It is better to follow a method in studying the lines, to start from the Life Line, then the Head Line and then the line of Fate etc.

4) If we find that the main lines on the hand are clear and strong and the chance lines are very few, we may say that the person is even-tempered and he will follow the natural course of his life. If, however, the chance lines are many and cross the main lines in various ways, it shows that the person is drawn in many directions and will change the map of his natural life.

5) We should also study the natural character of the lines in order to have the pure formation of the line. The line should be neat and very clear. It should not be too thin or too broad and should not look very pale. It should also be free from defects such as breaks, islands, forks, etc. We have therefore to study the formation, the colour and the defects of the line. We shall study them one by one.

Defects in the Line (Fig. 23)

Island (Fig. 23–1) : An island anywhere on the line weakens the line. It is an obstruction in the course of the line. The size and the length of the island show the extent of obstruction and its duration.

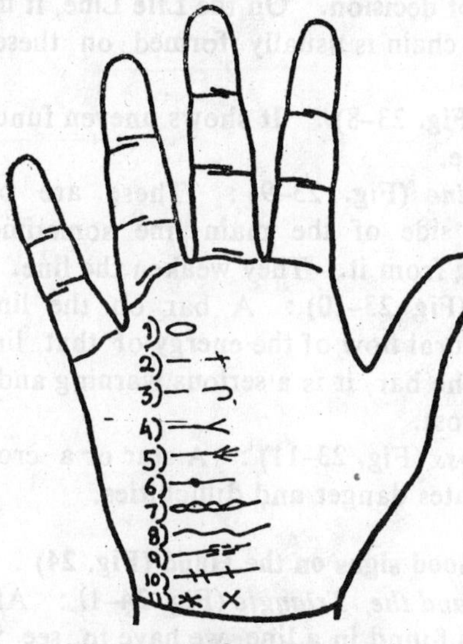

Fig. 23 : Defects in the Line
1) Island, 2) Break, 3) Broken end turning back, 4) Fork, 5) Tassel, 6) Dot, 7) Chained line, 8) Wavy line, 9) Capillary line, 10) Cross bars, 11) Star and Cross.

Break (Fig. 23–2) : It denotes obstacles and trouble. A break means stopping of the force running through the line. If the break is small, there is the possibility of the line joining again and the obstructed force will flow again. If the break is big, the danger is serious. If the broken end turns back, it is an alarming position (Fig. 23–3).

Fork (Fig. 23–4) : A fork at the end of the line indicates the diversified force of the line on which it is found. It is not a good indication except on the line of Head, where it shows talents. On the line of Life it shows loss of energy and vitality.

Tassel (Fig. 23–5) : It means several forks. It weakens the qualities indicated by the line.

Dot (Fig. 23–6) : It is an obstruction to the flow of energy.

Chained Line (Fig. 23–7) : If islands are placed one after the other, they form a chain. A chained line weakens the natural quality of the line. On the line of Heart, it shows changeability and weakness of affection and also the weak action of the heart. On the Head Line, it means weak mental power and lack of decision. On the Life Line, it means a weak constitution. A chain is usually formed on these three lines only.

Wavy Line (Fig. 23–8) : It shows uneven functioning and quality of the line.

Capillary Line (Fig. 23–9) : These are hairlike lines running by the side of the main line sometimes joining it, sometimes falling from it. They weaken the line.

Cross Bars (Fig 23–10) : A bar on the line completely obstructs the natural flow of the energy of that line. If there is a break after the bar, it is a serious warning and the effect of that line will be lost.

Star and Cross (Fig. 23–11) : A star or a cross anywhere on the line indicates danger and difficulties.

Good signs on the Hand (Fig. 24)

The Square and the Triangle (Fig. 24–1) : After studying the above defects found in a line, we have to see whether that defect has been offset by a square or a triangle. If a break in the line is compensated by a square or a triangle (Fig. 24–2) the intensity of the break is lessened. If an island is encircled by a square or a triangle, the effect of the island is lessened.

According to the Hindu system, there are several signs on the hand. These signs are described below.

1) A two-fish type formation on the hand shows a benevolent person (Fig. 24–3).

2) Signs like an umbrella, a palanquin or a lotus speak of those who lead a luxurious life and live like a king (Fig. 24–4).

3) A flag, pot and trident are indications of a very rich life (Fig. 24–5).

4) A swastic, sword and bow show a military position of a very high rank (Fig. 24–6).

5) A sign like a temple, a throne or a lake means a religious person (Fig. 24–7).

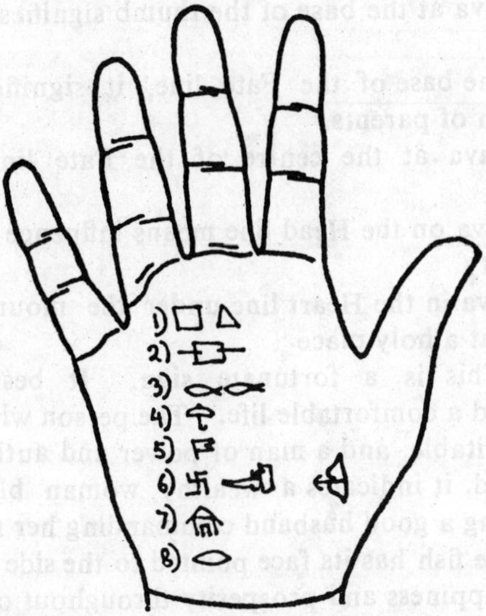

Fig. 24 : Good signs on the Hand

1) Square and Triangle, 2) A break protected by square, 3) Two Fish, 4) Umbrella, 5) Flag, 6) Swastik—Sword—Bow, 7) Temple, 8) Yava.

6) A garland, mountain and swastik are seen on the hand of a Mahatma.

When a person is born with a Rajayoga, one or more of the following signs are found on his hand :

Umbrella, fish, mountain, sword, flower, circle, palanquin, the letter 'M', cart-wheel.

Persons who are destined to live like a king have on their hand a conch, a palanquin, an umbrella, an elephant and a horse.

Wealth is also indicated by a rope-like line. Lines forming a pot, flag and banner indicate that the person will be benefited by trades such as in minerals or petrolium products.

Signs like a chain of triangle, a temple, a quadrangle and a pair of fish bestow occult powers.

Yava (an island-like formation) (Fig. 24–8) : This is usually found at the joints of fingers, on the middle or base of the thumb and at the rascette. It is a sign of a happy life.

a) A yava at the base of the thumb signifies the birth of a son.

b) At the base of the Fate line, it signifies mysterious birth or death of parents.

c) A yava at the centre of the Fate line shows love-intrigue.

d) A yava on the Head line means influence from another class of society.

e) A yava in the Heart line under the mount of Jupiter shows death at a holy place.

Fish : This is a fortunate sign. It bestows wealth, prosperity and a comfortable life. The person will be religious, wealthy, charitable, and a man of power and authority. On a woman's hand, it indicates a wealthy woman blessed with a son and having a good husband commanding her respect. It is said that if the fish has its face pointed to the side of the fingers, one enjoys happiness and prosperity throughout one's life.

Conch : This is a rare mark and the person possessing it will be a millionaire. It indicates all comforts in life, greatness, purity of life and a spirit of renunciation.

Formation of Lines

In appearance the lines should look lively, active and energetic and such lines show a happy disposition. On the contrary, dull and dismal lines indicate a non-active and lethargic life. They should be uniform throughout in appearance, depth and width. Shallow and feebly marked lines show a nervous constitution and low vitality.

At the first glance of the hand, the lines should create an impression that their pattern is normal with the usual number of main lines and also the accessory lines. If the hand shows the bare three lines, which are also poor and dull, it means a dull and dry life. In contrast, the pattern should not be too complicated ; a complicated pattern means tension and sensitivity. A many-lined hand shows ill-health and neurosis.

Lines on different types of hands

The same formation of lines on different types (shapes) of hands has different meanings. For example, a sloping Head line on a conic hand or a psychic hand is a natural position, whereas it is abnormal on a square hand. Similarly, a multiplicity of lines on a square hand is a matter of more serious concern than when found on a conic hand.

Rising and falling lines

Sometimes we find that a line rises from the main line. It shows periods of uplift and accentuates the power of the main line. Fallings or descending lines from the main lines show the opposite. These lines have importance on the line of Heart, while studying the problem of marriage. Rising lines show affection and harmony in marriage whereas descending lines show failure in married life.

General observations of the lines

1) Deep and shining lines indicate a wealthy life.

2) Shallow and faint lines indicate misery.

3) Thin, deep and attractive lines show a wealthy life and charity.

4) Distracted and broken lines indicate loss of health and wealth.

5) Lines with offshoots show worries and difficulties.

6) Lines which are not uniform but which are thin for some length and are thick thereafter and lines which do not follow their normal course but divert from the natural course, indicate an unusual life, loss of money and troubles.

Map of the hand (Fig. 25)

There are six important lines on the hand and eight less important lines. The important lines are as under :

1) The line of Life which embraces the mounts of Venus and Mars.

2) The line of Head which crosses the centre of the hand.

3) The line of Heart which runs parallel to the Head line at the base of the fingers.

The above three lines are present in all hands except in a few cases. Sometimes we find one line across the hand which may be a combination of the Head and Heart lines. These three lines usually start from the region of Jupiter and they exhibit the three basic principles, the spiritual, the mental and the physical.

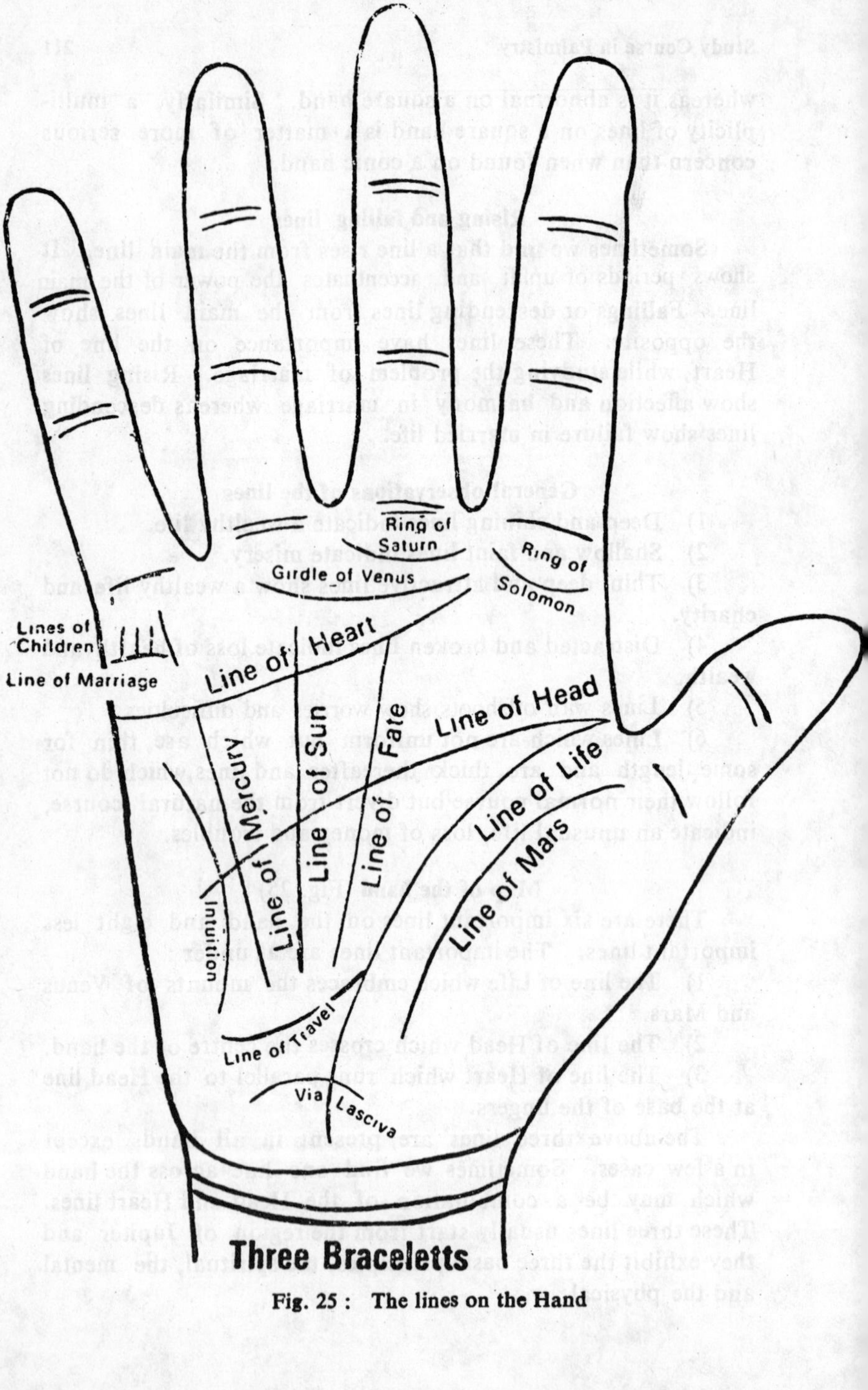

Fig. 25 : The lines on the Hand

4) The line of Mercury which starts low on the mount of Neptune and goes upto the mount of Mercury.

5) The line of Sun which rises generally on the plain of Mars and ascends to the mount of the Sun.

6) The line of Fate which starts from the wrist and goes to the mount of Saturn.

The above three lines are called after the mounts and these are lines of inspiration. The line of Saturn or the Fate line shows the sorrows or peace of mind of the person. The line of Sun denotes the brighter attitude towards life and the Mercury line shows a life in which there is understanding of others.

The eight less important lines on the hand are as under :

1) The line of Mars rises on the mount of Mars and within the line of Life. This line is usually called the Double line of Life. It gives an additional strength to the line of Life. When the lines of Life shows weakness or breaks, or accidents, this second Life line protects the person from the danger and the intensity will be lessened.

2) The Via Lasciva lies parallel to the line of Mercury. It shows succeptibility to physical excitement and indulgence in sensual pleasure. If excessively marked on the hand, it gives warning against alcoholism. This is sometimes seen in a curved position and runs from the mount of Moon to the mount of Venus.

3) The line of Intuition, which extends like a semi-circle from the mount of Moon to the mount of Mercury, strengthens the spiritual aspect of the sub-conscious mind and normally it is a healthy sign on the hand. However, in a weak hand, it shows superstitions and fanciful mysticism.

4) The line of Marriage is the horizontal line on the mount of Mercury. This line is found in all hands with a few exceptions. It shows marital relationship and the ability to live in sex partnership.

5) The Girdle of Venus, lying above the line of Heart and encircling the mount of Jupiter and the mount of Mercury, shows activity, enthusiasm and sex. It is a good line on a good hand and a bad line on a bad hand. To be good, it must be well traced and full. To be bad, it must be broken and poorly formed.

6) The three bracelets found on the wrist. They relate to longevity.

7) The lines of children seen on the line of Marriage and elsewhere on the hand.

8) The lines of travel found on the mount of Moon.

Other minor lines

1) The Ring of Solomon is found on the mount of Jupiter in a semi-circle and connotes wisdom.

2) The Ring of Saturn is found on the mount of Saturn and it enhances the Saturnian characteristics. It is a good sign on the hand of a woman and shows motherly wisdom.

3) Other lines of influence found all over the hand often appear and fade and show the hope that rises in the individual and also the frustration which he has to face. These lines show the events with amazing accuracy.

The Time factor on the hand (Fig. 26)

The most difficult part of the study of palmistry is to find out the exact period or age on the hand. The hand may show foreign travel or promotion in life, but the difficulty is in calculating the time at which the event may take place. However, we can calculate an approximate period with a margin of about two years on either side. There is a method of seven by which each line is divided. Figure 26 will make it more clear. Number seven has been considered as a mystic number and the importance of this number is indicated in several uses such as the seven wonders of the world, the seven heavens, the seven seas, the seven days of the week and the seven planets etc. The method of dividing the lines is as follows. Draw a straight line from the second joint of the thumb, from where the mount of Venus starts, across the hand upto the middle portion of the percussion. The point where this line intersects the line of Life is the 35th year, read on the line of life. Then from the percussion side beneath the little finger or the finger of Mercury, we have to draw a line which will cut the point on the line of Life and continue upto the middle mount of Venus. From this middle point on the mount of Venus we can draw lines towards

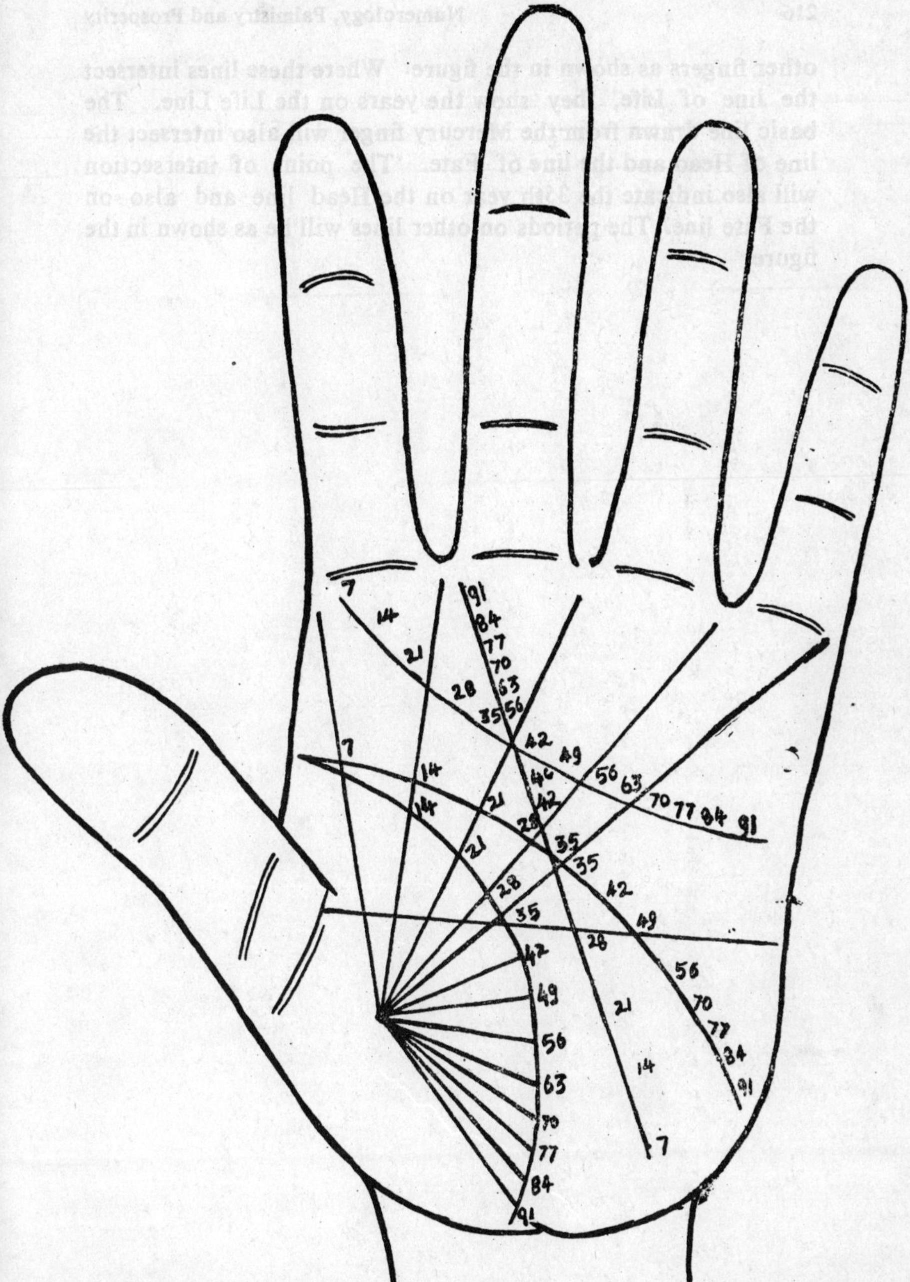

Fig. 26

other fingers as shown in the figure. Where these lines intersect the line of Life, they show the years on the Life Line. The basic line drawn from the Mercury finger will also intersect the line of Head and the line of Fate. The point of intersection will also indicate the 35th year on the Head line and also on the Fate line. The periods on other lines will be as shown in the figure.

CHAPTER 49

The Line of Life

Introduction

The line of Life is the map of the natural course of man's life. It is the first line that is developed in the embroyonic life. It usually shows the vitality and energy of the person. The length, the depth and the continuity of the line reveal the quality of the vitality. From the length of the line we can know the span of life. According to the Hindu system, before we start reading the hand, we must first find out the longevity of the person which we can know from the Life line. Since this line shows the existence of the man, we can never expect this line will be absent. However, one of the authors on this subject has stated that he has seen a hand without a Life line. In such a case, we can say logically that even if the person is living, he does not have the spirit and energy that is required to sustain life but lives on his nervous energy and is susceptible to nervous break-down. It is said that even the line of Mercury, if it is found on the hand but does not touch the Life line, is sufficient to sustain life. This Mercury line can compensate for the absence of Life line.

As a general proposition, we may consider that the longer the line of Life, the longer the man's life and the shorter the line of Life, the shorter his life. However, this is not always true. This is because the science of palmistry is a study of the combination of various factors on the hand and no one sign or line should be read independently.

If we study the route of the line of Life, we find that it first encircles the positive mount of Mars, then the mount of Venus and then the mount of Neptune. It, therefore, partakes all the qualities of these mounts. For the first few years, it is governed by the martian qualities such as dash, vigour, enthusiasm etc.

In the period of youth, it is governed by Venus indicating love and the mating period. At the end, the spiritual aspect of Neptune governs the Life line. This is how the changes go on developing in our life.

Normal development

Normally, this line should form a graceful curve and should look lively. It should be even throughout its course. It should be long, narrow and deep without any breaks or crosses. The colour should be deeper than the skin, transparent and lively. Such a formation promises a long and healthy life and an optimistic outlook. Such a person lives with good ideals and enjoys life even upto old age.

Deviation from the normal formation

1) If instead of the normal development of the line, one finds the line sweeping into the palm enclosing a greater portion of the mount of Venus (Fig. 27–a), it indicates excessive vitality and a greater sexual urge. The person enjoys happiness through his parents. He belongs to a high family and is healthy and lives long.

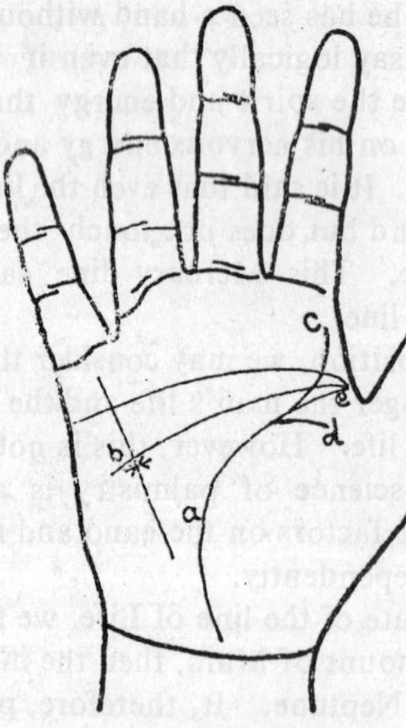

Fig. 27

2) If the Life line runs closer to the second phalange of the thumb and if there is a star at the intersection of the lines of Head and Mercury (Fig. 27–b), it shows childlessness and difficulty in child-bearing. Such a formation reduces the size of the mount of Venus and checks the operation of that mount. This makes the person cold, unsympathetic and lacking in sexual desires. This is an important formation which we have to take into consideration when studying the married life of the person.

Starting position

A good start for the Life line is from the bottom of the Jupiter mount, quite independent of the line of Head but still very near to it. The starting point of the line should be sharp and slightly pointing to the mount of Jupiter. Such a formation will give the line all the good aspects of the Jupiter mount, such as honesty, honour, prestige, etc. The closeness of the Life line with the Head line will give clarity of mind, good reasoning and understanding and the life of the person will be governed by these qualities. This also indicates the child's upbringing in a healthy and happy family. This formation also shows the happy life of the parents.

1) If the Life line starts well high on the mount of Jupiter, it shows a very ambitious nature and if it starts still higher on the mount, it shows dictatorship and cruelty (Fig. 27–c). Here comes the question of combining the characteristics of the mounts with the line of Life. If the person is a Jupiterian, his ambition will be for learning and a high position. If he is a Saturnian, the ambition will be for acquiring occult powers or to master medicine, science, mining, farming, etc. If he is an Apollonian, he will crave for success and fame in public life and also as an administrator, or even as an actor or an artist. If he is a Mercurian, his ambition will be in the business world or in scientific pursuits. We can apply the same logic if he is governed by other mounts.

2) If the line starts from the positive mount of Mars, it indicates struggle and hardship. It shows poor health and few opportunities in life (Fig. 27–d).

3) If the Life line at its start is closely connected with the Head line, it is a good formation and it shows good logic and

reasoning, even though he is somewhat sensitive. It also speaks of caution and prudence in practical life. The person is interested more in intellectual pursuits than in physical work.

4) If the lines of Life, Head and Heart join one another (Fig. 27–e), it is an unfortunate sign; the person lacks perception and creates difficulties and dangers for himself. Such a formation means that no line can have the freedom to show its characteristics, either moral, mental or instinctive. The person has a peculiar temperament and way of thinking. He is enthusiastic about love but usually loves a wrong person and finally meets with frustration.

5) If the Life line is connected with the Head line and forms a sharp angle, it means prudence.

6) If the Life line is joined to the Head line and both the lines run together for sometime, it shows extreme sensitivity, diffidence and timidity. In order to avoid these results the thumb should be powerful and should balance the defect.

7) If the Life line is connected with the Heart line at the start and if the Head line is poor or short, it always indicates accidents or sickness. The nature of the accident will depend upon the mount of the person by which he is governed. If he is a Jupiterian, the trouble will be high blood pressure; if a Saturnian, it will relate to legs; if an Apollonian, it will be connected with the eye; if a Mercurian, it will relate to bile and so on.

8) A fork at the start of the Life line means a sense of fidelity and justice.

9) A long fork deep into the mount of Jupiter shows realisation of ambition and a successful life.

10) Two or more forks at the beginning but below the line of Head and under the mount of Jupiter indicate honour to the parents which ultimately benefits the person. If however these forks are crossed by cross lines, they mean law–suits.

11) An island at the beginning shows mystery of birth.

Course of the Line of Life

The next thing we have to study about the Life line is its course. Normally the line should be of even thickness throughout the course. However, if we find that it is uneven, *i.e.*, sometimes thick and sometimes thin, it shows a moody and fickle-minded person. He is unsteady in thought and action. This is, however, due to ill-health as shown by the uneven line.

If the Life line is pale during its course, it means poor circulation at that age. A broad line anywhere in its course indicates sickness, feeble-mindedness and envy.

If the Life line is clear, evenly traced and thick, the person is good and fortunate. If during its course, the line inclines towards the Head line and then continues its normal course downwards without any hindrance, the person is wealthy and fortunate.

Usually, the line is chained at the beginning which shows delicate health in childhood. This delicate state will be over after the chain formation stops and the line takes its usual course.

Break in the Life Line

A break may be found anywhere during the course of the line. It can be of various formations such as a break that is narrow or broad or overlapping or hook-like, etc. Every formation has its own meaning. We may also find a bar, a dot or a hole in between the breaks.

A break indicates change in life. It may be caused by accident, sickness or through some shock. The exact cause can be ascertained from other signs on the hand.

a) *Overlapping break :* If we find a break in the line and if the lower part of the broken line begins before the break on the upper side, we may say that the break is over-lapping (Fig. 28–a). If the break is seen in one hand only, the over-lapping position guards against the danger. However, if it is found in both the hands, it is a warning of danger.

b) *Hook-like break* : If there is a break and if the upper line or the lower line turns inwards into the mount of Venus, the accident is likely to be fatal.

c) A break in the Life line with a break in the Fate at the same age, is most eminous and shows danger to one's life.

d) *Square on the break* : A square anywhere on the hand shows protection from danger. A danger shown by a break is offset by the square around the break (Fig. 28–b).

If a line descends from the mount of Saturn and touches

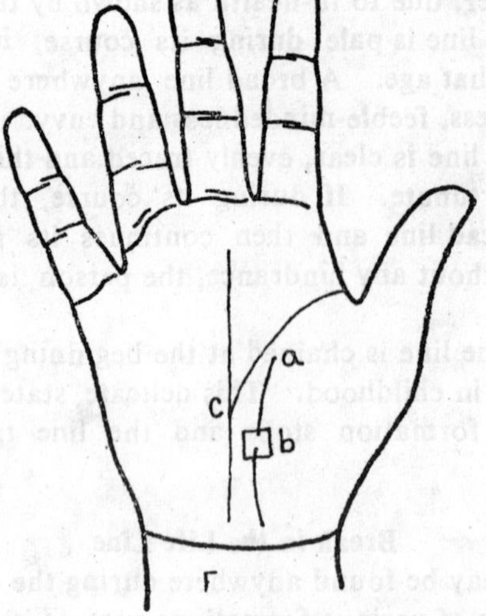

Fig. 28

the square, it means that the protection is from an accident and not from an illness.

e) If the Life line is broken and if the broken end is joined to the Fate line (Fig. 28–c), it shows good luck due to which danger is avoided.

f) A black spot at the end of a broken line is the worst sign and shows sudden death or assassination.

If the Life line shows good formation after the defect, the person will improve in his health. However, if after the defect in the line, the Life line looks thin or chained or shallow, the person will experience ill health till the end.

Rising and falling lines from the line of Life

During the course of the Life line we may find certain splits or sprouts either rising or falling from the line (Fig. 29–a). The rising lines show good health, riches and a change for the better.

a) A rising branch pointing towards the mount of Jupiter shows realisation of ambition, egoism and freedom in earlier age. It may mean an independent life either in a boarding house or college hostel.

b) If the split points out to the Saturn mount, it means marital success and financial stability.

c) If the split points out towards the mount of Apollo, it promises success, glory and wealth.

d) If the rising line points out to the mount of Mercury, it means success in scientific pursuits and or in business.

Sometimes we find these rising lines crossed by lines from the positive Mars or Venus mounts (Fig. 29-b). It means unhappiness, judicial separation from the spouse or a law-suit to that effect.

Falling lines or splits

Usually the falling offshoots show the weakening of the nervous system. But if the split joins the Fate line it means good health. Even though the Life line is short, the split line is indicates that the function of the Life line is handed over to the line of Fate. Thus the effect of the short Life line is nullified.

Ending of the Life line

The Life line may end at one of the four following places; on the mount of Venus, or the mount of Neptune, or the mount of Moon or on the Rascette.

If the Life line ends on the mount of Venus, it denotes a happy married life and a big family. The person is a good husband and also a good father.

If it ends on the mount of Neptune, it signifies a long life based on a spiritual foundation. The person is honest and truth-loving and finds joy in contemplation. He loves solitude and prefers loneliness.

If the Life ends on the mount of Moon, it shows love of travel and change in life. The persons likes to live near the sea or a water reservoir such as a lake. He may spend most of his life in foreign countries.

If the line ends on the rascétte, it signifies long life.

Life line ending in a fork

a) If the Neptunian line of Life ends in a fork and if one branch of the fork goes to the mount of Venus (Fig. 29-c), it means a clash between the married partners.

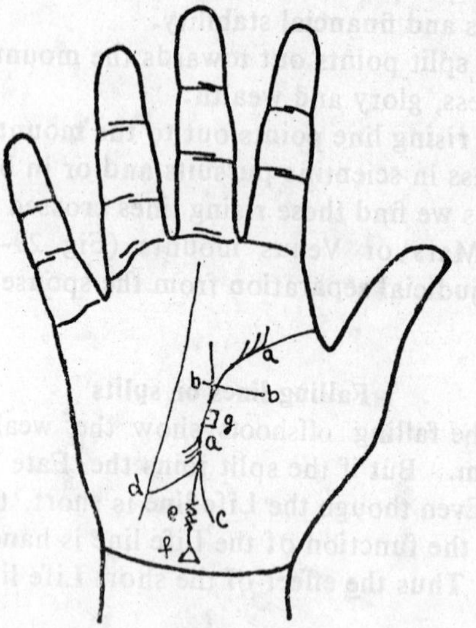

Fig. 29

b) A fork at the end of the Life line shows change in life, new environment or settlement in a foreign country if the fork is wide. A fork also shows financial difficulties in old age.

c) If one branch of the fork runs towards the line of Fate and merges into it, it shows dull ending of the Life (Fig. 29–d).

Life line ending in a cross (Fig. 29–e)

If the Life line ends in a series of crosses, it indicates a talented and lovable disposition. It also means a long period of ill-health.

Life line ending in a triangle : A triangle at the end of the Life line shows falsehood (Fig. 29–f).

Character of the Life Line

a) *Deep and well-cut line* : A deep and well-cut line of Life shows good supply of blood and ensures good health, vitality and vigour to the person. The person has the capacity to remain calm in moments of excitement and he can throw off worries easily. Robustness, self-confidence, energy, vigour and ability are the main attributes of the deep Life line.

b) *Narrow and thin line of Life* : This line shows less resistance, less robustness and less vitality. However, if the other main lines are deep and well-cut, this thin line indicates that the person will overstrain himself and will suffer ill-health.

c) *Broad and Shallow Life Line* : This Life line shows that the person is not robust and indicates lack of dash and push. He always suffers from small complaints and never feels fit. He needs to be loooked after either by relatives or friends. He can do only routine work without any high responsibility.

We have thus studied the starting point of the Life line, its course, its ending position and the character. We should also study the defects of the line, such as an island, a dot, cross bars etc.

We shall now see the influence or effects of some signs seen on the Life line.

a) A mole indicates serious disease or even an operation.

b) A triangle indicates that the person will support the families of relatives or friends. A small triangle speaks of property, land and agriculture.

c) A square is mark of protection. But if a square touches the Life line from inside, it shows imprisonment (Fig. 29–g).

d) A cross shows law-suits. A cross towards the end of the Life line shows poverty and ill-health in old age. Two crosses at the beginning of the Life line on the hand of a woman indicate immodesty.

e) A star means fatality or serious accident. If it is found right on the Life line, it means suicide. A star on the side of the mount of Venus and touching the Life line shows trouble from members of the family or close friends.

f) Circle : One circle on the Life line shows susceptibility to blindness of one eye. Two circles indicate total blindness.

g) A grill on the mount of Venus touching the Life line and another grill on the Head line also touching the Life line show change of religion.

Lines of Influence

We have also to take into consideration the importance of the lines of influence which are seen inside the line of Life. These influence lines are either vertical or horizontal.

Hindus have an elaborate system to interpret these lines and depend upon them for a large part of their work. The lines usually show the influence of members of the family or very close friends either for good or evil. The fewer the number of influence lines, the more self-reliant is the person. Such a person has few friends and even close relations do not influence him much. The absence of lines shows coldness and absence of response to the warmth of affection and attachment. It indicates a self-centred man. When the lines are deep and strong and well-coloured, they show powerful influence. If they are thin, shallow, chained or broken, they indicate that the influence is not so strong. If any influence line is deep in the beginning, then slowly becomes thin and fades away, it shows that it has lost its influence. We may come across the reverse marking also, in which case the influence will gradually grow strong. Vertical lines are not impediments or hostile to development. Cross lines show obstacles and worry us.

Vertical lines (Lines of Influence)

These vertical lines start either on the mount of Venus or on the mount of postive Mars.

1) A line starting on the mount of Venus and from the commencement of the Life line shows the influence of the parents or even the governess (Fig. 30–a).

2) If the influence line begins from the Life line at a later date on the hand, it shows the influence of the opposite sex or a love affair (Fig. 30–b).

3) If we find an island in the influence line, it means that the influence is not beneficial and it shows distinct disadvantage (Fig. 30–c).

4) An influence line from the positive mount of Mars on the hand of a woman shows the influence of the man over her.

5) An influence line on the positive Mars running along the line of Life for sometime and then ending directly on the Life line is an indication of an unfavourable attachment in early age which resulted in sorrow (Fig. 30–d).

6) If an influence line rising early ends in a star and has another line by its side but away from the Life line which grows shorter after the star, it shows the death of father or

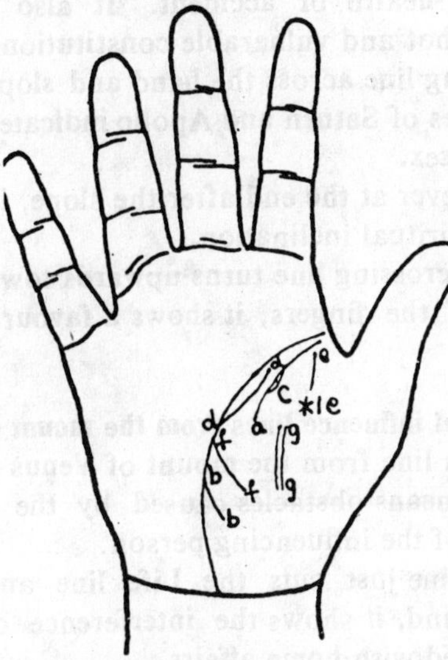

Fig. 30

mother at the age shown by the star or the death of a distant relative (Fig. 30–e).

7) A line of influence on the mount of Venus connected at the start to the line of Life, is a sign of marriage (Fig. 30–f). However, if there is an island in the line of Marriage, the marriage will take place without the sanction of law and convention.

8) A double influence line on the right hand is a sign of a happy marriage (Fig. 30–g).

9) If a sister line runs parallel to the Saturn line, the presence of the influence line on the mount of Venus also indicates a happy marriage.

10) An influence line, starting from the line of Life and suddenly curving away from it, means a broken engagement.

Horizontal influence lines from the positive mount of Mars

Many times we find horizontal lines starting from the mount of Mars or Venus and crossing the line of Life. These lines of influence may extend upto the percussion of the hand and may cut other main lines on the hand. In most cases these horizontal influence lines indicate trouble and worry.

1) A cross line from the mount of Mars cutting the Life

line indicates ill-health or accident. It also indicates blood pressure and a hot and vulnerable constitution.

2) A strong line across the hand and sloping down after crossing the lines of Saturn and Apollo indicates a bad influence of the opposite sex.

3) If however at the end after the slope, it turns upwards, it indicates a spiritual inclination.

4) If this crossing line turns upwards towards the mount at the base of the fingers, it shows a favourable and helpful influence.

Horizontal influence lines from the mount of Venus

1) A cross line from the mount of Venus and cutting the Life line only, means obstacles caused by the interference or the opposition of the influencing person.

2) If this line just cuts the Life line and does not go further in the hand, it shows the interference of the relatives usually connected with home affairs.

3) If this line cuts the line of Saturn, it shows loss due to the interference of the influencing person.

4) If this cross line cuts the line of Head, it shows interference with plans and ideas.

5) If it cuts the line of Heart, it shows interference with one's affection.

CHAPTER 50

The Line of Head

Introduction

The next line to be studied is the line of Head. This line indicates the brain power, mental power and intellectual abilities. If this line is well developed and powerful, it has the capacity to change the career of the person, according to his will-power. In such a case, the meaning attached to the signs and lines on the hand can be altered according to his strong desire. In fact, this line is the steering wheel of life.

This line is more changing and variable than the line of Life. In an extremely rare case we may find that this line is totally absent. In that case, it signifies a dull intellect and brain trouble. There are adequate grounds to prove that this line is associated with the intelligence of the person. Some experiments were conducted in which the hands of a number of college students, mentally deficient persons and schizophrenics were studied. Defects such as islands and breaks etc. were found and they were studied. It was observed that such defects were more common on the hands of abnormal persons. Abnormal shortness of the line is a very common feature in low and mentally defective persons.

The line of Head indicates the strength or weakness of the mind and the power of memory and concentration.

Position on the Hand

This line usually starts from the line of Life and goes to the other side of the hand in a slightly downward curve. This formation indicates a combination of calculation and imagination.

Normal Development

A good line of Head should be long, even and with an

attractive curve. The colour should be natural, that is, slightly deeper than the colour of the hand. It should be neither too broad nor too narrow, neither too deep nor too shallow. It should be without any defects such as breaks or islands. The line of Head should look as if it has divided the whole palm into two hemispheres, giving apparently a balanced outlook. It should normally start below the mount of Jupiter and slightly touch the line of Life at its beginning, and end between the mounts of negative Mars and the upper portion of the mount of Moon.

Starting position

Basically there are three starting positions as under: a) From the mount of Jupiter, b) from the line of Life and c) from inside the line of Life.

a) If the Head line starts from the mount of Jupiter but touches the line of Life, it shows a powerful mind (Fig. 31–a). It gives energy, determination and talent. The person has great ambition and sound reasoning power. He will actually control others but will not seem to control them. He is very cautious in his plans and is successful in administration.

Sometimes we may notice a Head line starting from the mount of Jupiter but slightly separated from the line of Life (Fig. 31–b). Such a person will have the same characteristics as mentioned above but with less power of control over others and diplomacy. He will be hasty and impetuous in his action and decision.

If the distance between the Life line and the Head line is too much at the start, it denotes fool-hardiness and overconfidence. It also means recklessness and conceit.

If the space between the two lines is small, it shows splendid energy, promptness and self-confidence. This formation is good for actors, barristers and preachers.

A Head line, which is separated from the Life line and which slopes down to the mount of Moon with a poor line of Heart, the first phalange of the thumb being short and broad, is indicative of obstinacy and a quarrelsome disposition. It also shows restlessness and sensitivity. Such persons are usually unhappy in their married life.

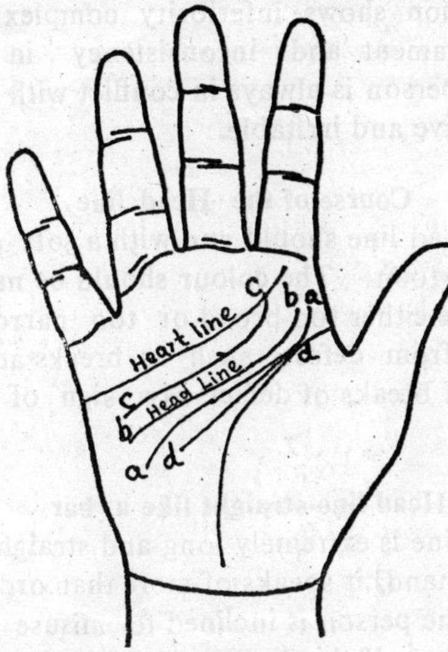

Fig. 31

A Head line starting from the mount of Jupiter but touching the line of Heart on the mount of Jupiter indicates a balanced mind and harmony in love and duty (Fig. 31–c).

Head line starting from the Life Line

If the line of Head is closely connected with the line of Life at the beginning (Fig. 31–d), it shows good logic and reasoning of the person even though he is somewhat sensitive. It also speaks of caution and prudence in practical life. Such a person is more interested in intellectual pursuits than physical work. If the Head line starts from the Life line but under the mount of Saturn, it denotes neglected education and late development of the brain.

A Head line closely connected with the line of Life and running together for some length indicates a negative aspect of free will. Such persons are influenced by the parents or by family members and their dominance will be to such an extent that these persons have no capacity to think and act independently. They do not have free expression and have fear complex. They underestimate themselves, distrust their own judgement and dislike responsibility.

Head line starting from inside the line of Life

This formation shows inferiority complex. It means a worrying temperament and inconsistency in thought and action. Such a person is always in conflict with his neighbour and is also sensitive and irritable.

Course of the Head line

A normal Head line should run with a soft curve and go to the mount of Moon. The colour should be natural and the line should not be either too broad or too narrow. The line should be free from defects such as breaks and islands. A Head line without breaks of defects is a sign of happiness or prosperity.

Head line straight like a bar

If the Head line is extremely long and straight going to the other side of the hand, it speaks of more than ordinary intellectual powers but the person is inclined to misuse these powers for selfish purposes. If this line turns up at the end, it shows avarice and a calculating and selfish nature.

If the Head line is straight but slanting, it shows cleverness. If with this formation, a branch goes to the mount of Mercury, it gives talent to the person.

A straight and clear Head line upto the middle of the hand and then curving towards the mount of Moon signifies a luxurious and happy life.

A straight Head line with a slightly upward curve on the mount of upper Mars shows unusual success in business.

Head line running close to the Life line for a while

It means brain fever.

Head line running close to the Heart line

This narrows the Quadrangle which signifies oppression, bigotry and meanness of moral tendency. As regards health, it shows asthmatic trouble.

Head line slightly sloping down to the mount of Moon

Such a line indicates intellectual faculties influenced by the imagination. The quality of the imagination will be influenced by the type of the hand. When the line slopes deeply on the mount of Moon, it indicates romance and idealism. If it ends in a fork, it promises literary talent.

If the Head line is joined to the Life line at its beginning and then it rises towards the line of Heart and then comes down and resumes its normal position, it shows blind passion. It also means an engagement or entanglement which does not result in marriage.

A short but straight Head line shows a very practical and materialistic attitude. The person will not believe anything which is not scientific and which is not acceptable to logic and reason. If the Head line is short, we should carefully study the line of Life. The short Head line may indicate a short life and the Life line will guide us in this respect.

One straight line which is a combination of Heart and Head line

Occasionally, we may come across a hand where we find only one line straight across the hand. We may be at a loss to know whether it is a Heart line or a Head line. In such a case, we should look at the location of the line, If it starts from or near the line of Life and goes straight across the hand, we may read this line as the Head line. In such a case, the line of Heart is absent. This one line formation shows a person who is cold, merciless, miserly and avaricious. If the colour of this line is red, it will make the person aggressive in his avarice. If the colour is yellow, he will be extremely mean in his acts.

Sometimes this one line may give us an impression that it is a combination of the Head and Heart lines. The joining of these two lines will result in a fusion of their strength. There is therefore a clash between the reason and logic shown by the Head line and the emotion and sentiment shown by the Heart line. It is therefore difficult for such a person to discriminate between moral and ethical codes of conduct on the one hand and finer sentiment and emotion of life on the other. He is very difficult to understand and is often misunderstood. He is very fickle in his moods and therefore unreliable in passion and love.

Rising branches from the Head line

1) If a branch goes to the mount of Jupiter (Fig. 32–a), it shows realisation of ambition. If this branch terminates in a star, it shows brilliant success.

2) If a branch first goes to the mount of Jupiter and then turns to the mount of Saturn, it signifies vanity and religious fanaticism. It also indicates deep thinking in philosophy.

3) If the rising branch goes to the mount of Sun (Fig. 32–b), it indicates success in talents. It also denotes riches.

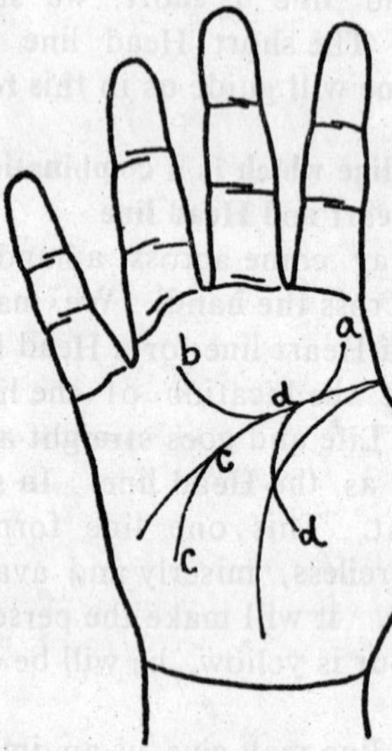

Fig. 32

4) If a branch goes between the third and the fourth finger, it shows scientific discoveries and achievements.

5) If one or two branches go to the mount of Mercury, they show prosperity in business and commercial or scientific pursuits.

6) If the branch goes to the mount of Moon (Fig. 32–c), it signifies mysticism, imagination and love of occult subjects.

7) A line from the Head line, joining the Heart line, foreshadows affection or fascination for someone.

Falling branches

1) A line descending from the line of Head indicates anxiety, worry and frustration.

2) A branch from the Head line going to the mount of Venus denotes a prominent love-affair against one's desire (Fig. 32-d).

Bars in the Head line

They indicate brain disorder or worries.

Breaks in the Head line

1) A break indicates a wound to the head or mental trouble.

2) A break at the starting of the Head line shows a short life.

3) A break in the Head line under the mount of Saturn shows early death. The death may be due to serious accident to the head. If this break is seen on both the hands, it indicates death on the scaffold.

4) A break in the Head line under the mount of Sun, shows sunstroke or trouble with the eyes or hydrophobia.

5) A Head line broken at the beginning, in the centre and at the end shows a poor and unhappy life.

6) If there are series of breaks in the Head line, they indicate continuous headaches and loss of memory.

Deflection of Head line towards different mounts

a) If, during its course, the Head line is attracted towards the mount of Saturn, the person will be influenced by the Saturnian qualities. In order to study the details of the characteristics of Saturn by which the person is influenced, we shall have to study the world by which he is influenced. For instance, if he is governed by the mental world, he will be attracted to the study of philosophy. If the second or the middle world is prominent, he may study mining or agriculture. If, however, the third world is dominant, he will think of saving money.

b) If the Head line is attracted towards the mount of Apollo, the man will be influenced by Apollonian ideas. Here also we can apply the same logic and find out his ideas which will be dominated by the prominent world shown on the hand. For example, if the mental world is ruling, he will be attracted towards pure art. If the middle world is powerful, he will strive for money. If the lower world is dominant, he will be more interested in display and show.

c) If the Head line is curving upwards under the mount of Mercury, his ideas will be governed by the Mercurian qualities. He will be business like and will be efficient in scientific pursuits.

A wavy Head line shows inconsistency in thought and action.

If during its course we find that the Head line is deflected towards the Heart line, the person is dominated more by emotions and sentiments than by reason and logic.

We should also study the thickness or thinness of the Head line during its course. If the line is deep in the beginning, then becomes thin during its course and then chained upto the end, it means that in the beginning the mind was strong but later on it became weak and nervous and finally was impaired.

End position of the line of Head

The next thing we have to study is the way the line of Head takes its position at the end. The ending of the line is equally important and we shall study the various formations one by one.

Head line turning up at the end

If the line turns up on the upper mount of Mars, it signifies overconfidence and egoism which results in serious trouble.

However, if the line turns back towards the mount of Venus before reaching the upper mount of Mars, it indicates cowardice.

Head line ending on the mount of Saturn

a) If it ends on the mount of Saturn, it shows death by a wound to the head.

b) If the line ends before touching the line of Heart, the wound to the head will not be fatal.

c) If the Head line only turns up towards the mount of Saturn, it shows death by mental paralysis.

Head line terminating on the mount of Uranus

It shows bias towards industrial life and also shows interest in machinery.

Head line terminating on the mount of Sun

If the Head line ends on the mount of Sun it means success in literary activities ; the person has a passion for fine arts. He gets riches and fame because of his intellectual capacity.

Head line terminating on the mount of Mercury

The person acquires tact and shrewdness which are the characteristics of Mercury. If this line reaches only upto the line of Heart but does not touch it, it indicates the art of mimicry. If this line ends in a star, it shows sudden death.

Head line ending on the negative (upper) mount of Mars

It shows a distrust of social environment, scepticism and a revolutionary attitude. The person will defend himself when attacked and will be brave but cool and calm in spirit.

Head line ending on the percussion

If this formation is accompanied by a good line of Mercury, it speaks of a good memory. It also shows good intellectual powers and a very good memory even in old age.

Head line ending on the mount of Moon

It shows good power of imagination and a love of travel. If at the end the Head line has a slight curve and then ends on the mount of Moon, the person will never lack any necessities of life.

Head line ending in a fork

a) If the Head line ends in a small fork, it shows versatility. It is an asset for artists and dramatists on the stage. Such persons take quick but impulsive decisions.

b) If the fork terminates on the mount of upper Mars, it shows a combination of a critical mind and an intuitive faculty.

c) If one prong of the fork goes deep into the mount of Moon, the person will deceive himself first and others afterwards. It also means double dealing and hypocrisy. A large and uneven forking shows trickery.

If both the prongs are strong, it shows the habit of falsifying.

d) A dropping line of Head with a fork on the mount of Moon, with mounts of Moon and Venus developed, indicates timidity, unscrupulousness, lack of a sense of responsibility and lack of patriotism. Such persons may even betray their country.

With the same formation as above, if one prong goes down to the mount of Moon, it shows lalent, diplomacy and clairvoyance.

e) One of the forks of the Head line going to the mount of Moon and the other to the mount of Mercury show the power to hypnotise.

f) If one prong goes to the mount of Moon and the other touches the line of Heart, it means that the person will sacrifice everything for his affection. If the line of Fate terminates on the line of Heart, it shows loss of career due to a love-affair.

If the Head line slopes down to the mount of Moon and ends in a star, it shows death or suicide by drowning.

g) An island at the end of the Head line shows a likelihood of a weaker memory in later life. It may also mean loss of memory.

Character of the line of Head

The next thing for our study is the character of the line of Head. By its study we can know the ability, the quality and also the power of concentration.

a) *A deep and well-cut line of Head*: This type of formation shows good memory, self-control, mental strength and health. The person is even-tempered and carries out his plans. He is firm in his decisions and pursues his aim. A person with a deep and well-cut line of Head accompanied by a strong thumb will accomplish any task in life.

b) *Thin and narrow line of Head*: A thin formation of the Head line indicates that the person is not mentally as strong as shown by the deep line. He lacks vigorous brain power and is mentally delicate. It also shows weak mental stamina. He may be clever but he finds it difficult to exert himself for a long time and soon gets mentally tired.

c) *A broad and shallow Head line*: It shows lack of force

and intensity. The person is not firm and resolute in his thought and actions. He also lacks courage, boldness and aggression. He has a very poor memory and cannot influence other people. He is very lazy and not fit for any intellectual work.

d) *Chain-like formation of the Head line*: This formation has practically the same meaning as the shallow and broad Head line. It shows serious mental strain but not necessarily insanity. It also shows lack of concentration and inconsistency in thought. At times the person is extremely thoughtful and reasonable, while at other times his behaviour is illogical and emotional.

e) *Wavy Head line*: It indicates lack of mental strength, perseverance and continuity of thought. If this wavy line inclines towards the mount of Mercury, it shows the morbid influence of the liver which creates melancholia and brain trouble. It also means nervous and bilious trouble.

Defects in the Head line

a) Deep, short and red cross bars indicate brain disorder, headaches and mental worries. These are usually seen on the hands of hyper-sensitive persons.

Islands

They indicate brain fevers. People who are spirit mediums have such islands. Such people think that they can get in touch with spirits at the time the island formations are seen on the hand. However, it is certain that the mind is not healthy and powerful during the period of the island.

Dot

Another defect which may appear on the Head line is the dot. It indicates some bacterial infection affecting the brain. We should study the line after the defect.

Double line of Head

It is very rarely found. This line indicates the capacity to plan and carry out big undertakings with ease and success. Such persons usually have a magnetic personality. The double line of Head shows tremendous mental power. Such persons have versatility, great command of speech and a peculiar power of playing and toying with human nature. They have great will and determination.

The peculiarity of the double line of Head is that it shows a dual personality and the person can play a double role in life like Doctor Jekyll and Mr. Hyde with great mental strain. He has his own philosophy and ideals which may show contradications. The upper Head line shows logic, reasoning and a cold nature whereas the lower line shows sentiments and emotions, which many a time control the person.

Signs on the line of Head

1) *Black spot* : Black spots on the Head line, with a fork in Life line at the start indicate serious brain trouble. Only one black spot means typhoid.

Black spots indicate toothache, if the mount of Saturn is powerful. However, if the mount of Venus is powerful, they indicate deafness. A black spot on the Head line, with a line from the upper mount of Mars to the mount of Jupiter also shows deafness.

If we find a black spot on the Head line and if the spot is joined by a line starting on a star from the mount of Venus, it indicates calamity and sorrow on account of the death of a loved one.

2) *White spot* : A white spot on the Head line under the mount of Sun and with cross bars on the line of Heart, indicates literary success.

3) *Cross* : It shows accident to the Head.

4) *Star* : It signifies wound to the head. If found on both the hands, it means a fatal wound.

5) *Circle* : It indicates blindness. If accompanined by cross on the line of Mercury on the upper side, it is a sure indication.

6) *Island* : An island in the line of Head under the mount of Saturn is a sign of deafness.

7) *Square* : It shows protection from illness or accident.

8) *Bars* : Bars on the line of Head mean headache.

9) *Mole* : A mole at the starting of the Head line means a luxurious life. A mole at the end of the Head line shows acquisition of conveyance.

A mole at the beginning, at the centre and at the end of the Head line gives all happiness and an executive position.

CHAPTER 51

The Line of Fate

Introduction

The line of Fate indicates the course of man's life from the standpoint of material success and shows whether he will prosper, whether he will have a hard time or whether things will come in an easy way. Many times, we say that a particular person is very lucky in life. But we should not forget that the line of Fate only indicates that the person will have a comfortable and successful life. He, however, will have to work for his career. Some people say that others are lucky whereas they are not. In this case, they forget that others are hard workers whereas they are not. On a practical basis, we can say that luck consists in seizing opportunities.

Absence of the Fate line

Sometimes we may find that this line is absent. It means an insignificant life. This is however not true in all cases, because a person without the Fate line may have a most successful life. The absence of the line only means that the person has succeeded by hard work and not just by sheer luck. According to the psychological interpretation, the presence or absence of the Fate line shows a sociable nature or an unsociable character. In other words, the line of Fate shows the social aptitude and behaviour of the person. It has been observed that this line is more markedly present on the hands of women than on the hands of men because women, in general, are more sociable than men.

The absence of this line indicates an uncompromising attitude. A sense of strong disagreement and dissatisfaction with the surroundings prevails. A feeling of frustration persists. There is always a craving for change and there is no stability in life.

Absence of the line of Fate can be counterbalanced by a good development of the mount of Jupiter or Mars or by a good line of the Sun.

A strong line of Fate emphasizes the Saturnian traits of wisdom, sobriety, studiousness, and an ability to think and to see both the sides of a coin. It indicates the course of life in regard to worldly affairs. It will tell us of the events in life and success or failure in relation to the capacity of the individual to adapt to the environment. This line is a line of prudence, restraint, virtue and simplicity. The most significant indication of a good line of Fate is that the owner is deeply involved in material achievements, and family obligations occupy his mind.

Position on the hand

This line usually starts from the base of the mount of Neptune or from the centre of the wrist, cuts its way upwards and terminates on the mount of Saturn. If shows a will to act and an energy to accomplish. It shows a steady but sure success in life. The person will get all normal dues and will lead a normal and successful life.

Starting position

There are various starting positions for the line of Fate but mainly it may start either from a) inside the line of Life or b) from the line of Life or c) from the centre of the palm or d) from the mount of Moon (Fig. 33).

Fate line starting from inside the Life line (Fig. 33–a)

If the Fate line starts from inside the line of Life or from the mount of Venus, it shows that the early life of the person has been hampered by the influence of his relatives. In this case the career of the person is ruled by the family members. If this line continues as a weak line throughout its course, the relatives will have full control of the man's life, The relatives may be either parents or the husband or the wife. When the Fate line comes out of the Life line, it is the period when the person will shake off the control of his relatives and exercise his own will. The period is calculated on the Fate line.

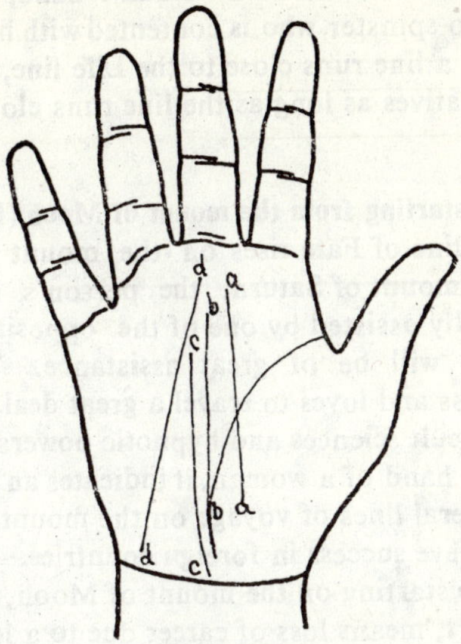

Fig. 33

Since the line starts on the mount of Venus, the person's life will be influenced by the Venusian qualities and he will be a lover of music and art. It also shows an outside love-affair which creates a scandal. If the Fate line ends in a fork on the mount of Saturn, it indicates an unhappy marriage. When the line of Fate starts from the mount of Venus and the line of Heart is sloping, it indicates that the person will be entangled in a love-affair with a person who is either married or is not free to marry.

Fate line starting from the Life line (Fig. 33–b)

It shows attachment to family members and prosperity with their help. However the person also works hard to get success in life.

Fate line starting from the centre of the hand (Fig. 33–c)

If the Fate line starts from the centre of the hand and from the wrist or from the mount of Neptune and proceeds straight to the mount of Saturn, it is a sign of fortune and success. The person will achieve success in life mainly by his own efforts. This also indicates a strong individuality but of the self-centred type.

If such a line is found on a woman's hand, it is the sign of a well-do-do spinster who is contented with her own environment. If such a line runs close to the Life line, it indicates the influence of relatives as long as the line runs close to the Life line.

Fate line starting from the mount of Moon (Fig. 33–d)

When the line of Fate rises on the mount of Moon and runs on to the mount of Saturn, the person's success in life will be materially assisted by one of the opposite sex. Sometimes the wife will be of great assistance. The person is generally restless and loves to travel a great deal. He is often interested in occult sciences and hypnotic powers. If this line is found on the hand of a woman, it indicates an early marriage. If there are several lines of voyage on the mount of Moon, the person will achieve success in foreign countries.

A Fate line starting on the mount of Moon, if it ends on the line of Heart, means loss of career due to a love-affair.

If the Fate line starts from the base of the mount of Moon and if the fingers of Jupiter and Apollo are long and conical, it shows a gift of intuition.

If the Fate line starts from the third rascette, it shows natural trouble and some intense grief.

A Fate line starting from the Plain of Mars or the mount of Uranus shows an uneventful early life. If however, this line penetrates into the the third phalange of the Saturn finger, it denotes a life full of unavoidable troubles and painful experiences.

A wavy line of Fate, which starts from the mount of upper Mars and terminates on the mount of Saturn, signifies imprisonment.

A straight and good line of Fate starting from the line of Heart shows good fortune in old age.

From the above it will be noticed that when the line starts higher in the hand, the later period in life will be one of smooth sailing. It should be specially mentioned that it is necessary to study both the hands in the case of this line. If the line begins low in the left hand but starts high in the right hand, it means that the natural course of life was favourable as shown in the left hand whereas some difficulties altered the original plan.

The difficulties may be due to health or family or friends' influence. For the defect we must look elsewhere on the hand. The absence of Fate line in the beginning, where it should normally start, will often be explained by some accidents to the parents. Since the early period covers childhood, it may not be through his fault that his life really started at a late age. If with this late rising of the Fate line, we come across some defects either in the Head line or the Life line, we may conclude that the late start in life was due to mental weakness or weak health.

Fate line starting from a fork

It shows the influence of a non-relative. If the line starts low in the hand but with a fork, it is a sign of adoption in early life (Fig. 34–a). This is especially true, if one prong goes deep into the mount of Venus. This later formation also shows separation from parents resulting in a law-suit. It also indicates travels undertaken under the influence of a member of the opposite sex. If this fork is wide apart, that is, one prong goes to the mount of Moon and the other to the mount of Venus (Fig. 34–b), it shows the influence of a member of the

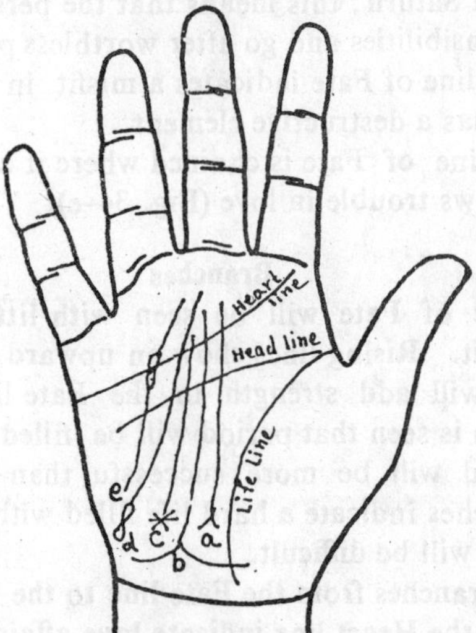

Fig. 34

opposite sex or a great love that has inspired the person to work hard for success.

Fate line starting from a star (Fig. 34–c)

A star at the beginning of the Fate line shows loss of fortune or great trouble to the parents.

Fate line starting with an island

It indicates mystery of birth. If the Fate line is very poor, it shows illegitimacy. If the Fate line starts with two islands forming the figure of '8' (Fig. 34–d), it shows the gift of intuition.

Course of the line of Fate

If the line of Fate starts in the centre of the hand and is of good character, it indicates good social habits. It also shows a receptive mind and great sympathy.

If the Fate line goes direct to the mount of Saturn and has branches rising upward, it is an indication of riches coming later in life.

Sometimes we may come across a Fate line which runs close to the line of Life for some time and then takes a turn towards the mount of Saturn; this means that the person will shirk his family responsibilities and go after worthless pursuits.

A short line of Fate indicates a misfit in the community. The person has a destructive element.

If the line of Fate is chained where it crosses the line of Heart, it shows trouble in love (Fig. 34–e).

Branches

The line of Fate will be seen with little lines rising or falling from it. Rising lines show an upward tendency of the career and will add strength to the Fate line. Whenever a rising branch is seen that period will be filled with hope and ambition and will be more successful than any other period. Falling branches indicate a hard life filled with discouragement and progress will be difficult.

Rising branches from the Fate line to the Heart line without touching the Heart line indicate love affairs which do not end in marriage. A rising branch towards the Jupiter mount and joining the Heart line signifies a second marriage.

Ending position of the line of Fate

a) Ending on the mount of Jupiter, it indicates a happy union and extraordinary success in life.

b) Ending on the centre of the mount of Jupiter means unusual distinction and power. He will climb up through his enormous energy, ambition and determination.

c) Ending beyond the palm and cutting the finger of Saturn, is not a good indication. It means everything going too far. For instance, if the person is a leader, his followers will not obey him and will most probably turn against and ruin him.

d) If, on a woman's hand, the line starts from the wrist and is straight, steady and ends deep in the mount of Saturn, it indicates a well-do-do spinster who has never married and who is satisfied with her environment.

e) Ending in a cross with a grill on the mount of Mercury, the line indicates a violent death due to some evil action of the person.

f) Ending on the mount of Sun shows celebrity.

g) A Fate line ending on the Head line means loss of career through lack of discrimination.

h) A Fate line ending on the line of Heart means loss of career due to a love affair.

Character of the line of Fate

a) *A very deep line of Fate* indicates 1) a believer in fate, 2) anxiety all through life and 3) perseverance in occupation.

b) *A thin and narrow line of Fate* indicates easy success in any undertaking.

c) *A broad and shallow line of Fate* means continued struggle.

d) *A chained line of Fate* shows misfortune and hard life.

e) *A wavy line of Fate* means changeable disposition and quarrelsomeness.

f) *A ladder-like Fate line* indicates obstruction in the carrer resulting in monetary losses.

Defects of the line of Fate

Usually, there are two places where the Fate line shows the greatest number of defects. The first is at the start which relates to childhood. The second is between the years 32 and 45, which is covered in the space between the Head and Heart lines. This period is the critical time in a business career and is the formative financial period in life.

1) a) A break shows a waiting period. It may mean a financial difficulty through a loss of job or business or it may mean a serious change in life. If the break is overlapping, the difficulties may not be keenly felt.

b) If the line of Fate is broken in the Quadrangle (between the lines of Head and Heart) and again starts from the line of Heart, it signifies that the fortune will be retrieved by the assistance of a member of the opposite sex.

c) If the overlapping line of the break ends on the mount of Jupiter, it denotes a second union of the person on the date of the break.

d) A strong line of voyage on the mount of Moon with a break in the Fate line shows a career abroad.

2) *Island*: An island on the Fate line with a star on the mount of Jupiter shows a guilty love-affair with one in a much higher position.

An island in the Fate line ending in a fork but between the lines of Head and Heart speaks of a divorce due to the person's leading astray an innocent girl.

An island at the beginning of the Fate line shows mystery of birth. Two islands, making a figure of '8' show gift of second sight (Fig. 34-d).

An island on the Fate line on the mount of Uranus, with a cross on the mount of Saturn, signifies rigorous imprisonment.

3) *Cross bars*: Cross bars on the line of Fate indicate obstacles in the career.

Double line of Fate

A double line of Fate is a good sign as it denotes two distinct carrers which the person will follow. It indicates an eventful life or a career influenced by someone else. It also means separate environments at home and in public life.

Lines of influence

Long and short lines running parallel to the Fate line show the influence of persons of the opposite sex. Whether the influence will be favourable or harmful will be determined by the course of the Fate line after the influence line.

The lines of influence may be either from the side of the mount of Moon or from the mount of Venus.

a) An influence line from the mount of Moon, running as a sister line for a short time means financial gains.

b) If the influence line starts high on the mount of Moon or from the negative mount of Mars and merges in the line of Fate, it shows intimacy or even a marriage.

c) If the line of influence does not touch the Fate line, the love affair may not end in marriage.

d) If the line of influence is cut before it reaches the Fate line by an influence line from the mount of Venus, it signifies family opposition to the marriage.

Signs on the Fate line

Cross : A cross attached to the line of Fate inside the Quadrangle (between the lines of Head and Heart) is a mystic cross and gives interest in occultism.

Star : It is not a good sign and shows danger or loss.

Triangle : A triangle on the Fate line indicates a monotonous life.

CHAPTER 52

The Line of Heart

Introduction

This line is so named because it reflects accurately the condition and operation of the heart, and also the sentiments and affections of the person. The Heart line represents the human personality in its most subtle aspect. From it we can know the nature of the conscience of the man, his expression of human elements, his sense of morality and social conduct and also his reaction to erotic life.

The course of the line of Heart covers all the mounts at the base of the fingers. It has close contact with the upper mount of Mars and the line of Head. Therefore the Heart line acquires all the characteristics of these mounts as well as the line of Head. It therefore acquires the ambition and the inspiration of the mount of Jupiter, the sobriety and wisdom of Saturn, the energy and the intelligence of Sun, the wisdom of Mercury, the steadfastness of the upper Mars and the higher influence of the line of Head. The length of the line shows the degree of the heart element present in the individual. It may be stated in a general way that too much of the line of Heart produces jealousy to a fault. Too short a line indicates a materialistic type of person who likes violence and not affection.

A Heart line devoid of branches through all its length, even though it may be well and clearly traced, speaks of want of affection and dryness of heart.

Absence of the Heart line

Absence of the line of Heart is rare. However, we may occasionally come across a hand with only one line crossing the hand below the mounts and we shall be at a loss to judge whether it is the Head or the Heart line, If it is at the place where the Head line usually starts, we can take it to be the Head line without the Heart line.

When the Heart line is absent, it speaks of a lack of sympathy and affectionate disposition and warns us of one who is cold-blooded and selfish and who desires personal success even at the expense of others. On a bad Mercurian, it means a natural temptation to be dishonest.

Normal position on the hand

A good line of Heart should start from the centre of the mount of Jupiter and should end on the percussion under the mount of Mercury. The starting should be sharp and not blunt and the termination should not be abrupt.

When the Heart line is placed very high on the hand and close to the fingers, it absorbs the qualities of the Girdle of Venus which has its normal place where the present Heart line is located.

A person with this type of Heart line is exceedingly calculating in love matters. If the Heart line is placed low on the hand, it does not absorb the qualities of the mounts. Such a person is emotionally dull, indifferent cold and selfish.

Starting position of the line of Heart

a) Rising from the mount of Jupiter, it indicates the sentimental side to affection. To this man, love is an adoration and to love a person in poverty is attractive.

b) Rising between the Jupiter and Saturn fingers, it indicates a love that is practical and based on common sense.

c) Rising from the mount of Saturn, it indicates sensualism in affection and pleasure from sexual relation.

d) If the Heart line encircles the mount of Jupiter, it shows a marvellous faculty for occultism.

e) If the Heart line curves down on the mount of Jupiter, it shows frustration in love.

f) If the Heart line starts from the Life line, it shows a strong sex impulse and the determination to gratify it.

Heart line starting from a fork

a) A fork on the mount of Jupiter signifies a successful married life.

b) A fork at the edge of the mount of Jupiter with three prongs signifies good fortune.

Course of the line of Heart

During the course of the line of Heart we have to study how the line is reflected, how long it runs in this course, the character of the line during the change in this course and the age at which it occurs. This analysis helps us to know the events on the line as well as the age at which they occur.

a) *Heart line rising towards the mounts*: If during its course the Heart line inclines towards any mount, it suggests a person who has the qualities of that mount.

b) *Gap or distance between the Heart line and the Head line* : 1) If the gap between the two lines is large by virtue of the Heart line shifting towards the mounts, it shows an obstinate and extrovert person. He will grab things by force.

It also means a loose moral character.

2) If the Heart line is nearer the Head line, the person is avaricious, selfish and cold-hearted. If the gap is small, it is a sign of unhappiness in affection.

3) If in addition to item 2 above, the Head line is connected to the Life line over a long stretch, it signifies stiffness and formality in manner. If in addition to the small gap between the Head and Heart lines, the line of Mercury is poor and wavy, it leads to asthma and hay fever.

c) *Short line of Heart* : A short and straight Heart line is a sign of brutal and selfish sexual tendency.

d) *Long Heart line* : A long, clear and well-traced Heart line gives lasting affection. The longer the line, the earlier the sex development.

e) *Falling lines* : Lines falling from the Heart line were read by old palmists as love ending in sorrow and disappointment. Falling lines under the mount of the Sun indicate versatility.

If the falling lines reach the line of Head but do not cut it, it shows that the man's life is greatly influenced by the opposite sex.

Dropping lines towards the mount of Uranus cause financial setbacks and losses to the person and lead to disputes and disappointments.

Branches of the Heart line

The branches of the Heart line implement or strengthen inherent qualities and basic character. From the direction, position and approach of the branches, it is possible to ascertain the direction of the growth and its susceptibility to outside influences, both material and abstract.

a) Branches pointing straight in the direction of the thumb speak of riches and affluence of the person (Fig. 35–a).

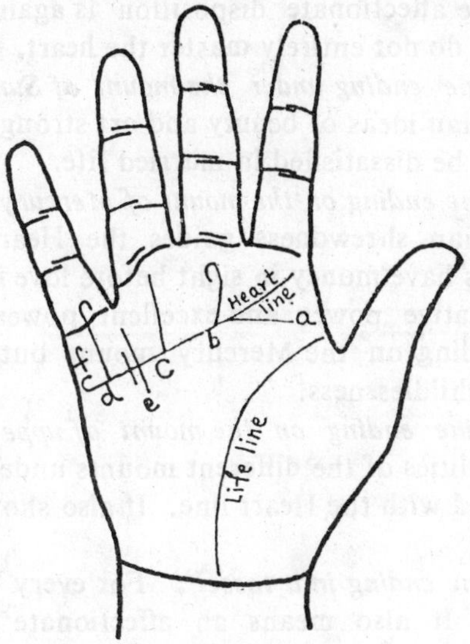

Fig, 35

b) A branch, straight upward and reaching the mount of Saturn and then turning back abruptly, indicates misplaced affection (Fig. 35–b).

c) A descending line from the mount of Sun and touching the Heart line gives a high and unexpected rise in the position of the person (Fig, 35–c).

d) A straight branch ending in a hook on the finger of Mercury is a sign of accident that will cripple the person. The accident will generally affect the legs (Fig. 35–d).

e) Two vertical lines one short and another long, cutting the Heart line show danger of falling from the roof of the house (Fig. 35–e).

Ending position of the Heart line

1) *Ending under the mount of Saturn* : It indicates that a) the Heart line which started with the right sort of affection soon changed into coldness and dislike of mankind peculiar to Saturn and b) the life span is not more than 25 years. c) It also shows heart and stomach troubles.

2) *Heart line ending in Head line* : It means that the head overrules the heart, and reason and logic are more powerful than sentiments and emotions. If the Heart line regains its usual course, the affectionate disposition is again revived and worldly interests do not entirely master the heart.

3) *Heart line ending under the mount of Sun* : It means that the Apollonian ideas of beauty and art strongly attract the person, who will be dissatisfied in married life.

4) *Heart line ending on the mount of Mercury* : It means that the Mercurian shrewdness guides the Heart line. The man must always have money in sight before love is recognised. It also shows creative power and excellent power of mimicry. A Heart line ending on the Mercury mount but without any branches shows childlessness.

5) *Heart line ending on the mount of upper Mars* : In this case the qualities of the different mounts under the fingers are not associated with the Heart line. It also shows attraction for a Martian.

6) *Heart line ending in a tassel* : For every prong there is a love affair. It also means an affectionate and prolific character.

7) *Heart line ending in a hook on the mount of Mercury* : It shows danger from an elephant (Fig. 35–f).

Character of the Heart line

a) *Deep line of Heart* : A deep-cut line of Heart, even and well coloured, shows strong and constant affection and a person reliable in love. He is brave and fearless.

b) *Narrow and thin line of Heart* : The person is narrow-minded, cowardly, timid, unsympathetic and has no real affection for anyone.

c) *Broad and shallow line of Heart* : The person is fickle-minded and sentimental. He falls violently in love but quickly transfers his affection to the next attractive person he comes across.

d) *Chained line of Heart* : It shows a strong flirting disposition and ups and downs in life.

If the Hear t line is chained and the fingers are knotty or spatulate with a sloping line of Head and with a cross on the top phalange of the Saturn finger, there is a change of religion.

Defects in the Heart line

a) *Island* : i) For every island, there is a guilty intrigue, ii) An Island under the mount of Saturn shows a love-affair which interferes with the career prospects of the person. iii) An island in the Heart line under the mount of Sun shows eye trouble or heart trouble.

b) *Break* : It Indicates a broken engagement or problem in affection. A Heart line, broken in three places and with a sphere-like formation at the termination of the line under the mount of Mercury, shows danger of drowning.

A break under the mount of Saturn is a sign of broken loveaffair, not due to the fault of the lovers but due to fate.

A Heart line broken at several places shows danger of falling from a height as from a tree or a mountain.

Double line of Heart

It means deep affection ending in sorrow. For men it shows special vigour whereas for women it means exemption from female trouble.

Signs on the line of Heart

a) *Triangle* : It indicates income and improvement in financial position. A triangle attached to the line of the Sun and the line of Heart indicates a period of unusual enjoyment of wealth.

b) *Cross* : A cross on the Heart line at the intersection of the Fate line shows pecuniary trouble due to love affairs.

CHAPTER 53

The Line of Apollo (Sun)

introduction

The line of Apollo is the central of the three vertical lines on the hand. This line is usually regarded as capable of giving unexpected fortune and success more through chance or accident. But chance and accident will always be backed by an inherent capacity, understanding, optimism and learning. There is always talent behind this fortune or success.

The line of the Sun presents a happy personality without much labour or strain. It represents the capacity to command circumstances that are favourable and happy.

Absence of the line of Sun gives late recognition to the person even though he is talented and artistic. A good line of Fate will compensate for the absence of the Sun line.

Starting of the line of Sun

According to the Indian tradition it starts on the mount of Sun and descends down upto the wrist. But according to the western system it starts from the bottom of the hand and rises upwards upto the mount of Sun. As we are following the Western system we shall study the line accordingly.

Starting from the line of life (Fig. 36–a)

It shows success in art and literature and also good fortune. Relatives will help the person. Success is shown in all fields, in one's profession, finance, marriage and health.

Starting from the line of Fate (Fig. 36–b)

It adds to the success promised by the line of Fate.

Starting from the racette or the mount of Neptune (Fig. 36–c)

The talent of the individual leads him to fame and fortune. It is one of the best origins for the line of Sun to have.

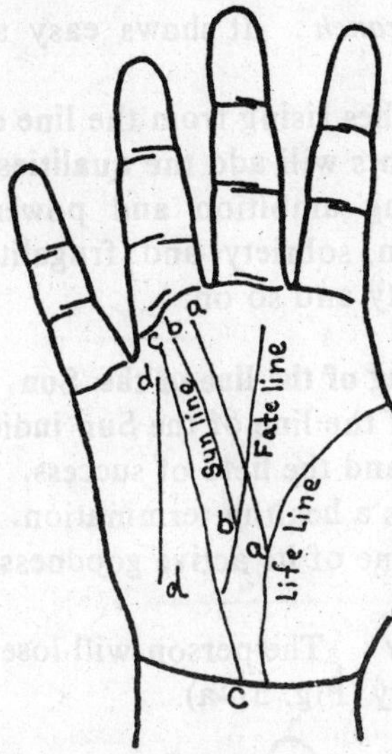

Fig. 36

Starting from the mount of the Moon (Fig. 36–d)

It promises success and distinction largely dependent upon the help of others.

Starting with an Island

An island at the starting point of the line of the Sun gives success due to a guilty love. It also shows a brilliant future for the illegitimate child born of one in a high position.

Starting from the mount of Uranus

It may mean either celebrity or notoriety. The person is aggressive in the quest of fame and fortune.

Course of the line of the Sun

a) *Long and uncrossed line of the Sun* : It shows riches, fame and reputation.

b) *Strong on the mount of the Sun* : It means getting protection and favour from great personalities.

c) *Rising lines* : They make the success more certain.

d) *Falling lines* : They mean that great effort is necessary to achieve success.

e) *Without any branch* : It shows easy success in one's career.

Branches : Branches rising from the line of the Sun and going to different mounts will add the qualities of that mount. Jupiter will give strong ambition and power of leadership, Saturn will give wisdom, sobriety and frugality and Mercury will give business ability and so on.

Ending of the line of the Sun

The termination of the line of the Sun indicates the source and direction of fame and the field of success. A clear straight formation of the line is a healthy termination. Any tendency to curve deprives the line of its active goodness and may result in malefic significance.

a) *Ending in a dot* : The person will lose his reputation after a life of prosperity (Fig. 37–a).

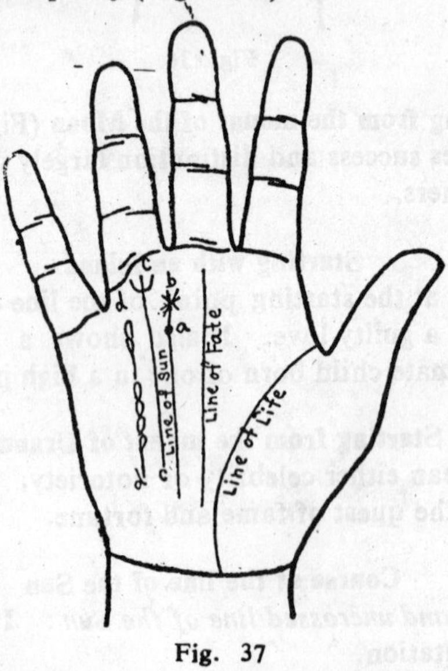

Fig. 37

b) *Ending in a star* : It means brilliant success and a dazzling career (Fig. 37–b).

c) *Ending in a cross* : It means absolute ruin of the reputation of the person. It indicates poor judgement and several mistakes in the course of life.

d) *Ending in an island*: It means loss of money and reputation.

e) *Ending in a fork*: A single fork means success only in one direction.

f) *Ending in a trident*: It indicates celebrity and wealth from intellectual work (Fig. 37–c).

Character of the line of the Sun

a) *Deep*: It is the exaggeration of the vital force shown by the line of Sun. It may mean heart trouble.

b) *Narrow and thin line of the Sun*: This line will reduce the creative power of the individual.

c) *Broad and shallow*: The person will like only pretty things, he will be fond of art but will not attempt any great production himself.

d) *Chained line of the Sun* (Fig. 37–d): It shows poor success in the conquest of fame and fortune. He does not realise his shallowness and most of his efforts are wasted in talk.

e) *Wavy line of the Sun*: It shows lack of concentration. The person may be clever but he will be erratic, unstable and unreliable.

Defects in the line of the Sun

a) *Island*: It means loss of position and name.

b) *Bars*: The bars hinder the career due to envious rivals.

c) *Breaks*: They are indicative of either temporary money losses or changes affecting one's private or domestic life.

Double line of the Sun

A sudden appearance of the double line of the Sun gives unexpected luck through lottery or shows a windfall or a love marriage bringing good luck.

Signs on the line of the Sun

a) *Triangle*: It shows a period of enjoyment and reputation.

b) *Cross*: A cross touching the line towards the mount of Mercury is a sign of poor business capacity.

c) *Star*: It shows brilliant and lasting success.

d) Two parallel lines on either side of the straight and deep line of the Sun show untold fortune and glory.

CHAPTER 54

The Line of Mercury

Indroduction

This is the most controversial line on the hand. There are various opinions regading its function as well as its starting point.

a) According to some scholars, it is better if this line is absent on the hand so that the person can enjoy good health. According to them, the point where it touches the Life line is the end of life.

b) According to some, it starts from the bottom of the hand whereas according to others it starts from the mount of Mercury and descends.

c) Some say that this line shows the constitution of the person, and some say that it shows business ability.

d) This line is also known by various names such as the line of the liver, the line of health, the line of hepatica and the line of Mercury.

Absence of the line of Mercury

It denotes a quick mind and an alert disposition. There are very few lines on the hand and the person does not suffer from inevitable diseases or disorder of the liver.

Starting position of the line of Mercury

1) *Starting from the mount of Venus* (Fig. 38–a) : A wavy line of Mercury starting from the mount of Venus shows immorality due to excessive passions.

2) *Starting from the line of Life* (Fig. 38–b) : Mercury line starting from the Life line and the Quadrangle being narrow due to the Heart line curving towards the line of Head, the person suffers from fainting fits due to bad digestion.

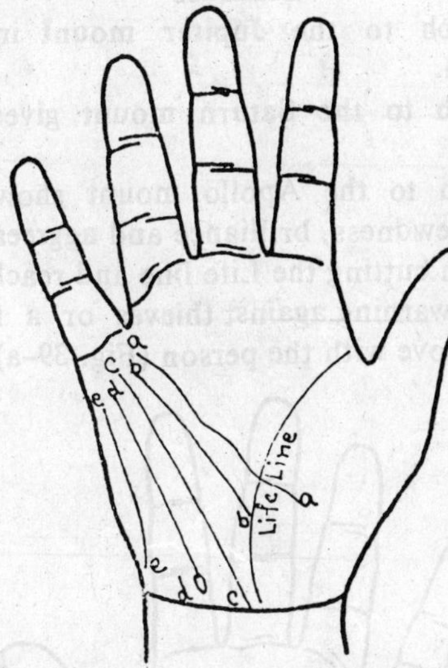

Fig. 38

3) *Starting from the bracelet* (Fig. 38–e) : It shows excellent business success and frequent travels.

4) *Starting from an island* (Fig. 38–d) : It indicates somnambulism.

5) *Starting from near the percussion* (Fig. 38–e) : It signifies a changeable and extreme nervous disposition. It also gives a gift of clairvoyance.

Course of the line of Mercury

1) If the line first points to the mount of Apollo and then takes its course towards the mount of Mercury from near the line of the Head, the person earns wealth but has to spend much.

2) If the line starts from the Life line and forms a triangle with the Head line, it means success and brilliance.

Rising branches : They assure good health and great business success.

Falling branches : They also assure success but the person will have to work hard.

Branches

1) A branch to the Jupiter mount indicates success through ambition.

2) A branch to the Saturn mount gives sobriety and wisdom.

3) A branch to the Apollo mount shows a successful career due to shrewdness, brilliance and aggreeable manners.

4) A branch cutting the Life line and reaching the mount of Venus gives a warning against thieves or a fraud by those who intimately move with the person (Fig. 39–a).

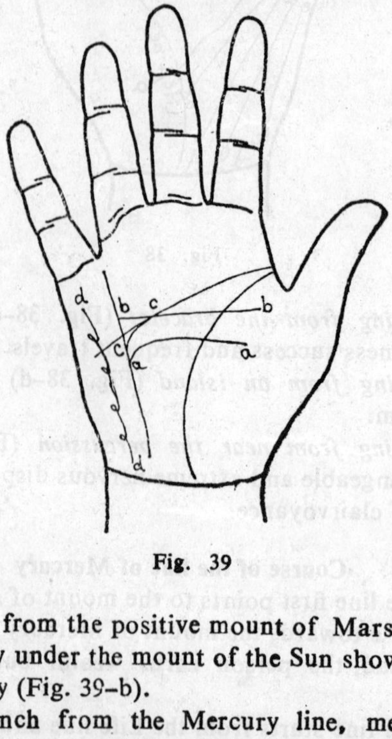

Fig. 39

5) A line from the positive mount of Mars touching the line of Mercury under the mount of the Sun shows purchase of landed property (Fig. 39–b).

6) A branch from the Mercury line, merging into the Head line, indicates succession conferred by a will (Fig. 39–c).

Ending position of the Mercury line

a) *Ending on the Heart line* : It denotes heart trouble.

b) *Ending on the Head line in a fork* : It shows an aptitude for occultism.

c) *Ending on the mount of Mercury* : It means friendship with famous people.

d) *Ending in a grill* : It indicates failure in life either due to poor health or dishonesty.

Character of the Mercury line

a) *Deep line* : It is an asset. However, if this deep line of Mercury touches the lines of both the Heart and the Head but is absent in the Quadrangle, it shows brain fever.

b) *Broad and Shallow* : It denotes a delicate stomach.

c) *Straight and thin* : It signifies stiffness of manner.

d) *Chained line* : It is an indication of poor success in business. It also indicates the inflammation of gall duct.

e) *Twisted line* : It shows a thief and a cheat and one with an evil mind (Fig. 39–d).

Defects of the line of Mercury

a) *Island* : It shows financial difficulties and affliction of the vocal organs.

b) Dots, bars, breaks in the Mercury line indicate either trouble of the liver, or indigestion or weak health. These signs also show impediments in business.

Double line of Mercury

It indicates more than one business, inheritance, unprincipled avarice and a strong animal aptitude.

Signs on the line of Mercury

a) *Circle* : It denotes minor misfortunes during hunting or driving.

b) *Cross* : A cross near the line but not on it denotes serious changes in life. A cross on the line is a warning of coming danger. A cross towards the termination of the line of Mercury with a circle on the line of Head shows blindness.

c) *Star* : It means unexpected luck. It also means the person will have not more than one child. A star close to the line of Mercury and inside the Big Triangle indicates blindness.

CHAPTER 55

Minor Lines on the Hand

The Girdle of Venus

Introduction

The Girdle of Venus is usually associated with highly sensitive and intellectual persons who are changeable in moods, and feel easily offended and touchy over small things. The Girdle of Venus (see fig. 25) denotes a highly strung and nervous temperament. Persons with this mark are capable of rising to the highest pitch of enthusiasm over anything that engages their attention but they are rarely twice in the same mood.

The Girdle of Venus also indicates those vicious habits which are generally developed at the time of puberty.

In a large percentage of hands in which the Girdle of Venus is found, the palm will be crossed by innumerable lines running in various directions. This proves that the person is intensely nervous and has nervous excitability.

Position of the Girdle of Venus

It is a broken or unbroken kind of semi-circle rising between the first and the second fingers and ending between the third and the fourth fingers.

Course of the Girdle of Venus

a) When it connects the mounts of Jupiter and Mercury, it indicates refinement of passions and occult wisdom.

b) If it crosses both the lines of Fate and the line of the Sun, inordinate passion and pursuits of sensual pleasures may stand in the way of success.

Ending position of the Girdle of Venus

a) *Touching the Marriage line* : It means that the happiness of the marriage will be marred due to peculiarities of temperament. The person is exacting and hard to live with and he expects many virtues in his wife.

Character of the Girdle of Venus

a) *Very deep* : If it cuts either the line of Fate or the line of the Sun, it will spoil the good qualities of those lines.

b) *Thin* : If it cuts either of the lines of Fate or the Sun, the person has wit and love of literature.

c) *Thick* : It gives increased momentum to whatever special character is found on the hand.

Double or triple Girdle of Venus : It shows lust and intemperance.

Signs on the Girdle of Venus

a) *Star* : A star on a double or multiple Girdle of Venus is a sure indication of venereal disease from which there will be no recovery.

b) *Cross* : A cross on the Girdle under the mount of Saturn shows a tendency for suicide by poisoning.

CHAPTER 56

The Line of Marriage

Introduction

This is the most important line among the secondary or minor lines. Marriage is very important in everybody's life and much of the happiness in life depends upon harmony in married life.

Everybody is curious to know about the nature and character of his life partner, whether the partner will be from a rich family, whether their love will continue to the end etc. It is therefore necessary that this aspect of marriage should be carefully studied from the hand. The line of Marriage is one of the indications on the hand showing marriage relations and this line should be combined and studied in relation to various other factors on the hand which indicate life partnership.

The Marriage line is also called the line of Affection or the line of Union. If we use this line as indicating marriage and make it a hard and fast rule, it will lead to constant error. This is because marriage does not affect every person in the same way. Some persons do not take marriage seriously. On such hands we may not notice any marriage line. According to the Hindu system, the left hand of men and the right of hand of women should be studied in this regard.

Absence of the line of Marriage

The absence of the Marriage line does not mean that the person will have no sex relationship. It often means a cold determined nature of one who has little faith in the higher responsibility of sex life.

Age factor : The spacing of the Marriage line in relation to the line of Heart and the base of the finger of Mercury can give a fair idea of the time of marriage or of a particular attachment. The distance between the line of Heart and the base of the Mercury finger can be considered as a span of 50 years. The centre point therefore is 25. The age factor, however, may differ from place to place or country to country, since the notion of early marriage or late marriage varies in different parts of the world. The nearer the line to the line of Heart, the earlier the marriage and *vice versa*.

Position of the line of Marriage on the hand

The line of Marriage lies on the mount of Mercury and runs from the percussion side towards the inside of the palm and reaches upto the middle of the mount of Mercury. This line is horizontally placed between the line of Heart and the base of the Mercury finger.

a) *A single line* : A single line of Marriage, running straight and parallel to the line of Heart, indicates a happy and healthy married life or partnership.

b) *Two lines* : If two marriage lines run parallel to each other, the person has two affairs of equal intensity. The line nearer to the Heart line shows the earlier affection and the upper one shows the later one.

c) *Many lines* : They indicate susceptibility to attachments. If these lines are deeper at the end, the earlier affairs have not gone out of the person's life.

Starting position of the line of Marriage

a) *Starting with a fork* (Fig. 40–a) : It means delay brought about by financial difficulties, ill-health or travel abroad.

b) *Fork at both ends* (Fig. 40–b) : It shows a period of separation due to travels which may cause concern, anxiety and pain. This is not indicative of legal separation.

c) *Starting with an island* : It means illegitimate relationship before marriage. It can also mean delay in marriage or separation of the couple at the commencement of married life.

Course of the line of Marriage

1) *Pointing towards the line of Heart* : It means disunity and constant quarrels.

2) *Marriage line turning to the line of Heart and resting on it* : It signifies widowhood (Fig. 40–c).

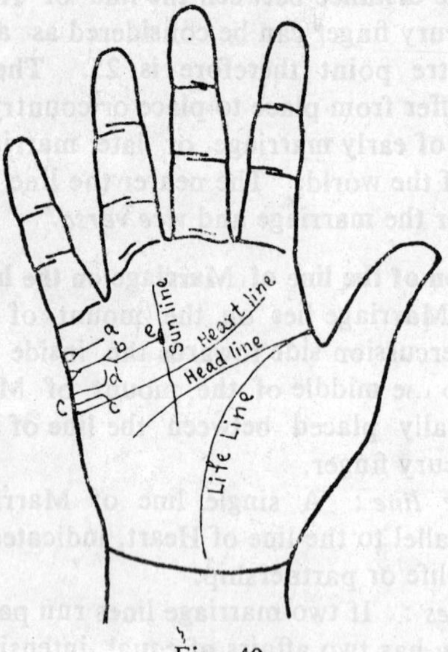

Fig. 40

Branches

Rising branches from the line of Marriage indicate rise in position after marriage. Falling branches indicate sorrow.

a) A branch to the mount of Sun shows brilliant marriage with one of distinction and exalted position.

b) Fine lines from the Marriage line crossing the entire palm indicate a struggle to get freed from married life and to effect divorce. These fine lines mean that there is seldom hope of reconciliation.

Ending position of the line of Marriage

a) *Ending in a fork*: It means married happiness destroyed through the interference of others.

b) *Marriage line curving upward* (Fig. 40–d) : It means that the person is not destined to marry.

c) *Branch from a fork ending on Sun line* (Fig. 40–e) : If the line of Marriage ends in a fork and a line from the fork joins an island on the Sun line, there is separation accompanied by a scandal, disgrace and loss of position.

d) *Ending in an island*: It means that married life ends in disaster and separation. If there is an island at the end of the Marriage line with another island at the base of the second phalange of the thumb, the marriage takes place between near relatives.

Character of the line of Marriage

a) *Long line* : It means longer life to the partner. With a cross on the mount of Jupiter, it means a happy married life.

b) *Deep line* : It shows harmony in married life.

c) *Thin line* : It means a cold nature and unhappiness.

d) *Broad, shallow or chained line* : It shows an indifferent nature.

Defects in the line of Marriage

a) *Island* : It shows unhappiness as long as the island lasts.

b) *Splits* : They indicate divided interest of the partners.

c) *Cross bars* : They show unusual complications in married life.

d) *Breaks* : They show interruptions in married life.

Signs on the line of Marriage

1) *Dots* : They mean impediment in love. A black spot not on the line but on the mount of Mercury shows conjugal misery.

2) *Cross* : It shows difficulties in the attachment.

3) *Square* : It means protection from any difficulty regarding marriage.

4) *Star* : It means a shock through the death of the partner.

CHAPTER 57

The Lines of Children

Introduction

To tell accurately the number of children from the hand requires a more careful study than is usually given to the pursuit of hand reading. In the first place, a thorough knowledge of all the places on the hand which indicate children is necessary. For instance, a person with a very poor development of the mount of Venus is not so likely to have children as a person with the mount fully developed.

The lines of children on the hand of yogis and sadhus or monks indicate disciples and on the hands of nuns they mean monasteries and holy places where they reside.

Position on the hand

The lines of children are the fine upright lines on the line of Marriage (Fig. 25). From the position of these lines and by their appearance, we can make out accurately whether such children will play an important role in the life of the person. It will also indicate whether the children will be strong or delicate, whether they will be male or female.

Character of the lines of children

In general, we may say that broad lines denote males and fine and narrow lines indicate females. Strong lines denote strong and healthy children and faint and wavy lines show weak and delicate children.

Straight lines show sons and delicate lines show daughters.

If one of the lines is outstanding, it shows the rise of the child to great heights in life. If two lines rise from the same point, they represent twins.

Other places on the hand showing children

Please see the separate chart at the end of the book.

CHAPTER 58

The Line of Intuition

Introduction

The presence of this line adds greatly to the intuitive faculties of the person. The person seems to receive impressions for which he cannot account and takes correct decisions which he cannot explain. The line of Intuition adds to the faculty of sensitiveness, which develops shrewdness in arriving at correct opinions. This line is usually seen on the hands of spirit mediums.

This line is usually found on psychic and conic hands. On a Mercurian hand, the presence of this line creates a tricky and deceptive person. He may exploit intutive faculties to make money. If in addition to the line of Intuition, there is a mystic cross on the hand, the person has an unusual aptitude for occult science.

Position of the line of Intuition

This line is seen in a curved form and rises on the mount of Moon and goes towards the mount of Mercury. It occupies the same position as the line of Mercury but it is distinguished from it by its curve formation.

Starting of the line of Intuition

1) The higher it starts on the mount of the Moon, the more the intuitive faculty will be under the control of the person.

2) If the line starts from an island, it shows the gift of clairvoyance and also a habit of somnambulism.

Course of the line of Intuition

a) If the line makes a triangle with the line of Head and the line of Fate, a strong aptitude for occult sciences is indicated.

b) If during its course the line is crossed by an influence line from the line of Life, there will be opposition from relatives and friends to the study of occultism.

Branches

1) A rising branch from the line of Iutuition to the mount of Jupiter will make the person ambitious to achieve something with his intuitive faculties.

2) If the rising branch merges into the line of Fate, the exercise of the intuitive faculties will assist the career of the person.

Ending position of the line of Intuition

a) *Ending in a Star* : It indicates great success from the exercise of the intuitive faculties.

b) *Ending on the mount of Mercury* : The person has intuition of a high order and has the gift of prophecy.

c) *Ending on the negative mount of Mars* : It shows high hypnotic power.

Signs on the line

A cross on the line with a badly marked mount of Mercury indicates a humbug clairvoyant and a charlatan.

CHAPTER 59

Travel Lines

Introduction

There are mainly two types of lines on the hand which are known as the lines of travel. One is a small line falling out of the line of Life and going to the mount of Moon (Fig. 41–a), and the other is a cross line on the mount of Moon (Fig. 41–b). This second line usually starts from the percussion and runs towards the interior of the palm.. If the line is long, the person will go on a long voyage and *vice versa.*

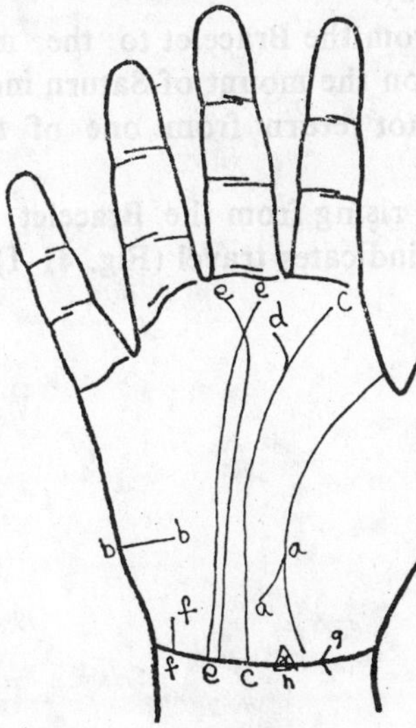

Fig. 41

Ending position of the line of Travel

This ending position is in relation to the horizontal line on the mount of Moon as shown in fig. 41–b.

a) If this voyage line turns up at its end and points out to a certain mount, the person will gain by the voyage.

b) In case the line of Voyage turns up and joins the line of Heart, the person will come across some one who will influence his affections.

c) If the line joins the line of Head, the influence will be of a business nature.

Signs on the travel line

a) An island on the line of Voyage shows danger from water.

b) A star on the line shows a fatal accident.

Other lines on the hand showing travels

1) A line from the Bracelet going to the mount of Jupiter shows a successful travel (Fig. 41–c).

2) If the above line changes its course at the end and goes to the mount of Saturn, the person will not return from the voyage (Fig. 41–d).

3) Two lines from the Bracelet to the mount of Saturn crossing each other on the mount of Saturn indicate two travels but the person will not return from one of the travels (Fig. 41–e).

4) A small line rising from the Bracelet and going upto the mount of Moon indicates travel (Fig. 41–f).

CHAPTER 60

The Line of Mars

Introduction

This line signifies resistance, vitality and divinity. It is also called the Double Line of Life. The presencc of this line certainly gives good health and material wealth. There is no difficult situation from which the person is not protected. He can venture in life and will be successful in climbing great heights.

However, the main drawback in having this line is that the person lacks patience; he is irritable and is constantly involved in quarrels. His ardour and energy create a state of auto-stimulation. He develops a taste for alcohol and a tendency to indulge in it.

The person is usually involved in love affairs very early in life and he is also fortunate in his married life. He has strong faith in what may be called divine help at the time of urgent need. Slowly he turns from materialism to spiritualism.

Position on the hand

Normally the line of Mars runs close and parallel to the line of Life. It starts on the mount of Mars and travels upto the wrist, covering the mounts both of Mars and of Venus. The mount of Venus gives the qualities of sympathy, kindness, steadfastness and love.

Starting position

1) The starting point of the line of Mars denotes the beginning of a great love affair at the time it corresponds to the line of Life.

2) If the line starts from a fork, it shows a love affair at an early age.

Course of the line of Mars

1) *Running too close to the line of Life* : It shows an irritable temperament and a love of litigation and quarrels.

2) *Running full length to the line of Life* : It means that the marriage partner will be in more affluent circumstances than the person.

3) The line of Mars touching the Life line at the beginning and also at the end : If the line of Mars makes a figure of string and bow after touching the line of Life at the beginning and at the end, it means that the husband lives in the house of his wife.

Branches

1) *Branch to the mount of Moon* : Such a branch is seen on the hands of travellers who indulge in wine and women.

2) *Rising line merging in the line of Head*: This is accentuation of mental strength. If the branch cuts the line of Head, overstrain injures the brain power.

3) *Rising line merging in the line of Fate* : This ensures an upward lift in life. However, if the branch cuts the line of Fate or the line of the Sun or both, the career is checked through adverse qualities of the mount of Mars. It also indicates marital unhappiness due to the unfaithfulness of the person.

Ending position of the line of Mars

a) If the line of Mars is forked at the end and one branch goes to the mount of the Moon, it indicates intemperance and brutal insanity.

b) If the line ends only in a fork, it shows a tendency to murder.

Character of the line of Mars

Deep : If the line is as deep and strong as the line of Life, it speaks of tremendous vitality and aggression

CHAPTER 61

The Line of Via Lasciva

Introduction

There are two positions of Via Lasciva on the hand (Fig. 42–a, 42–b).

a) Sometimes it starts as a line parallel to the line of Mercury. In that case, it works as a sister line to the Mercury line and the defects in the Mercury line, if any, are nullified by the presence of Via Lasciva.

b) It may also start on the mount of Venus and run to the mount of the Moon in a semicircular way. This line shows the lower instinct of man and his animal appetite. This line is a menace to the career of the person.

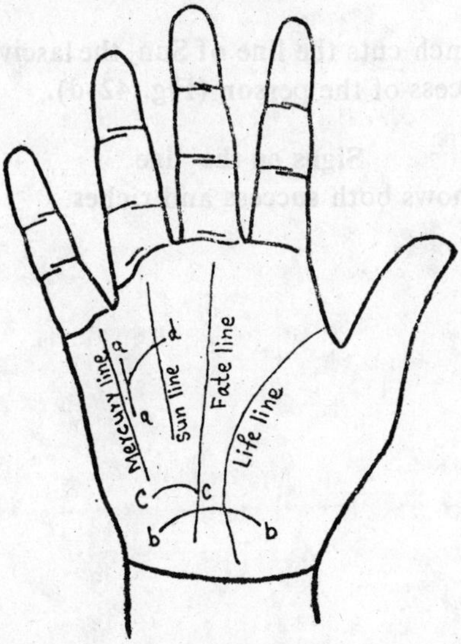

Fig. 42

Starting position

1) *Starting from the mount of Venus* : If it starts from the mount of Venus and goes to the mount of the Moon, in a loop-type formation, it emphazises coarser instincts and sexual craving.

2) If it starts from the line of Fate or the line of Mercury and goes to the mount of the Moon, unbroken and uniformly constituted, it shows healthy brain qualities. It also means journeys both on land and on sea. This formation, with a good mount of Venus, shows favours from women (Fig. 42–c).

3) If it starts from the plain of Mars (mount of Uranus) and runs parallel to the line of Mercury, it indicates sensuality and a passionate thirst for money.

Ending of the line of Via Lasciva

1) If it ends on the mount of Mercury, it shows zest in business and a clever politician. It gives luck and eloquence.

2) If it is formed at the end only, it means impotence.

Branches

a) If a branch runs and cuts the line of marriage which ends in a fork, the lasciviousness of the person will rule his married life.

b) If a branch cuts the line of Sun, the lascivious tendency will ruin the success of the person (Fig. 42–d).

Signs on the line

Star : It shows both success and riches.

CHAPTER 62

Bracelets

Introduction

According to the Hindu system, the Bracelets show longevity and good luck. They are also called Dragon's lines. If there are three bracelets, they are called the Magic Bracelets. If there are four such Bracelets, they are called the Royal Bracelets. Of all these, it is the first one which is nearer to the palm, which has greater importance. A star on this Bracelet is identified as the Dragon's Head. A clear line running from the second Bracelet into the mount of Venus is the Dragon's Tail.

When a bracelet is placed high on the hand and closer to the palm, it is an auspicious indication. It means noble aspirations and noble and elevated ideas. The presence of three Bracelets of good colour gives tranquility of mind, with good health and wealth. These three Bracelets will even compensate a short line of Life.

If the first Bracelet on the hand of a woman curves too much inside the palm, it shows difficulties in child-bearing.

Position on the hand

It is found below the palm and near the wrist. According to the Hindu system, each Bracelet speaks of a life of about 30 years.

Course of the first Bracelet

If the Bracelet rises in the centre, it indicates delicacy of the abdomen in women.

Branches

Rising lines : They indicate journeys, either on land or on the sea. The journeys are either long or short according to the length of the lines.

a) *Rising line to the mount of Jupiter* (Fig. 41–c) : It shows a rise in life, success in law and high position. It also indicates a long journey.

b) *Rising line to the mount of Saturn* : It shows elevation to some high position connected with science or religion. Two lines from the Bracelet to the mount of Saturn crossing each other on the mount indicate two travels but the person will not return from one of the travels (Fig. 41–e).

c) *Rising line to the mount of Sun* : It shows riches, honour, literary success and fame. It also means good reputation through people in high position and travels in tropical countries.

d) *Rising line to the mount of Mercury* : A straight line to the mount of Mercury gives sudden and unexpected wealth and life in a foreign country.

Character of the Bracelet

a) A poorly marked Bracelet indicates extravagance.

b) A chained first Bracelet shows a life of hard labour but with good fortune at the end.

c) A broad and shallow Bracelet speaks of a poor constitution.

Signs on the Bracelet

1) *A clear angle* (Fig. 41–g) : It shows unexpected wealth by inheritance and position and honour in old age.

2) *Cross* : A cross on the centre of the first Bracelet indicates a hard life which ends in tranquillity and fortune. Unexpected gains through legacy are also denoted.

3) *Star* : A star on the centre of the first Bracelet is the Dragon's Head and indicates fortunes by inheritance in old age.

4) *A triangle with a cross in it* (Fig. 41–h) : It shows a large fortune through inheritance.

CHAPTER 63

Useful Charts

After going through a study course in palmistry, it is necessary for every student of palmistry to grasp certain subjects in greater detail. I, therefore, produce a few charts which give information at a glance about certain aspects in our daily life. I request the students to learn these charts by heart so that they can guide their friends in the proper direction. It is not necessary that all the signs and lines described and produced in the chart should be present. Two or more signs or lines on the hand will confirm the finding.

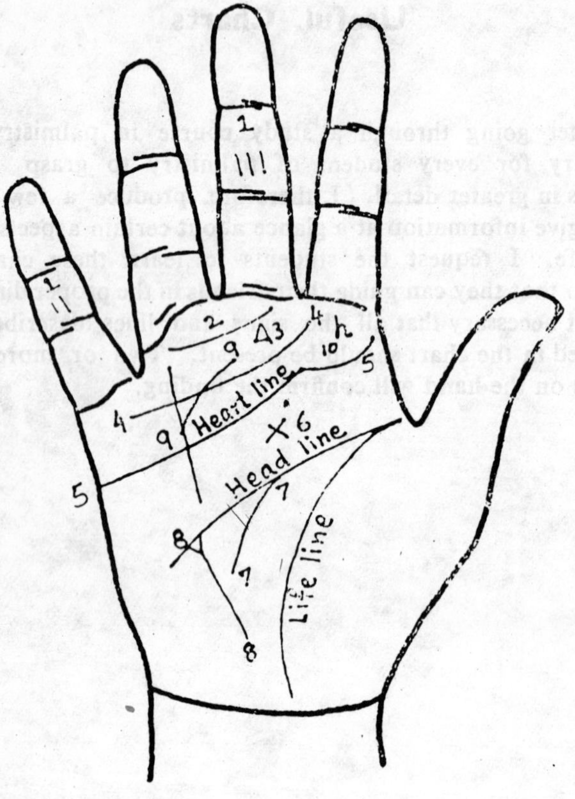

Fig. 43

Interest in Occultism
Fig. 43

1) Two or three lines on the second phalange of Saturn or the Mercury finger.
2) A single Girdle of Venus.
3) A triangle on the mount of Saturn.
4) A line connecting Jupiter and Mercury mounts.
5) The Heart line encircling the mount of Jupiter.
6) A mystic cross between the Heart and the Head lines and under the mount of Saturn.
7) A branch from the Head line going to the mount of the Moon.
8) The Mercury line ending in a fork on the Head line.
9) A rising line from the Sun line to the mount of Saturn.
10) The sign of Saturn on the mount of Jupiter.

Other signs showing interest in occultism but not shown in figure 43

11) A Mercurian with a line of Intuition.
12) The Heart line encircling the mount of Mercury.
13) A pointed tip to the Mercury finger.
14) The first phalange of the Saturn finger developed.
15) A rising branch from the Mercury line to the Jupiter mount.

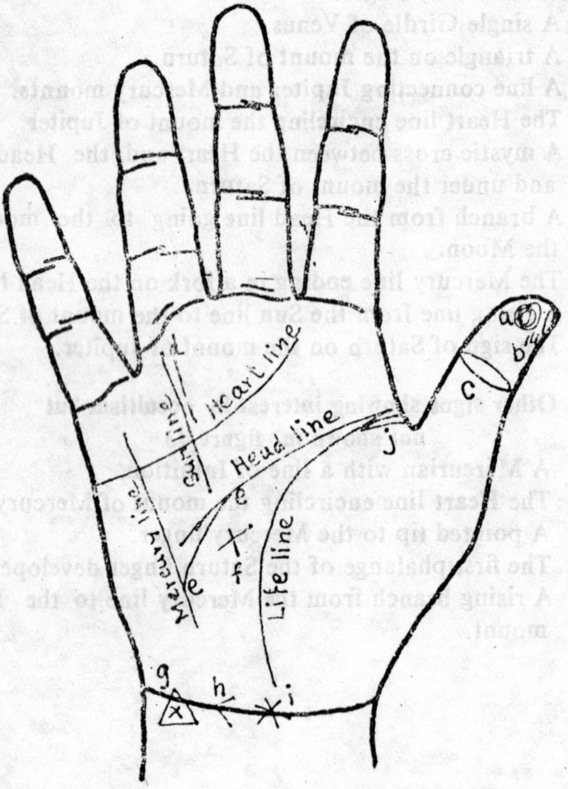
Heart line
Head line
Sun line
Mercury line
Life line
a
b
c
e
f
g
h
i
j
x

Fig. 44

Inheritance

Fig. 44

a) Whorl on the thumb.
b) Small vertical lines near the nail of the thumb.
c) Sign of the lotus or yova on the first joint of the thumb.
d) Influence line running parallel to the Sun line.
e) Rising line from the Mercury line merging in the Head line.
f) Cross in the Big Triangle(Head line, Life line, Mercury line).
g) Cross in a triangle on the Bracelet.
h) Sign of an angle on the Bracelet.
i) Star or cross on the first Bracelet.
j) Life line connected by other lines at the start.

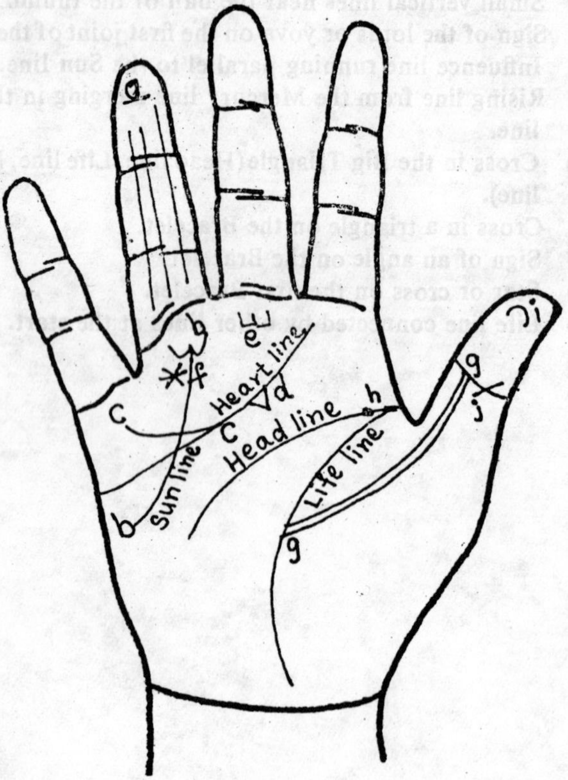

Fig. 45

Riches and Wealth
Fig. 45

a) Many lines on Apollo finger going from the bottom to the top.
b) The Sun line starting from negative Mars and ending in a trident.
c) Line from the mount of Mercury touching the line of Heart.
d) Triangle attached to the Heart line in the Quadrangle.
e) Sign of Trident on the mount of Saturn.
f) Star on the mount of Apollo.
g) Two lines from the first phalange of the thumb to the Life line.
h) Mole on the Head line at the beginning.
i) Sign of a rainbow on the first phalange of the thumb.
j) Prominent and slanting line on the first joint of the thumb.

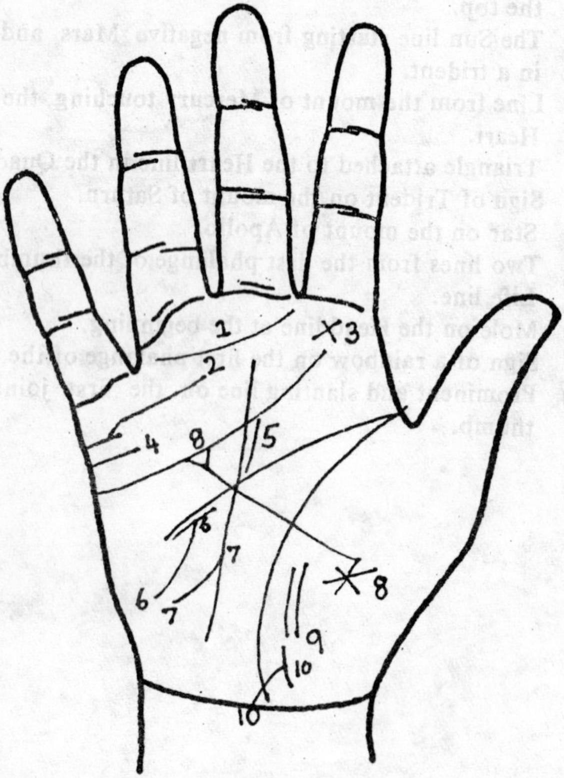

Fig. 46

Happy Marriage
Fig. 46

1) Single Girdle of Venus
2) Branch from Marriage line to the mount of the Sun.
3) Cross or star on the mount of Jupiter.
4) Straight line of Marriage.
5) Sister line to the Fate line.
6) Line of Influence from the mount of the Moon joining a small line running parallel to the Head line.
7) Influence line from the mount of the Moon merging in the Fate line.
8) Line from a star on the Venus mount ending in a fork on the Heart line.
9) Double lines of Influence on the mount of Venus.
10) Line from Bracelet going to a vertical line on the mount of Venus and a cross on the mount of Jupiter.

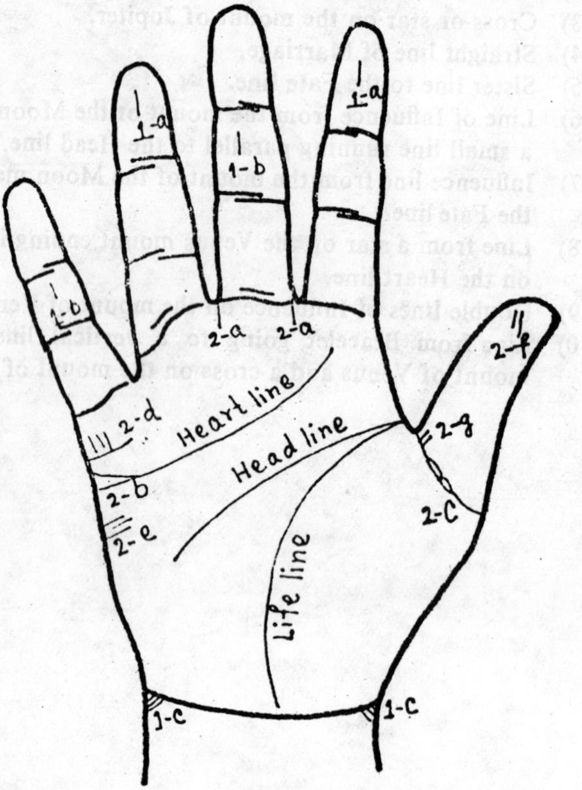
1-a
1-b
1-a
1-b
1-a
2-a
2-a
2-d
Heart line
Head line
2-b
2-e
Life line
2-g
2-f
2-C
1-C
1-C

Fig. 47

Children
Fig. 47

1) *Children and grand children*
   a) Vertical line on the first phalange of the Jupiter finger or the Sun finger.
   b) Vertical line on the second phalange of the Saturn finger or Mercury finger.
   c) Falling branches from the first Bracelet and from the other side of the hand.
2) *Children*
   a) Two clear vertical lines on either side of the mount of Saturn.
   b) The line of Heart forked on the mount of Mercury.
   c) Number of Yova on the second joint of the thumb.
   d) Presence of lines of children.
   e) Small lines on the upper mount of Mars.
   f) Vertical lines on the first phalange of the thumb.
   g) Lines at the base of the thumb.

Other lines not shown in the figure
   i) Red lines on the hand of a woman.
   ii) Sign like a trident, a pot, a lotus or a fish.

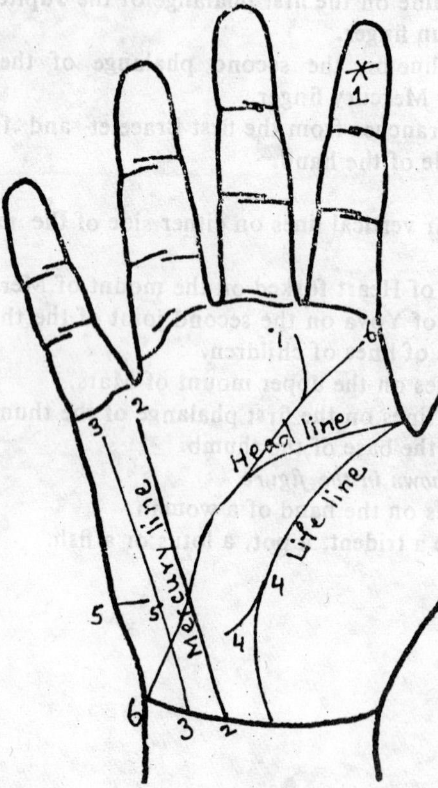

Fig. 48

Travel and Voyage

Fig. 48

1) Star on the first phalange of Jupiter finger.
2) Mercury line starting from the Rascette (Bracelet) without touching the Life line.
3) Rising branch from the Bracelet and going to the mount of Mercury.
4) Line from the Life line going to the mount of the Moon.
5) Horizontal line on the mount of the Moon.
6) Line from the Bracelet starting from near the percussion and going to the mount of Jupiter.
7) The line in item 6 above changes its course at the end and goes to the mount of Saturn.

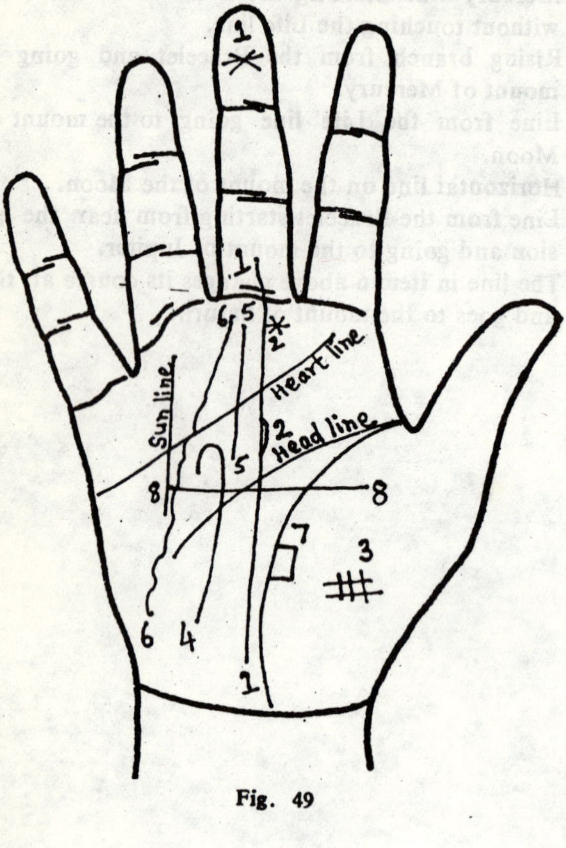

Fig. 49

Imprisonment
Fig. 49

1) Fate line cutting the third phalange of the Saturn finger with a star on the first phalange of the Saturn finger.
2) Island in the Fate line on the mount of Uranus and a star on the mount of Saturn.
3) Grill on the mount of Saturn or Venus.
4) Fate line turning backward into the hollow of the hand and towards the mount of the Moon in a semicircle.
5) Fate line starting from inside the Quadrangle.
6) Crooked line of Fate starting from the mount of the Moon and terminating on the mount of Saturn.
7) Square touching the Life line from inside.
8) Influence line from the positive Mars touching the Sun line with a cross on the mount of Saturn.

Intuition Fig. 50

1) Triangle on the mount of the Moon.
2) Line of Intuition.
3) Fate line starting from two islands forming a figure of eight.
4) Intuition line ending in a star.
5) Rising branch from the line of Intuition going to the mount of Jupiter or the Sun.
6) Mercury line forming a small triangle with the lines of Head and Life.

Other signs not shown in the figure

7) A Mercurian.
8) First phalange of Jupiter finger better developed.
9) Fate line starting from the base of the mount of the Moon with long fingers of Jupiter and Apollo.

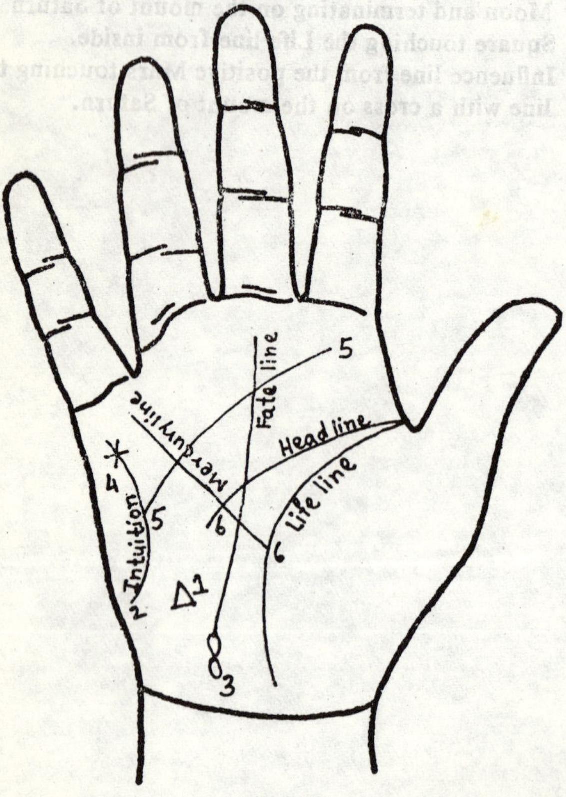

Fig. 50